Guide to the National Park Areas:
EASTERN STATES

Also by David L. Scott and Kay W. Scott

Guide to the National Park Areas: Western States

Guide to the National Park Areas:
EASTERN STATES

Fourth Edition

by
DAVID L. SCOTT *and*
KAY W. SCOTT

A Voyager Book

The
Globe
Pequot
Press

Old Saybrook, Connecticut

Text photographs and Facilities and Activities chart reprinted courtesy of the National Park Service.

Cover Photo: H. Abernathy / H. Armstrong Roberts
Cover design by Schwartzman Design
Text and map design by Nancy Freeborn

Library of Congress Cataloging-in-Publication Data

Scott, David Logan, 1942–
     Guide to the National Park areas. Eastern states / by David L. Scott
and Kay W. Scott. — 4th ed.
         p.   cm.
     "A Voyager book"
     ISBN 1-7627-0062-9
     1. National parks and reserves—East (U.S.)—Guidebooks. 2. National parks and reserves—Puerto Rico—Guidebooks. 3. National parks and reserves—Virgin Islands of the United States—Guidebooks. 4. East (U.S.)—Guidebooks. 5. Puerto Rico—Guidebooks. 6. Virgin Islands of the United States—Guidebooks. I. Scott, Kay Woelfel. II. Title.
E160.S448 1997
917.3—dc21   97-5384
                                                                              CIP

Manufactured in the United States of America
Fourth Edition/First Printing

This text is printed on recycled paper.

CONTENTS

MARYLAND

MASSACHUSETTS

MICHIGAN

Chimney Rock in Cumberland Gap National Historical Park, Kentucky (opposite page)

INTRODUCTION

Any discussion of America's national parks is likely to cause most people to automatically think of one or more well-known national parks such as Acadia, Grand Canyon, Grand Teton, Olympic, Rocky Mountain, Great Smoky Mountains (by far the most visited national park), Yellowstone, or Yosemite. These are eight of our most spectacular, visited, and photographed national parks. Literally hundreds of additional beautiful and interesting areas are operated by the National Park Service, however, even though most are not officially designated as national parks. The system of parks includes national monuments, historical parks, military parks, historic sites, reserves, seashores, lakeshores, battlefields, and recreation areas. The National Park Service administers areas that include seashores to walk, parkways to drive, rivers to float, and majestic redwoods to admire. Each area offers something special that is worth seeking. How about a visit to the fort that was the site of the first engagement of the Civil War? Have you tried camping on a pristine barrier island of the Atlantic Ocean where you can take morning strolls on the beach and pick up shells and sand dollars? Would you enjoy a visit to an old Spanish fort constructed in the 1600s? How about a stroll around the Virginia farm where George Washington was born?

More than 350 areas are administered by the National Park Service, but only about 15 percent of these are officially designated as national parks. Generally national parks are relatively large in area and contain a variety of resources. Other areas administered by the National Park Service designated have a more limited size and scope. The different designation doesn't make these areas any less rewarding to visit. In fact you are likely to discover that these other areas are less well known, less crowded, and offer much to see and do. On several occasions we were the only members of ranger-guided walks, and we once experienced a wonderful campfire program with only six other visitors. These experiences become a trip's most memorable events.

As these books are being revised, we have spent twenty-two summers touring the national parks. We have visited all of the states and have seen most of the parks. We have driven the length of the East Coast from Key West, Florida, to the northern tip of Newfoundland. (We did take a ferry from Nova Scotia to Newfoundland.) We walked Boston National Historical Park's Freedom Trail and Boston African American National Historic Site's Black Heritage Trail on a beautiful Fourth of July. We have spent a day walking along the endless beach of Georgia's Cumberland Island National Seashore and several nights camping in Maine's Acadia National Park. We have driven the Blue Ridge Parkway from Great Smoky Mountains National Park in North Carolina to Shenandoah National Park in Virginia. We fought mosquitoes in Cape Hatteras National Seashore, rain at Allegheny Portage Railroad National Historic Site, and traffic at Independence National Historical Park. We have seen the sights, walked the trails, talked with the park rangers, and visited with other lovers of nature.

The idea for this series of books occurred to us during the fifth summer of our travels. Each time we headed in a new direction we found ourselves trying to decide which areas of the National Park Service to visit and, once there, attempting to determine which particular points of interest and activities held the most promise for our limited time. We discovered that we often delayed trips to areas we should have visited earlier and spent time driving to parks that were found to have little interest. In addition, after arriving at a park, we were often unsure of which campgrounds to use or what activities and facilities were available.

Our hope is that these books will assist others in avoiding these same pitfalls. We have tried to include enough information to allow readers to decide which parks to visit as well as how long to allow to adequately discover the major features of each park. For most areas, we have tried to provide information on why the area was set aside, a summary of the history and/or geology of the area, activities for visitors, facilities such as availability of food service and overnight accommodations, campgrounds and their facilities, and possibilities for fishermen. In the limited space allotted to each area, we believe that this is the information most useful to the majority of visitors. (If camping facilities or fishing opportunities do not exist at a site, there will not be separate headings for these activities at the end of that particular entry.)

For those who are new to visiting the national parks, a few introductory comments may be helpful. Some areas charge for entrance, and nearly all charge for camping. Fees vary, and the most developed areas are typically the ones that charge. These same developed areas are also generally the ones that are most crowded. If you plan to camp at Acadia National Park, you need to arrive early. In such cases, it is often best to drive as close as possible the day before you plan to arrive. In the morning, rise with the sun and head for the park.

For your own benefit, don't overlook the small park areas. Big, busy parks are out of necessity often set up to process visitors on a production-line basis, but many of the small, less frequently visited parks offer a real personal touch.

We want to thank a great many individuals at the various National Park Service areas for reading and correcting initial drafts of the manuscript. We have tried to incorporate as many of the suggested changes as possible. The material in these books is believed to be accurate. The National Park Service, however, is constantly altering the areas under its jurisdiction, and no doubt there will be changes even before you buy this book. Budget limitations have resulted in the closing of certain facilities as funds for maintenance and personnel have been cut or, at least, have not kept up with visitation growth. In some cases, closings are temporary; in other instances, they appear permanent.

David L. Scott
Kay W. Scott
Valdosta, Georgia

KEY FOR
MAP SYMBOLS

—————— Roads

- - - - - - - Dirt Roads

· · · · · · · · · · · Trails

— · · — · · — · · State Border

Park Area

Rivers / Water

⬠ Visitor Center

▲ Camping

■ Building

● Locator / Town

⊼ Picnic Area

✘ Ruins / Historic Site
(as noted on individual maps)

ALABAMA

STATE TOURIST INFORMATION
(800) 252–2262

HORSESHOE BEND NATIONAL MILITARY PARK

11288 Horseshoe Bend Road
Daviston, AL 36256
(205) 234–7111

Horseshoe Bend National Military Park comprises 2,040 acres and was authorized in 1956 to commemorate the site where General Andrew Jackson's forces broke the power of the Creek Indian Confederacy and opened the Old Southwest to settlement. The park is located in east-central Alabama, 12 miles north of Dadeville and U.S. 280 via State Highway 49.

Following the spread of the Creek Civil War to frontier settlements in 1813, Andrew Jackson mobilized the Tennessee Militia for a full-scale campaign into the heart of the Mississippi Territory. After a series of engagements with Jackson's forces, many of the Upper Creek braves fled to a refugee town called Tohopeka, inside a great bend of the Tallapoosa River known as the "Horse's Flatfoot." Here they hoped to be protected by the river, the magic of their religious leaders, and a sturdy log barricade. On March 27, 1814, Jackson's forces attacked the "horseshoe" and killed most of the 1,000 Creek warriors. The victory resulted in the transfer of more than 20 million acres of Indian land to the United States, and set Jackson on the road to national fame.

The visitor center contains exhibits on Creek culture, frontier life, and the Creek War of 1813–14. From here, a 3-mile road loops through the park, where trails and markers help interpret the battlefield. A 2.8-mile nature trail begins near the overlook, a short distance from the visitor center. Demonstrations are given periodically during summer months.

FACILITIES: Restrooms and water are in the visitor center. A nice shaded picnic area across from the visitor center has drinking water and tables. Restaurants and lodging are available in Dadeville and Alexander City.

CAMPING: No camping is permitted in the park. Wind Creek State Park, 6 miles south of Alexander City via State Highway 22, offers camping, fishing, swimming, and a marina.

FISHING: Visitors may fish for catfish, crappie, sunfish, and bass in the Tallapoosa River, which flows through the park. State fishing laws apply, and an Alabama license is required.

LITTLE RIVER CANYON NATIONAL PRESERVE

P.O. Box 45
2201 East Gault Ave. North
Fort Payne, AL 35967
(205) 845–9605 and 845–9239

Little River Canyon National Preserve comprises 13,699 acres and was authorized in 1992 to protect the natural, recreational, scenic, and cultural resources of the Little River Canyon. The preserve is located in northeast Alabama on Lookout Mountain in Cherokee and DeKalb counties. It is best reached via State Highway 35 between the towns of the Fort Payne and Gaylesville.

The Little River has carved a deep canyon on its journey from Lookout Mountain. The area encompassing the preserve contains spectacular terrain including waterfalls, canyon rims and bluffs, sandstone cliffs, and forested uplands. The preserve provides numerous recreational opportunities for camping, hiking, fishing, canoeing, mountain biking, swimming, climbing, and hunting. Canyon Rim Drive (State Highway 176) provides access to many spectacular overlooks and undeveloped trails along the west rim of the canyon. This is the most visited part of the preserve.

No federal facilities are presently in the preserve.

FACILITIES: DeSoto State Park (205–845–0051 or 800–568–8840), at the north end of the preserve on County Highway 89, offers some facilities. These include meals, limited groceries, and lodging, including cabins and a resort lodge. Full facilities are available in surrounding communities.

CAMPING: Primitive camping is permitted in the preserve. DeSoto State Park (see above) offers seventy-eight developed campsites with water and electrical hookups.

FISHING: Fishing is permitted in the Little River. An Alabama license is required.

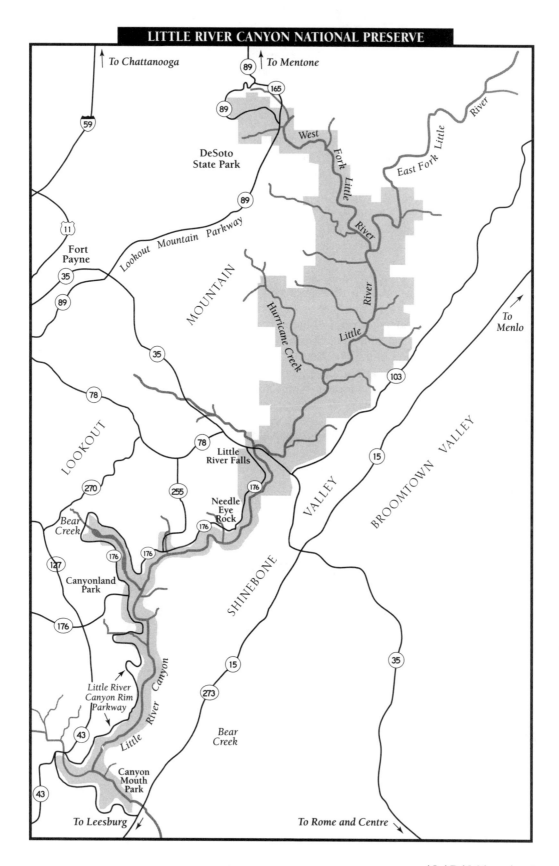

LITTLE RIVER CANYON NATIONAL PRESERVE

To Chattanooga

To Mentone

89

165

89

West

DeSoto
State Park

Fork

East Fork Little

River

Little

11

River

Fort
Payne

89

35

MOUNTAIN

89

Lookout Mountain Parkway

Little

River

Hurricane Creek

To
Menlo

35

103

78

LOOKOUT

78

Little
River Falls

VALLEY

15

BROOMTOWN VALLEY

270

255

176

Bear
Creek

Needle
Eye
Rock

127

176

176

176

SHINEBONE

Canyonland
Park

176

15

35

Little River Canyon

Little River
Canyon Rim
Parkway

15

273

Bear
Creek

43

Canyon
Mouth
Park

43

To Leesburg

To Rome and Centre

RUSSELL CAVE NATIONAL MONUMENT

3729 County Road 98
Bridgeport, AL 35740
(205) 495–2672

Russell Cave's 310 acres were incorporated into the National Park System in 1961 to preserve a cave shelter revealing an archaeological record of human habitation from 7000 B.C. to about A.D. 1000. The park is located in the northeastern corner of Alabama. From Bridgeport and U.S. 72, turn north on County Road 75 to Mount Carmel and then right on County Road 98 to the entrance. The park is about 8 miles from Bridgeport.

About 9,000 years ago, groups of nomadic Indians first began to occupy Russell Cave. These early Indians lived in the cave shelter only during the autumn and winter and subsisted by hunting game and gathering plants. Successive groups inhabited the cave until A.D. 1000.

Archaeological excavations, which first began here in 1953, have uncovered broken pottery, spear and arrow points, and animal and human skeletal remains. These items reveal the thousands of years of habitation in the cave shelter.

The visitor center, open year-round, contains exhibits to help interpret the monument. An exhibit of the archaeological excavation is in the cave shelter, but entrance into cave passages is allowed only with written permission of the superintendent. A slide program is in the cave shelter, and interpretive programs are presented in the visitor center audiovisual room upon request. Demonstrations on the life of the ancient Indians are also presented upon request. The monument sponsors a day of special events on the third Saturday in April that includes programs on Native American culture, demonstrations, and programs on archaeology.

FACILITIES: No food or lodging is available in the park. Both are in South Pittsburg, Tennessee, and Stevenson, Alabama. Restrooms and drinking water are in the visitor center. A small picnic area is available, but fires are not permitted.

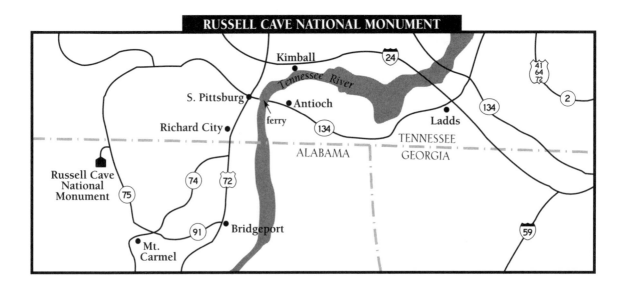

CAMPING: No camping is permitted in the monument. Camping is available in Stevenson and at a small private campground near the park. DeSoto State Park at Fort Payne, Alabama, Cloudland Canyon State Park near Trenton, Georgia, and TVA's Nickajack Dam Recreation Area are within 50 miles of Russell Cave.

TUSKEGEE INSTITUTE NATIONAL HISTORIC SITE

P.O. Drawer 10
Tuskegee, AL 36083
(334) 727–6390

Tuskegee Institute National Historic Site comprises seventy-five acres and was authorized in 1974 to memorialize a famous college for black Americans founded by Booker T. Washington. The site is located in eastern Alabama in the north-west corner of the city of Tuskegee. When approaching on Interstate 85, exit on State Highway 81 South and turn right on Old Montgomery Road.

Booker T. Washington was six years old when the Civil War broke out. After gaining his freedom following the war, he held a number of jobs before graduating with honors from Hampton Institute in 1875. In 1881, he moved to Tuskegee to create Tuskegee Normal and Industrial Institute. From an initial state appropriation of $2,000 and classes in a dilapidated church, Booker T. Washington moved Tuskegee Institute through a period of growth and improvement until his death in 1915. The main campus has subsequently expanded to 161 buildings that house nearly 5,000 students, faculty, and staff. For further information on Booker T. Washington, see Booker T. Washington National Monument (Virginia) elsewhere in this book.

Information, audio-visual programs, and guide maps to the campus are available at the visitor orientation center at the George Washington Carver Museum. Many of the Institute's buildings constructed during the tenure of Booker T. Washington are still standing. Most of these are built of brick made on the campus by students, and many of the historic buildings were designed by R. R. Taylor, the first black graduate of MIT and a Tuskegee faculty member. Of particular interest are the Washington family home, The Oaks (tours available), and the Carver Museum.

FACILITIES: Food service is available on campus, and lodging may be found in the city of Tuskegee.

CAMPING: No camping is permitted at the site. Wind Creek State Park is northwest of Tuskegee, near Alexander City.

Tuskegee Institute National Historic Site

CONNECTICUT

STATE TOURIST INFORMATION
(800) 282–6863

WEIR FARM NATIONAL HISTORIC SITE

735 Nod Hill Road
Wilton, CT 06897
(203) 761–9945

Weir Farm National Historic Site is comprised of sixty acres and was authorized in 1990 to preserve the home, studio, and landscape of American Impressionist painter Julian Alden Weir. The historic site is located in southwestern Connecticut in the towns of Ridgefield and Wilton. From State Highway 7, take State Highway 102 west to Old Branchville Road, to 735 Nod Hill Road. The visitor center is the red house on the right past Pelham Lane. Parking is available on the left opposite the visitor center.

Julian Weir (1852–1919) was one of many American art students who studied in Paris during the years following the Civil War. It was here where he made friendships and was exposed to exhibitions that would strongly influence his future work. After returning to the United States, the painter pursued his own work in portraits and still lives while serving as an art instructor in New York City. It was not until after moving to this farm that he began to paint outdoor scenes in an impressionist style. Branchville-inspired landscapes painted by Weir and several colleagues are considered exceptional examples of the American impressionist movement.

Julian Weir purchased the 153-acre farm in 1882, in anticipation of his upcoming marriage. He built a studio, enlarged the house, and eventually expanded the farm to 238 acres. He was to spend nearly four decades entertaining artist colleagues such as John Twachtman, Albert Pinkham Ryder, and Childe Hassam. Weir's daughter, Dorothy, married sculptor Mahonri Young (Brigham Young's grandson) in 1931, and the couple resided at the farm until Mahonri Young's death in 1957.

The visitor center, located in the Burlingham House, features an introduction to the site including an exhibit of historical photographs, a twenty-minute-long video, and a laser disc showing Weir's paintings. The visitor center is open daily from 8:30 A.M. to 5:00 P.M. from June 1 through November 30. During the winter season it is open only on weekdays. Scheduled tours of Weir's studio are available Wednesday through Saturday at 10:00 A.M. (Wednesday through Friday during winter). The site also contains Young's Studio (tours at 10:00 A.M. Thursdays and Saturdays from April 1 through November 30), an icehouse, and barn. Guided landscape tours are offered Saturday and Sunday at 2:00 P.M. April 1 through November 30. Visitors may also follow a self-guided tour of twelve historic painting sites where they can compare art reproductions with the vistas that inspired them.

FACILITIES: Restrooms and drinking water are available. Lodging and food are available nearby.

CAMPING: No camping is permitted at the site.

FISHING: No fishing is available at Weir Farm National Historic Site.

DISTRICT OF COLUMBIA

DISTRICT TOURIST INFORMATION
(202) 789–7000

The District of Columbia contains more than 300 National Park Service units comprising thousands of acres. These units consist of such diverse areas as parkways, parks, a national cemetery, and the White House. Only the more popular areas are included in this section. Chesapeake and Ohio Canal National Historical Park, which offers boat trips from Georgetown, is discussed separately in the Maryland section. The concessioner-operated Tourmobile service stops at most major points of interest with unlimited reboarding permitted on the same day a ticket is purchased (202–554–7950). Because of limited parking and long walking distances between sites in downtown Washington, the Tourmobile is a worthwhile addition to a trip, especially if it is to last only a day or two. For information on particular units, write National Capital Region, 1100 Ohio Drive S.W., Washington, DC 20242 (202–619–7222).

National Park Service campgrounds are available in surrounding areas. These include Catoctin Mountain Park (Maryland), Greenbelt Park (Maryland), and Prince William Forest Park (Virginia).

1. **Constitution Gardens:** A fifty-two-acre park constructed during the American Revolution Bicentennial sits on what was once the site of War Department office buildings. An island in a lake in the gardens contains a memorial to the fifty-six signers of the Declaration of Independence (202–426–6841).

2. **Ford's Theatre National Historic Site** (511 Tenth Street, N.W.): This restored theater, the scene of President Abraham Lincoln's assassination, is maintained as a living memorial. A theater and museum in the basement provide an 18-minute narration on the highlights of Lincoln's life, and a number of objects owned by Lincoln and his family are exhibited. Periodic talks on the assassination are presented in the theater where visitors may view the presidential box where Lincoln was shot. Across the street is the house where Lincoln died the next morning. The museum and house are open daily from 9:00 A.M. to 5:00 P.M. (theater

closed for matinees at noon on Thursdays, and 2:00 P.M. on Sundays), and guided tours are available (202–426–6924).

3. **Frederick Douglass National Historic Site** (1411 W Street, S.E.): Frederick Douglass was America's leading nineteenth-century black spokesman, and this restored brick house served as his home from 1877 to his death in 1895. The house is open for free guided tours daily from 9:00 A.M. to 4:00 P.M. The visitor center contains exhibits and audio-visual programs (202–426–5960). Advance reservations are required for groups numbering ten people or more.

4. **John F. Kennedy Center for the Performing Arts** (New Hampshire Avenue at F Street, N.W.): This national cultural center opened in 1971 and contains various theaters, opera house, concert hall, and restaurants. Free guided tours are available from 10:00 A.M. to 1:00 P.M. daily (202–416–8340).

5. **Lincoln Memorial** (foot of Twenty-third Street, N.W., at Arlington Memorial Bridge): Work on this huge seated figure of Abraham Lincoln commenced in 1914. The figure is surrounded by thirty-six marble columns, and Lincoln's Second Inaugural and Gettysburg addresses are inscribed on the great marble walls. Interpretive services are provided daily from 8:00 A.M. to midnight (202–426–6841).

6. **Lyndon Baines Johnson Memorial Grove on the Potomac:** a nineteen-acre memorial to the thirty-sixth president located on the south side of the Potomac River overlooking the Capitol. The grove contains 500 white pines. Open dawn to dusk (703–285–2601).

7. **Mary McLeod Bethune Council House National Historic Site** (1318 Vermont Avenue, N.W.): headquarters of the National Council on Negro Women established by Mary McLeod Bethune in 1935. Born in 1875, Ms. Bethune served as advisor to four U.S. presidents and was a leader in black women's rights movements. Open Monday through Friday, 10:00 A.M. to 4:30 P.M., and Saturday and Sunday by appointment (202–332–1233).

8. **National Mall:** This landscaped park with its rows of elms extends from the Capitol to the Washington Monument. Within its 146 acres visitors will find footpaths, bike trails, and refreshment stands. The mall is bordered by a number of interesting buildings, including those of the National Gallery of Art (open 10:00 A.M. to 5:00 P.M. Monday through Saturday, noon to 9:00 P.M. on Sunday) and the Smithsonian Institution (open 10:00 A.M. to 5:30 P.M.).

9. **Old Post Office Tower** (corner of Pennsylvania Avenue and Twelfth Street N.W.): a part of the Old Post Office completed in 1899. Tours of the tower provide an excellent view of the city from the third-highest point in Washington. The tour also goes past bells presented by Great Britain to the United States in 1976. The bells ring only on special occasions. Tours take about fifteen to twenty minutes and begin at the building's main level. A variety of restaurants and shops are inside the renovated interior (202–606–8691).

10. **Old Stone House** (3051 M Street, N.W., in Georgetown): Built in 1765, this is the oldest existing house in Washington and a fine example of pre-Revolution architecture. The site offers guided tours, living-history demonstrations, and interpretive exhibits (202–426–6851).

11. **Rock Creek Park:** This 1,750-acre woodland in northwest Washington contains a diverse selection of natural, historical, and recreational resources. Activities include hiking, tennis, golf, softball, picnicking, horseback riding, and bicycling. The nature center provides exhibits, a planetarium, and nature programs; nearby are self-guiding nature trails. Pierce Mill is a restored gristmill built around 1820 (202–426–6829).

12. **Sewall-Belmont House National Historic Site** (144 Constitution Avenue, N.E.): This house, which dates to the early 1700s, has been headquarters for the National Women's Party since 1929. The house commemorates the party's founder and women's suffrage leader, Alice Paul. The house is open Tuesday through Friday, 10:00 A.M. to 3:00 P.M.; Saturday noon to 4:00 P.M. It is closed Sundays, Mondays, and holidays (202–546–3989).

13. **Theodore Roosevelt Island:** This eighty-eight-acre island has been preserved as a wildlife sanctuary to commemorate our twenty-sixth president's devotion to conservation. No vehicles are permitted on the island, which can be reached by footbridge from a parking area on the Virginia shore. Access to the parking area is from the northbound lane only of the George Washington Memorial Parkway. The island contains trails and an impressive 23-foot-tall statue of Theodore Roosevelt; it is open from 9:30 A.M. until sundown (703–285–2601).

14. **Thomas Jefferson Memorial** (south bank of Tidal Basin): This circular structure, built in a style introduced in this country by Thomas Jefferson, was dedicated in 1943 as a memorial to our third president, the principal author of the Declaration of Independence. Interpretive services are available year-round from 8:00 A.M. to midnight (202–426–6841).

15. **Vietnam Veterans Memorial** (Constitution Ave. and Twenty-first Street N.W. near Lincoln Memorial): This memorial was dedicated in November 1982 as a symbol of the nation's honor and recognition for the men and women who served in the Vietnam War. It is a special tribute to and inscribed with the names of more than 58,000 individuals who died or are missing in Vietnam. The memorial was built with $7 million in private funds, with its design decided through a national competition. A life-size statue of three servicemen was added in 1984, which, along with a flagstaff, forms an entrance plaza to the memorial. Directories providing the locations of individual names are available at the memorial. The memorial is open 24 hours a day. Staff members are available at the memorial from 8:00 A.M. to midnight (202–426–6841).

16. **Washington Monument** (Constitution Avenue at Fifteenth Street, N.W.): This 555-foot monument, built as a memorial to our first president, was first opened to the public in 1888. Visitors may take an elevator to the 500-foot level or walk the 897 steps. The monument is open daily from 9:00 A.M. to 5:00 P.M., September through March; 8:00 A.M. to midnight, April through August (202–426–6841).

17. **White House** (1600 Pennsylvania Avenue, N.W.): The White House has been the residence of all U.S. presidents except George Washington, who selected the site upon which it stands. The house is open for tours from 10:00 A.M. to noon, Tuesday through Saturday. A ticket system is in effect March through October. Tickets are issued on a first-come basis starting at 8:00 A.M. on the Ellipse. The White House is closed during official functions (202–208–1631).

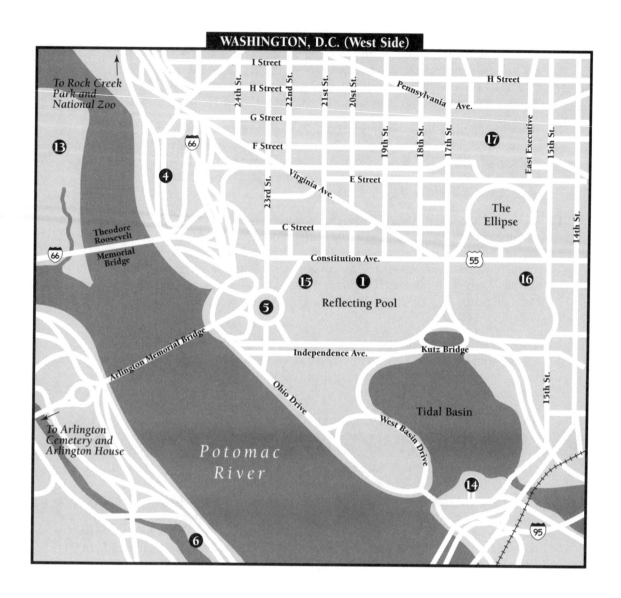

To Rock Creek Park and National Zoo

I Street

H Street

24th St.

22nd St.

21st St.

20st St.

G Street

F Street

66

4

23rd St.

Virginia Ave.

19th St.

18th St.

17th St.

Pennsylvania Ave.

H Street

East Executive

15th St.

13

17

E Street

C Street

The Ellipse

14th St.

Theodore Roosevelt Memorial Bridge

66

Constitution Ave.

55

15

1

16

5

Reflecting Pool

Arlington Memorial Bridge

Independence Ave.

Kutz Bridge

To Arlington Cemetery and Arlington House

Ohio Drive

West Basin Drive

Tidal Basin

15th St.

Potomac River

14

6

95

WASHINGTON, D.C. (East Side)

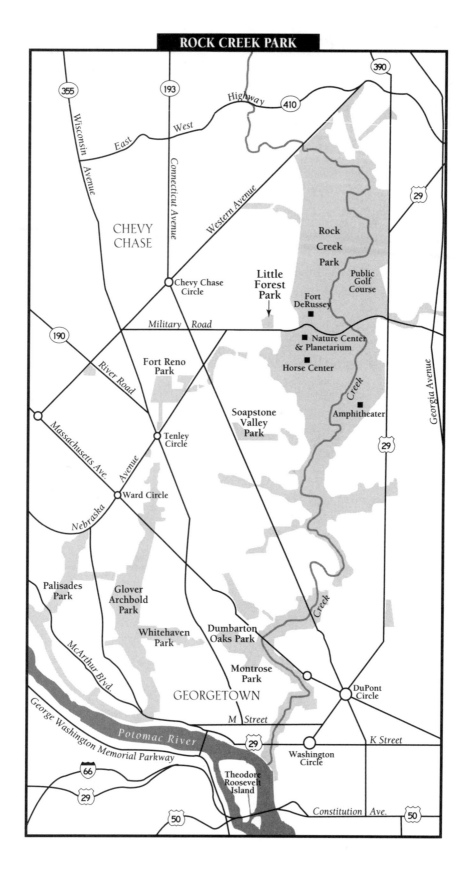

ROCK CREEK PARK

CHEVY CHASE

Rock Creek Park

Public Golf Course

Little Forest Park

Fort DeRussey

Nature Center & Planetarium

Horse Center

Soapstone Valley Park

Amphitheater

Fort Reno Park

Palisades Park

Glover Archbold Park

Whitehaven Park

Dumbarton Oaks Park

Montrose Park

GEORGETOWN

Theodore Roosevelt Island

Washington Circle

DuPont Circle

Chevy Chase Circle

Tenley Circle

Ward Circle

Wisconsin Avenue

Connecticut Avenue

Western Avenue

Military Road

River Road

Massachusetts Ave.

Nebraska Avenue

McArthur Blvd.

George Washington Memorial Parkway

Potomac River

M Street

K Street

Constitution Ave.

Georgia Avenue

East West Highway

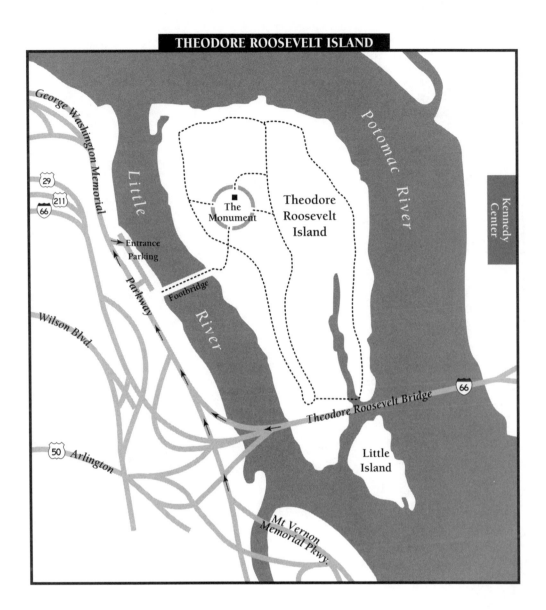

THEODORE ROOSEVELT ISLAND

George Washington Memorial

29

211

66

Little

Parkway

River

Wilson Blvd

Entrance
Parking

Footbridge

The
Monument

Theodore
Roosevelt
Island

Potomac River

Kennedy
Center

Theodore Roosevelt Bridge

66

50 Arlington

Little
Island

Mt Vernon
Memorial Pkwy.

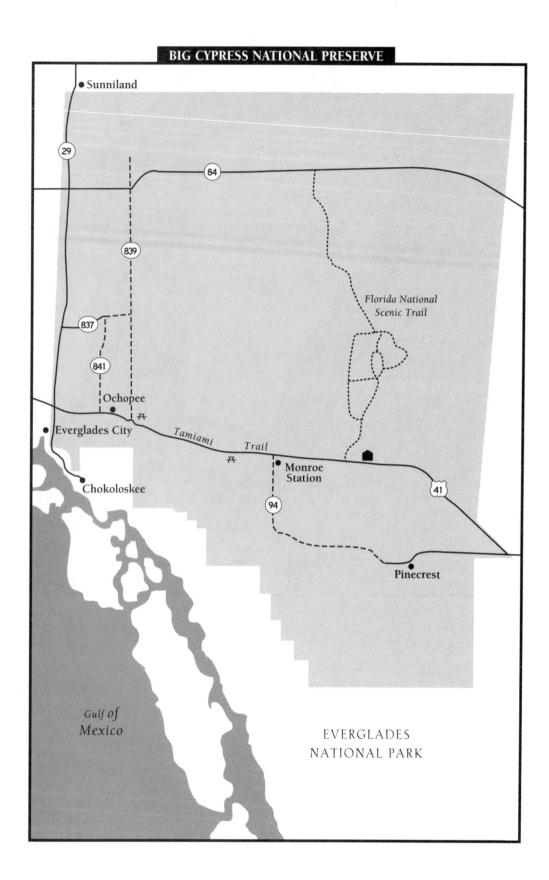

BIG CYPRESS NATIONAL PRESERVE

Sunniland

29

84

839

Florida National
Scenic Trail

837

841

Ochopee

Everglades City

Tamiami

Trail

Monroe
Station

Chokoloskee

41

94

Pinecrest

Gulf of
Mexico

EVERGLADES
NATIONAL PARK

FLORIDA

BIG CYPRESS NATIONAL PRESERVE
HCR 61
Ochopee, FL 33943
(941) 695–2000

Big Cypress National Preserve comprises 728,000 acres and was authorized in 1974 to preserve an area that is rich in subtropical plant and animal life as well as critical in providing fresh water to the Everglades. The preserve is located in southwestern Florida, adjoining the northwest section of Everglades National Park. Access is via U.S. Highway 41, State Highway 29, and Interstate 75.

Big Cypress Swamp is big in the sense that it encompasses 2,400 square miles in subtropical Florida. The area includes not only what is popularly considered a swamp but also sandy islands of pine, mixed hardwood islands, dry prairies, and mangrove forests. Unfortunately, few giant cypress trees remain, although about one third of the swamp is covered with dwarf pond cypress.

The area was opened to commercial exploitation in 1928 with the opening of the Tamiami Trail. In addition to a lumber boom in the 1930s and 1940s, Big Cypress attracted hunters, fishermen, guides, and cattlemen. Florida's first producing oil well was drilled near here in 1943. Later, in the 1960s, developers began draining the Big Cypress and selling land. It was this development and the resulting threat to the Everglades' watershed that prompted establishment of Big Cypress National Preserve.

Big Cypress contains a variety of plant life and wildlife. The latter includes herons, egrets, alligators, wild turkeys, deer, mink, bald eagles, red-cockaded woodpeckers, and the unique wood stork. Big Cypress is home to several endangered Florida panthers.

Big Cypress Visitor Center, 55 miles east of Naples on U.S. 41, is the main visitor contact station. The center has an information desk, wildlife exhibits, and a fifteen-minute-long orientation film about the preserve. It is open daily from 8:30 A.M. to 4:30 P.M. Primary access to the preserve is by U.S. 41.

FACILITIES: Food service and accommodations are in Naples and Everglades City. The town of Ochopee has food service during the winter tourist season. The National Park Service offers no facilities.

CAMPING: One privately owned campground in the preserve is at Ochopee. A developed campground with tables, grills, flush toilets, and showers is in Collier–Seminole State Park. Other campgrounds are in Everglades City and Naples and on Alligator Alley. The National Park Service provides six primitive campgrounds on U.S. 41 and on Loop Road (Highway 94). No water or restrooms are available.

FISHING: Bass, bluegills, and catfish are three of several species that may be taken from canal waters. A Florida license is required.

BISCAYNE NATIONAL PARK
P.O. Box 1369
Homestead, FL 33090–1369
(305) 247–7275

Biscayne National Park was authorized as a national monument in 1968 (redesignated as a national park in 1980) and comprises more than 180,000 acres (only 8,800 of which are land) of reefs and water surrounding a north–south chain of forty-four islands. The park is located in extreme southeastern Florida, south of Miami and east of Homestead. The mainland section and Convoy Point Visitor Center are reached via North Canal Drive (Southwest 328th Street) from Homestead and U.S. Highway 1.

Biscayne National Park is one of the few areas administered by the National Park Service in which the center of attraction is water and the life it supports. The tropical climate combined with extraordinarily clean, clear water produces an unusual diversity of trees, ferns, vines, flowers, shrubs, and the wildlife they support. Offshore, along Biscayne's reefs, more than 200 species of colorful fish can be seen. Brown pelicans, terns, and herons inhabit the bay. On the mainland, a mangrove forest provides a breeding ground for marine animals and acts as a buffer against the winds and waves of hurricanes.

Main access to the park is at Convoy Point, where park headquarters and the visitor center are located. The visitor center is open daily (times vary according to season) with exhibits and a schedule of activities. A park concessioner offers glass-bottom-boat trips, guided boat trips to the keys, and snorkeling tours to the reefs from Convoy Point (305–230–1100). A picnic area is near the visitor center.

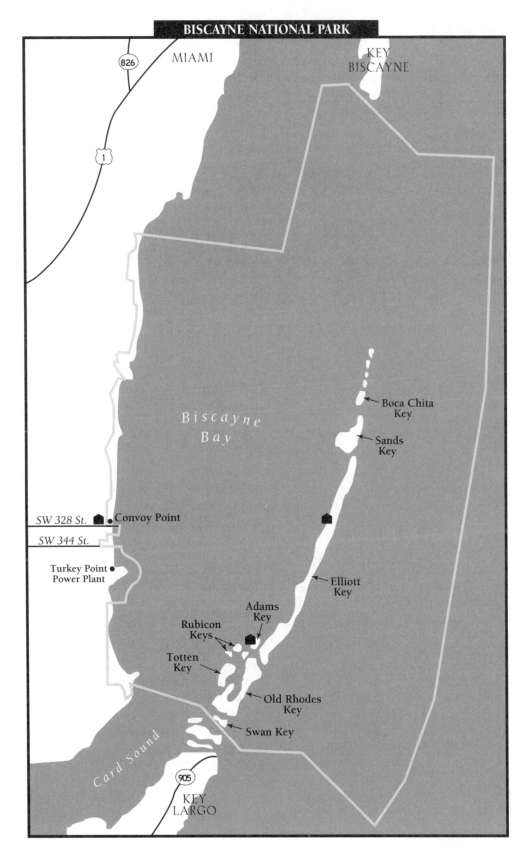

MIAMI

KEY
BISCAYNE

826

1

Biscayne
Bay

Boca Chita
Key

Sands
Key

SW 328 St. Convoy Point

SW 344 St.

Turkey Point
Power Plant

Elliott
Key

Adams
Key

Rubicon
Keys

Totten
Key

Old Rhodes
Key

Swan Key

Card Sound

905

KEY
LARGO

Offshore, Elliott Key has a nature trail, freshwater showers, drinking water, free boat docks with sixty-eight boat slips (first-come basis), and overnight camping. Adams Key is open for day use only and offers free docking, a picnic area, restrooms, and a nature trail. Sands Key features a popular offshore overnight anchorage area. Boca Chita Key has free docking, picnic facilities, saltwater restrooms, and overnight camping, but no fresh water is available. A lookout tower is open on weekends.

FACILITIES: Homestead, Miami, and the Florida Keys offer a wide range of food and lodging. Snorkeling and scuba-diving gear are rented or sold in surrounding locations.

CAMPING: Elliott Key has a campground with thirty-five sites and a group campsite, each with picnic tables and grills. Drinking water, restrooms, and showers are available. Boca Chita Key has a camping area with grills, picnic tables, and saltwater restrooms. No fresh water is available. Both campgrounds are accessible only by private boat. Everglades National Park, John Pennekamp Coral Reef State Park, and other area state parks offer year-round camping.

FISHING: A variety of saltwater fish can be caught here. Florida state licensing requirements apply to park waters.

CANAVERAL NATIONAL SEASHORE

308 Julia Street
Titusville, FL 32780
(407) 267–1110

Canaveral National Seashore comprises 57,627 acres and was established by Congress in 1975 to preserve one of the few remaining wilderness areas on Florida's Atlantic Coast. The seashore is located midway down Florida's east coast along a 24-mile stretch of beach beginning approximately 18 miles south of Daytona Beach and ending at the north end of the Kennedy Space Center.

Amid the hustle and bustle of Florida tourists and the launch area of America's space effort, Canaveral National Seashore provides a sanctuary for plants, wildlife, and man. The seashore is actually a by-product of the space program in that the National Park Service became involved in managing a portion of Merritt Island that was not needed for the Kennedy Space Center. Another section, Merritt Island National Wildlife Refuge, is managed by the U.S. Fish and Wildlife Service.

More than 310 species of birds have been recorded on the island, including egrets, gulls, herons, pipers, osprey, sandpipers, terns, and an occasional bald eagle. Manatees are seen in Mosquito Lagoon and Indian River; whales and dolphins can sometimes be spotted offshore. On the island are armadillos, bobcats, raccoons, and rattlesnakes. Crabs, loggerhead turtles, and green sea turtles frequent the beach.

Apollo Beach to the north and Playalinda Beach to the south can be reached by road. Klondike Beach between Apollo and Playalinda is reached by foot, bicycle, or horseback, and offers considerably more solitude. Although ocean temperatures are relatively mild all year, the surf can be rough; swimmers should be aware of potential riptides and should watch for stinging jellyfish, including the Portuguese man-of-war. Boat-launching sites provide boating access to both Mosquito Lagoon and Indian River.

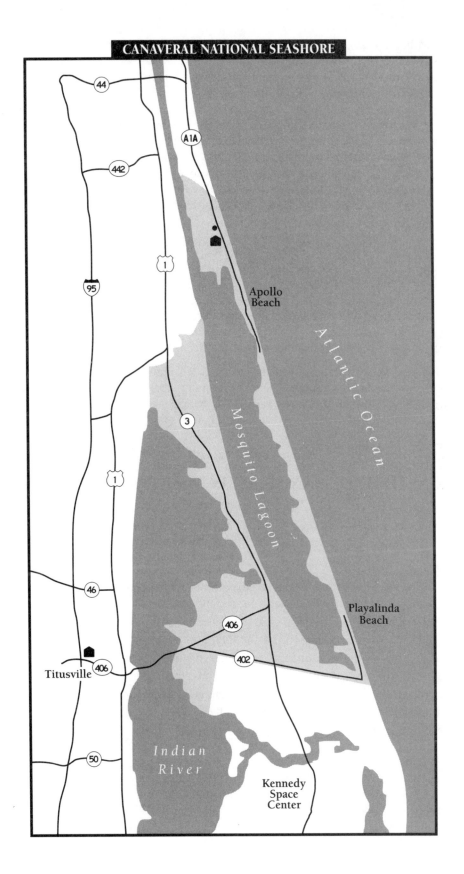

CANAVERAL NATIONAL SEASHORE

Apollo
Beach

Atlantic Ocean

Mosquito Lagoon

Playalinda
Beach

Titusville

*Indian
River*

Kennedy
Space
Center

The seashore's headquarters is located in Titusville at the intersection of Julia Street and Hopkins Avenue (Highway 1). The wildlife refuge's headquarters is on Highway 402/406, 4 miles east of Titusville. Here visitors can obtain information on the area, including handouts on wildlife, vegetation, and seashells. Within the seashore and wildlife refuge are drives and hiking trails to provide a more intimate experience. In the wildlife refuge, Black Point Wildlife Drive (thirty to forty-five minutes) wanders through pine flatwoods and a marsh where visitors may observe waterfowl and wading birds. Oak Hammock Trail (thirty minutes) is a loop trail through a hardwood hammock. In the Apollo Units a self-guiding trail at Turtle Mound (fifteen minutes) provides a viewpoint of the Atlantic Ocean and Mosquito Lagoon. A 2½-mile self-guiding canoe trail goes through lagoons and backcountry waters of Mosquito Lagoon. The canoe trip takes two to three hours and is especially beautiful during fall, winter, and spring months.

FACILITIES: Restrooms and drinking water are available at the headquarters buildings. There is no running water elsewhere within the seashore section. Food and lodging are in communities surrounding the seashore.

CAMPING: Limited backcountry camping is permitted on Klondike Beach from November 1 to April 30, with access from Apollo Beach. Backcountry camping is available in Mosquito Lagoon throughout the year. A free permit is required and must be obtained at the seashore's information center at Apollo Beach. A number of private campgrounds are nearby.

FISHING: The brackish water of Indian River and Mosquito Lagoon is ideal for mullet, redfish, and trout. Freshwater impoundments in the interior of the island offer largemouth bass and bream. Surf fishing in the break zone yields bluefish, whiting, and pompano. A Florida license is required for freshwater and saltwater fishing.

CASTILLO DE SAN MARCOS NATIONAL MONUMENT

1 Castillo Drive
St. Augustine, FL 32084
(904) 829–6506

Castillo de San Marcos National Monument comprises twenty acres and was established in 1924 to preserve a unique relic of the Spanish presence in Florida and a specimen of a vanished style of military architecture and engineering. The fort, built over the period 1672 to 1695 and modernized in the eighteenth century, replaced the last of nine successive wooden forts, which, since 1565, affirmed the Spanish title to Florida and protected Spanish ships returning to Europe via the Gulf Stream. The monument is located in northeastern Florida, in downtown St. Augustine, adjacent to Highway A1A. (See also Fort Matanzas National Monument in this section.)

St. Augustine was settled by the Spanish in 1565. Things remained relatively quiet until the English founded Charleston in 1670. The two nations then began a rivalry that soon brought about the construction of masonry Castillo de San Marcos. Although the fort was never captured, it came under British rule when Spain ceded Florida to England in 1763. After being

CASTILLO DE SAN MARCOS NATIONAL MONUMENT AND FORT MATANZAS NATIONAL MONUMENT

1

A1A

16

ST.
AUGUSTINE

Castillo De San Marcos
National Monument

214

Anastasia
State Park

207

312

A1A

Anastasia Island

Atlantic Ocean

Matanzas River

1

95

Fort Matanzas
National
Monument

A1A

204

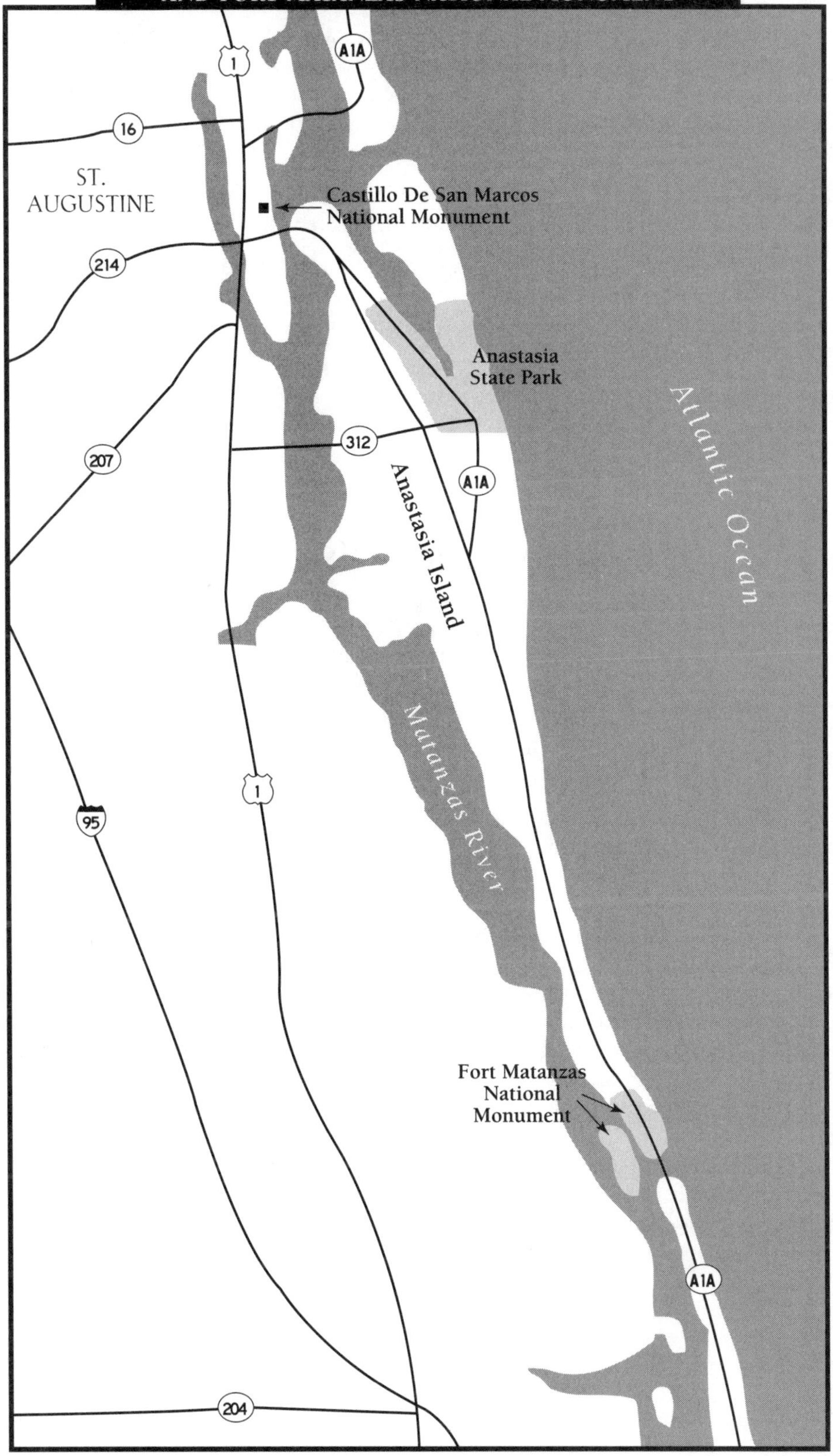

used as a British base of operations during the American Revolution, the fort reverted to Spain in 1784 before being ceded to the United States in 1821.

The fort is open daily except Christmas Day, and a nominal fee is required for entrance. Talks by park rangers and living-history programs are offered periodically. After passing through the fort's entrance, begin your tour at the small museum on the left. A pleasant experience for visitors is just relaxing on one of the benches or on the large grass area surrounding the fort and watching pleasure boats sailing on the river.

FACILITIES: Restrooms and water are available in the fort. In addition, souvenirs and camera supplies are sold by a concessioner. Food and lodging are within easy walking distance.

CAMPING: No camping is permitted within the monument grounds, and no overnight parking is allowed in the parking lot adjacent to the fort. Anastasia State Park provides campsites with tables, flush toilets, and showers a short distance south of town on A1A. A nice beach area is across the road from the state park.

FISHING: Fishing is permitted from the seawall; catches include a variety of saltwater fish. A saltwater fishing license is required.

DE SOTO NATIONAL MEMORIAL
P.O. Box 15390
Bradenton, FL 34280
(813) 792–0458

De Soto National Memorial contains thirty acres and was authorized in 1948 to commemorate the 1539 Florida landing of Spanish explorer Hernando De Soto. The memorial is located in west-central Florida, 5 miles west of Bradenton via Highway 64 on Tampa Bay.

In 1538 the De Soto expedition left the Spanish port of San Lucar in search of gold in the New World. After landing somewhere on the west coast of Florida, a group of more than 600 men started up the Florida peninsula on a four-year trip, which would take them through most of the southern states. The expedition was beset with problems, and many of the men died or deserted. In 1542 De Soto died, and the remaining members, tired of the search for gold, struck out for Mexico. Although no gold had been found and many viewed the expedition as a failure, the men learned much about the New World that was to prove useful to those who followed.

The visitor center contains exhibits and an audio-visual program to help interpret the De Soto trip. From January to April park employees provide demonstrations and talks. There is a ½-mile self-guiding nature trail with signs describing the flora and fauna of the area. The park is open daily from 9:00 A.M. to 5:00 P.M. There is no entrance fee.

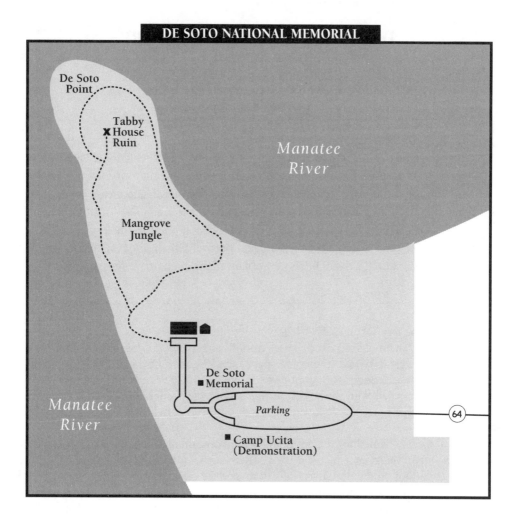

DE SOTO NATIONAL MEMORIAL

De Soto Point

Tabby House Ruin

Manatee River

Mangrove Jungle

De Soto Memorial

Manatee River

Parking

64

Camp Ucita (Demonstration)

FACILITIES: No food or lodging is available inside the park. Restrooms and drinking water are at the visitor center.

CAMPING: No camping is permitted at the memorial. Myakka River State Park, southeast of Bradenton via U.S. 41 and Highway 72, offers campsites with tables, grills, drinking water, flush toilets, and showers. Private campgrounds are in Bradenton.

FISHING: A variety of saltwater fish may be caught in Tampa Bay from the shore or from boats. Possible catches include mackerel, cobia, snapper, grouper, sea bass, redfish, and speckled trout. A fishing license is required. A copy of regulations may be picked up in the visitor center.

DRY TORTUGAS NATIONAL PARK

P.O. Box 6208
Key West, FL 33041
(305) 242–7700 (Everglades National Park)

Dry Tortugas National Park contains 64,657 acres (fewer than forty acres of which are land). Initially a wildlife refuge, it was added to the National Park System in 1935 to preserve a nineteenth-century brick and masonry fort built to help control the Florida Straits and protect the Gulf Coast. The area was redesignated in 1992 as a national park to protect both the area's historical and natural features. The park is located 68 miles west of Key West in the Dry Tortugas and is accessible only by boat or seaplane, both of which are available in Key West and Marathon. Private boats can obtain nautical charts at numerous locations in Key West.

Construction on the Dry Tortugas' Fort Jefferson commenced in 1846 as part of a United States program to build a chain of seacoast defenses from Maine to Texas. The fort's 50-foot-high and 8-foot-thick walls were designed to provide space for 450 guns around an area large enough to garrison 1,500 men. Although work continued for nearly thirty years, Fort Jefferson was never finished. During the Civil War, the structure was occupied by federal forces and was used as a prison, but in 1874, a hurricane followed a second outbreak of yellow fever and resulted in its abandonment.

The Dry Tortugas (named for the abundant sea turtles and absence of fresh water) are in an ideal location for development of coral reefs. These reefs, in turn, support a wide variety of marine life, including multicolored sea fans, four species of sea turtles, and colorful fish. Sea birds such as magnificent frigate birds, masked boobies, and sooty and noddy terns nest in the Tortugas. Frequent droughts, storms, and a saline soil support a limited number of hardy land plants.

Fort Jefferson is open during daylight hours only. Contact the superintendent at Everglades National Park for a list of licensed operators. An orientation video program explaining the fort's significance is shown inside the visitor center. Tours of the monument are self-guided, although rangers are available to answer questions.

FACILITIES: A grass picnic area with grills and tables is available. Restrooms are at the dock. No other facilities, including water, are provided.

CAMPING: Camping is permitted year-round in a designated area. No drinking water is available, and garbage must be carried away. Group camping requires a permit from the superintendent at Everglades National Park.

FISHING: Waters within and surrounding the monument contain good saltwater fishing for which a Florida saltwater fishing license is required. Fishing is permitted from the pier and shore between the north and south coaling docks. Fishing is prohibited within the moat and within 100 feet of the moat wall. Fishing licenses must be obtained on the mainland.

EVERGLADES NATIONAL PARK

P.O. Box 279
Homestead, FL 33030
(305) 242–7700

Everglades National Park comprises more than 1 1/2 million acres and was established in 1947 to preserve a large subtropical wilderness with extensive freshwater and saltwater areas, open prairies, and mangrove forests. The park is located across the southern tip of Florida with access from State Highway 9336. The entrance station is 11 miles southwest of the town of Homestead.

The Everglades is a fragile subtropical paradise containing a rich mixture of plants and animals along a freshwater river that is at times 6 inches deep and 50 miles wide. The lush park sits atop a limestone bed and competes for water with the fast-growing developments of southern Florida. The park is best known for its bird life, which includes roseate spoonbills, flamingos, egrets, white herons, pelicans, cranes, hawks, and falcons. The Everglades' most famous resident is the alligator.

The first stop should be the visitor center near the park entrance. Here visitors will find exhibits, audiovisual presentations, informational talks, and a schedule of interpretive activities.

The 38-mile drive from the entrance station to Flamingo (an activity area) passes a number of short walking trails (some on elevated boardwalks) that present a better picture of the land. Among the trails (each one about 1/2-mile long) and sights along the road are the following: The Anhinga Trail offers special exhibits and an excellent opportunity to see wildlife along a slow-moving freshwater, marshy river; Gumbo Limbo Trail winds through a junglelike grove of tropical trees and small plants; Pineland Trail circles through pinelands on a bed of limestone; Pa-hay-okee Overlook Trail leads to an observation platform; Mahogany Hammock Trail enters a dark, junglelike hardwood hammock; and West Lake Trail winds through mangrove trees along the edge of a large, brackish lake.

At Flamingo, a second visitor center contains exhibits that interpret the wildlife and environment around Florida Bay. The area also includes self-guiding trails, conducted walks, interpretive talks, boat tours, and boat rentals. A third visitor center is 2 miles southwest of the entrance station at Royal Palm.

On the park's north side, a public transportation system (fee charged) takes visitors into the Shark River slough. For reservations, call Shark Valley Tours (305–221–8455). Boat tours of the Ten Thousand Islands area of the park leave from Everglades City. For information write Sammy Hamilton, Jr., Box 119, Everglades City, FL 33923.

FACILITIES: At Flamingo, the Flamingo Lodge, Marina and Outpost provides 120 rooms and twenty-four cottages. Rates are lower in summer. For information, write Flamingo Inn, c/o TW Services, Flamingo, FL 33030 (813–695–3101 or 305–253–2241). Also in Flamingo are a marina, store, gift shop, restaurant, and service station. Some services are seasonal; contact the concessioner for availabilities. A variety of accommodations and food can be found outside the park in Florida City and Homestead.

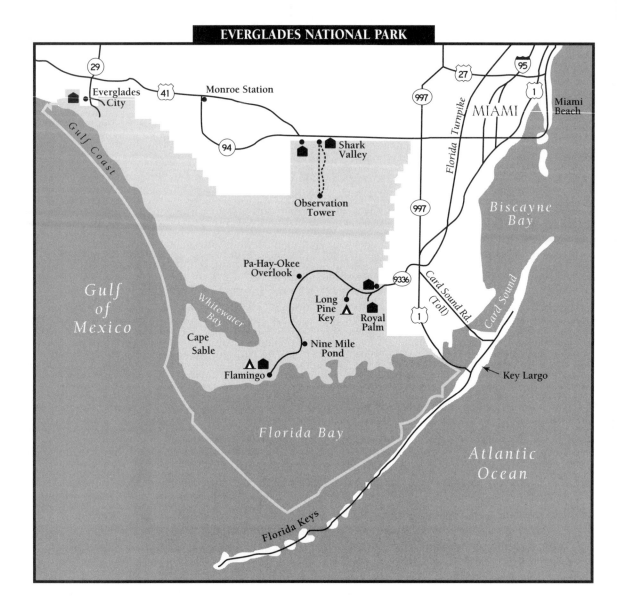

CAMPING: Long Pine Key (107 spaces), Flamingo (237 spaces, sixty walk-in tent sites, four group sites), and Chekika (twenty spaces, one group site) offer tables, grills, water, dump station, and flush toilets. Flamingo also has cold-water showers and Chekika has hot showers. Thirty-two backcountry locations offer primitive sites (non-fee backcountry use permits required).

FISHING: In bays and estuarine waters, spotted sea trout, mangrove snapper, redfish, tarpon, snook, and bonefish can be found. Largemouth bass, bluegill, and other species live in the freshwater streams, ponds, and pools. A license is required for freshwater and saltwater fishing.

FORT CAROLINE NATIONAL MEMORIAL

12713 Fort Caroline Road
Jacksonville, FL 32225
(904) 641–7155

Fort Caroline National Memorial was authorized in 1950 to commemorate the historic French settlement of La Caroline in the present United States. The park, which comprises 139 acres, is located in northeastern Florida within Jacksonville and can be reached via State Highway 10, Monument Road, and Fort Caroline Road.

In June 1564 an expedition of 300 French Huguenots anchored in Florida's St. Johns River. Here they established a colony named La Caroline in honor of King Charles IX of France. The colony included a triangular earth-and-wood fort. The intent was to establish a French presence in the New World and provide a Huguenot haven from the religious wars in France.

In September 1565 the Spanish established St. Augustin during its effort to rid Florida of the French. In an attempt to strike first, the French set sail to attack, but caught by an untimely storm, they were shipwrecked. Taking advantage of the loosely guarded fort, the Spanish attacked and claimed La Caroline for their own, renaming it San Mateo. The French massacre was avenged two years later by a Frenchman, once a Spanish galley slave, who led a successful attack on San Mateo and burned it to the ground.

Although the fort's original site is believed to have washed away after the river channel was deepened in 1880, a model of the fort has been constructed based on a sixteenth-century sketch by a French artist with the expedition. A visitor center is open daily from 9:00 A.M. to 5:00 P.M. except Christmas Day.

FACILITIES: No food or lodging is available at the park, but drinking water and restrooms are located in the visitor center.

CAMPING: No camping facilities are available at the memorial. Nearby camping at Little Talbot Island State Park provides forty sites with electricity, tables, flush toilets, and hot showers. This park is located northeast of Jacksonville on Highway A1A.

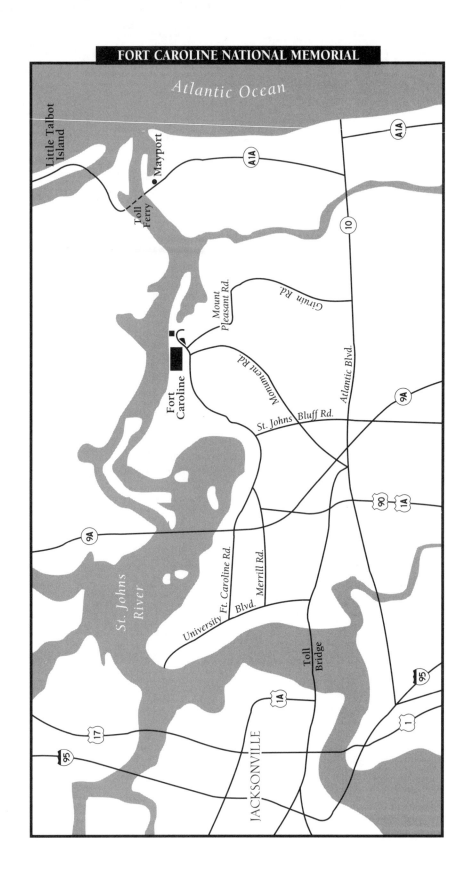

Atlantic Ocean

Little Talbot Island

Mayport

Toll Ferry

A1A

A1A

10

Mount Pleasant Rd.

Gruin Rd.

Monument Rd.

Atlantic Blvd.

Fort Caroline

St. Johns Bluff Rd.

9A

9A

90

1A

University

Ft. Caroline Rd.

Blvd.

Merrill Rd.

St. Johns River

Toll Bridge

95

1A

17

1

95

JACKSONVILLE

FORT MATANZAS NATIONAL MONUMENT

c/o Castillo de San Marcos National Monument
1 Castillo Drive
St. Augustine, FL 32084
(904) 471–0116

Fort Matanzas National Monument comprises nearly 300 acres and was established in 1924 to preserve the most important auxiliary defense of St. Augustine and a unique specimen of a vanished style of military architecture and engineering. The monument is located 14 miles south of St. Augustine via Highway A1A. (For an area map, see Castillo de San Marcos National Monument in this section.)

Matanzas (meaning "slaughters") Inlet received its name from the 1565 Spanish massacre of nearly 250 Frenchmen (see story of Fort Caroline National Memorial). The Spanish built a succession of wooden watchtowers there beginning in 1569 to look out for vessels approaching the inlet and St. Augustine. Following a British siege of St. Augustine in 1740, including the blockade of Matanzas Inlet, the governor decided to have a strong, stone tower built to guard the inlet. The fort was completed in 1742, twenty-one years before Spain ceded all of Florida to England. Florida was under Spanish domination again during thirty-seven years before cession to the United States in 1821.

A small visitor center on Anastasia Island is open from 8:30 A.M. to 5:30 P.M. (except Christmas Day). Here visitors will find a few exhibits explaining the history of the fort and can view an eight-minute-long video about the park. A free ferry carries passengers to the fort, where they can walk through the fort and learn of its history. A public beach area is directly across Highway A1A.

FACILITIES: Restrooms and drinking water are provided in the visitor center. Meals and lodging are nearby along Highway A1A.

CAMPING: No camping is permitted at the monument. Anastasia State Park, just south of St. Augustine, offers camping with tables, grills, water, flush toilets, and showers. A beautiful public beach is directly across the highway from the state park.

FISHING: The visitor center fronts the Matanzas River (a saltwater inlet) where fishing along the shoreline is permitted. Fishing for drum, whiting, and sheepshead is fair.

Canaveral National Seashore (next two pages)

GULF ISLANDS NATIONAL SEASHORE

1801 Gulf Breeze Parkway
Gulf Breeze, FL 32561
(904) 934–2600

Gulf Islands National Seashore is comprised of nearly 96,000 mostly underwater acres in Florida and Mississippi and was authorized in 1971. The seashore has both mainland units and offshore islands and keys with white sand beaches and historic forts and ruins. The Florida section includes six units near Pensacola; the Mississippi section is discussed in the Mississippi chapter of this book.

Although the great glaciers of the ice ages did not cover this section of the country, some experts theorize the glaciers strongly influenced Florida's coastline. According to one theory, as large masses of ice went through phases of buildup and melting, they had the effect of raising and lowering the sea level, thus forming the barrier islands of this park.

The park's most developed area is around Fort Pickens. Tours of the early-nineteenth-century fort are conducted daily March through October, and exhibits are available nearby at the park museum. Also in this section are nature trails, supervised swimming beaches, and fishing access. A swim beach is at Johnson Beach on Perdido Key. At Naval Live Oaks, visitors may walk through a heavily forested plantation of live oaks that was placed under protective management in 1828 to provide timbers used in building naval ships. The main visitor center for the national seashore in Florida is at Naval Live Oaks. On the mainland, on board the Pensacola Naval Air Station, a group of historic fortifications may be toured. A visitor contact station with exhibits, sales area, restrooms, and trails is located at the Fort Barrancas on board NAS *Pensacola.*

FACILITIES: A store with grocery items is located in the Fort Pickens area. Restrooms and drinking water are also available in this section. Picnic areas are at Naval Live Oaks, Fort Pickens, Santa Rosa, Okaloosa, Fort Barrancas, and Perdido Key. Snack bars are at Santa Rosa Key, Perdido Key, and in the Fort Pickens area.

CAMPING: In the Fort Pickens area, a campground (200 sites, one group campsite) offers tables, grills, water, flush toilets, coin laundry, sanitary station, and some sites with hookups.

FISHING: Surf fishing with possibilities for pompano, ling, mackerel, and sea trout is allowed along the beach where there are no swimmers. A saltwater fishing license is required in both Florida and Mississippi.

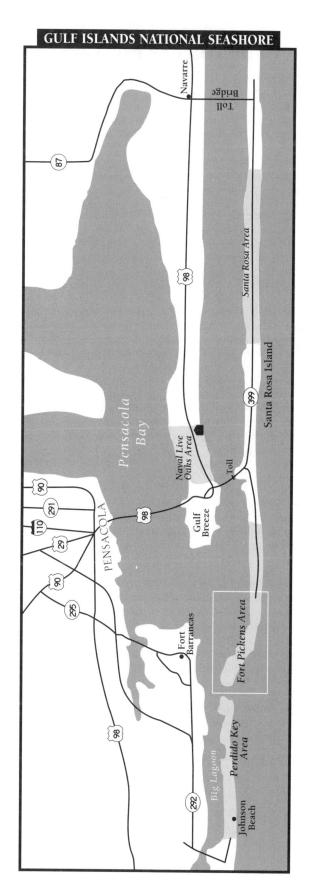

GULF ISLANDS NATIONAL SEASHORE

Navarre

Toll Bridge

87

98

399

Santa Rosa Area

Santa Rosa Island

Pensacola Bay

Naval Live Oaks Area

Toll

90

291

98

110

29

Gulf Breeze

PENSACOLA

90

295

Fort Barrancas

Fort Pickens Area

98

Big Lagoon

Perdido Key Area

292

Johnson Beach

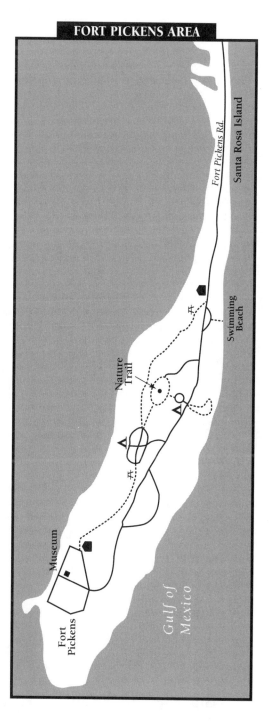

FORT PICKENS AREA

Fort Pickens Rd.

Santa Rosa Island

Swimming Beach

Nature Trail

Museum

Fort Pickens

Gulf of Mexico

TIMUCUAN ECOLOGICAL AND HISTORICAL PRESERVE

12713 Fort Caroline Road
Jacksonville, FL 32225
(904) 641–7155

The Timucuan Ecological and Historical Preserve was established in 1988 to preserve certain wetlands and historic and prehistoric sites in the St. Johns River Valley, Florida. The park, which comprises about 46,000 acres of saltwater and freshwater wetlands and associated upland islands, is in Jacksonville, centered on the St. Johns and Nassau rivers and the Intracoastal Waterway.

One of the newest National Park Service areas in Florida, the Timucuan Preserve protects significant coastal wetlands and over 400 years of history in northeast Florida. More than half of the preserve's acreage is wetlands. This sensitive ecological community provides a home and nursery for many varieties of fish and wildlife, stores water, helps control erosion, and serves as a natural filter for man-caused pollutants. The wetlands play host to several rare or endangered species, such as the West Indian manatee, colonial wood stork, peregrine falcon, bald eagle, and gopher tortoise.

The preserve contains significant historical sites representing important chapters in America's history. The sites include the archaeological remains of the first inhabitants of the preserve, the Timucuan Indians, for whom the preserve is named. Fort Caroline National Memorial (and main visitor center of the preserve), a separate National Park Service area within the boundaries of the preserve, commemorates early French and Spanish colonial settlement and struggles in the area.

Under continual development, the preserve also has operational areas at Kingsley Plantation, which is open daily and features a small visitor center and ranger-led guided tours and programs. Kingsley is the oldest plantation site in the state and includes remains of twenty-five of the original thirty-two slave quarters. The Theodore Roosevelt Area near Fort Caroline encompasses about 600 acres of Florida before development. Open daily, the area has hiking trails and weekend programs.

Much of the land within the boundaries of the preserve is privately owned, and federal development is limited. The management and success of this partnership park involves the assistance and cooperation of a variety of landowners. Visitors are reminded to respect private property owners' rights and to ask permission before visiting any land not designated as public.

FACILITIES: No food or lodging is available at the park. Drinking water and restrooms are at Fort Caroline and Kingsley Plantation, and restrooms are at the trailhead of the Theodore Roosevelt Area.

CAMPING: No camping facilities are available in the park. Nearby, Little Talbot Island State Park provides forty sites with electricity, tables, flush toilets, and hot showers. The park is located along the ocean on Highway A1A. Also close by Huguenot Memorial and Kathryn Abbey Hanna parks, both administered by the city of Jacksonville, provide camping, swimming, picnicking, and fishing.

FISHING: Fishing is not permitted in the ponds at the Theodore Roosevelt Area but is allowed along Chicopit Bay and elsewhere in the preserve subject to state regulations.

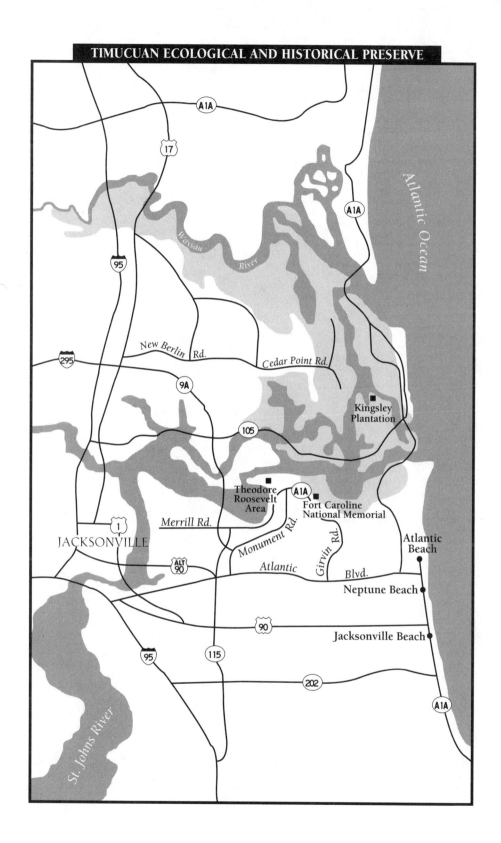

GEORGIA

STATE TOURIST INFORMATION
(800) 847–4842

ANDERSONVILLE NATIONAL HISTORIC SITE
Route 1, Box 800
Andersonville, GA 31711
(912) 924–0343

Andersonville National Historic Site comprises 475 acres and was authorized in 1970, incorporating both the national cemetery (still active) and the prison site as a unit of the National Park System. Andersonville today is a memorial to all who have been prisoners of war in defense of the United States. The site is located in southwestern Georgia, 9 miles northeast of Americus via State Highway 49. (The Jimmy Carter National Historic Site in Plains is just 21 miles southwest of Andersonville.)

Andersonville Prison (officially called Camp Sumter) was built in 1864 when Confederate leaders decided to move a large number of Federal prisoners from Richmond, Virginia, to an area of greater security and more abundant food. Although originally designed to hold 10,000 men, more than 32,000 prisoners were confined here in the summer of 1864. During fourteen months of existence, more than 12,000 men died here of disease, malnutrition, and exposure. A small structure (the "dead house") outside the prison was used to accumulate the bodies of prisoners that were to be carried by wagons to the cemetery for burial.

Monument in Chickamauga Chattanooga National Military Park (opposite page)

The park is open daily from 8:00 A.M. until 5:00 P.M. A visitor center, located at the main entrance, houses a museum with exhibits, an audio-visual presentation, and files containing the records of more than 45,000 Andersonville prisoners and POW burials, as well as recent burials. The POW museum is at the prison site and houses exhibits and audio-visual programs on POWs from all other wars. Sections of the stockade have been reconstructed. Park interpreters are on duty to answer visitor questions. A guide brochure and a cassette tape for touring by car are available at the visitor center.

FACILITIES: No food or lodging is at the historic site, but both are available in the vicinity. Restrooms and drinking water are in the visitor center and near the picnic area.

CAMPING: No camping is permitted at the site, but there are several local campgrounds available. Georgia Veterans Memorial State Park, between Americus and Cordele on U.S. 280, offers campsites with tables, grills, flush toilets, and showers.

CHATTAHOOCHEE RIVER NATIONAL RECREATION AREA

1978 Island Ford Parkway
Atlanta, GA 30350
(770) 399–8070

Chattahoochee River National Recreation Area was authorized by Congress in 1978 to preserve a series of land units along 48 miles of the Chattahoochee River for natural, scenic, recreational, and historical values. Presently, 4,243 acres are under management of the National Park Service; the proposed total acreage is 6,800. The Chattahoochee River National Recreation Area is in northern Georgia, beginning directly below Buford Dam and terminating 10 miles north of Atlanta.

The Chattahoochee River is generally cold, clear, and slow-moving as it flows 436 miles from the mountains of northern Georgia to the Gulf of Mexico. Surrounded by colorful plants and trees, the river corridor provides opportunities for fishing, hiking, floating, picnicking, and just relaxing. The banks and meadows surrounding the river support typical wildlife found in this region such as beaver, chipmunk, fox, raccoon, and squirrel.

The Chattahoochee River National Recreation Area is rated Class I and/or II in river difficulty. This section of the Chattahoochee has a few riffles, small waves, and rapids, with some obstructions (rocks and downed trees) that require minimum scouting and some maneuvering ability. Rafts and canoes can be rented from the park concessioner (Chattahoochee Outdoor Center at Johnson Ferry and Powers Island units) or from commercial entrepreneurs outside the park. A shuttle service for floaters is available through the park concessioner for Johnson Ferry, Powers Island, and Paces Mill units (404–395–6851).

There are a number of trails in the various units of the recreation area. In the Cochran Shoals Unit, a fitness trail has exercise stations and is a popular jogging path. In the Vickery Creek Unit, trails lead to a gorge with ruins of pre–Civil War textile mills and a dam. On the west side of the Sope Creek Unit, a loop trail leads to old homesites, a small fishing lake, and ruins of a paper mill.

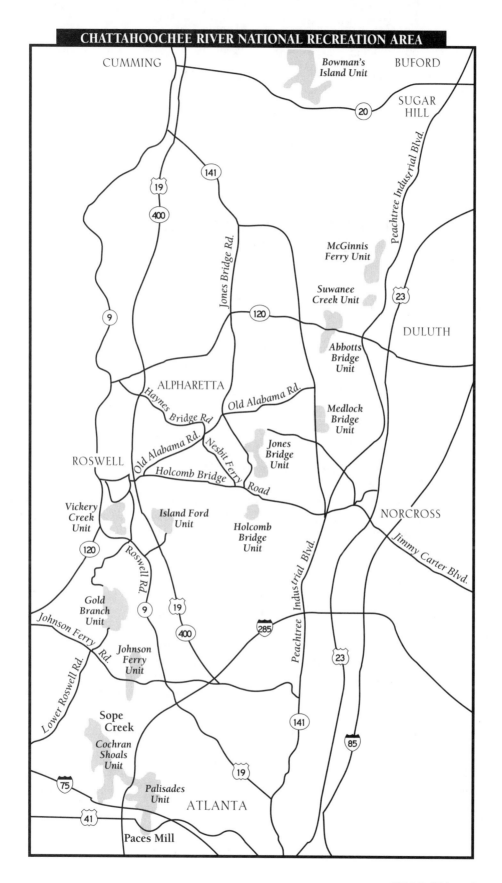

FACILITIES: Food and lodging are available in the metropolitan areas surrounding the park.

CAMPING: Overnight camping in the recreation area is not permitted. U.S. Corps of Engineers campgrounds are located around Lake Sidney Lanier. Other nearby campgrounds are located at Stone Mountain Park and Georgia state parks.

FISHING: The Chattahoochee River provides catches of bream, bass, catfish, and trout. A current Georgia license with trout stamp is required.

CHICKAMAUGA AND CHATTANOOGA NATIONAL MILITARY PARK

P.O. Box 2128
Fort Oglethorpe, GA 30742
(706) 866–9241

Chickamauga and Chattanooga National Military Park comprises 8,100 acres and was established in 1890 to preserve two Civil War battlefields on which Confederate troops tried to stop the Union advance toward Atlanta. The park's various separate units are located in northwestern Georgia and southern Tennessee, in and around the city of Chattanooga.

Following the battle of Stones River in January 1863, Federal forces began preparations for an attack on the Confederate rail center at Chattanooga. To avoid the entrenched Confederate army, the Union general flanked the city and forced the withdrawal of Southern troops. Upon receiving reinforcements, however, 66,000 Confederates met and defeated the Federals at Chickamauga. Two months later, with 36,000 additional men, Union troops under the command of Ulysses Grant were able to drive Confederate forces off Lookout Mountain and Missionary Ridge and take control of Chattanooga. Chattanooga then became Sherman's base for his march to Atlanta.

At Chickamauga Battlefield, a visitor center on U.S. 27 contains exhibits, a gun museum, a twenty-six-minute multimedia program (fee charged), and leaflets for a 7-mile self-guiding auto tour. Tour-stop markers, monuments, and plaques are located along the road. A walking tour on Lookout Mountain will direct visitors to the most important points in this section of the park. Near Point Park, the Ochs Museum and Overlook provides exhibits and pictures of the battle. A visitor center in this section of the park has a seven-minute audio presentation on James Walker's painting *The Battle of Lookout Mountain* and an assortment of publications. Park rangers give guided walks, historical talks, and demonstrations during summer months.

FACILITIES: Food and lodging are available in Chattanooga. Restrooms and water are in the visitor centers.

CAMPING: No camping is permitted in the park. Georgia's Cloudland Canyon State Park, approximately 20 miles southwest of Chattanooga via Interstate 59 and State Highway 136, offers camping facilities.

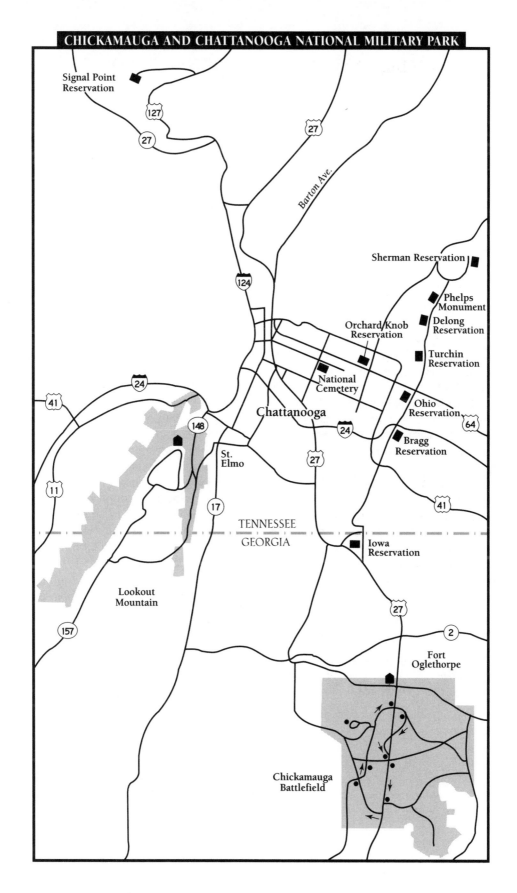

CUMBERLAND ISLAND NATIONAL SEASHORE

P.O. Box 806
St. Marys, GA 31558
(912) 882–4335

Cumberland Island National Seashore was established in 1972 to preserve 36,545 acres of freshwater lakes, magnificent beaches and dunes, and saltwater marshes on one of Georgia's largest coastal islands. The park is located in southeastern Georgia, approximately 30 miles north of Jacksonville, Florida, via Interstate 95 and Georgia Highway 40. Access is only by ferry from the town of St. Marys, Georgia.

Cumberland Island (named after an English duke) is a sandy island measuring 16 miles long by 3 miles wide at its widest point. The island is separated from the Georgia mainland by a mile or more of salt marsh and river. The hardwood forest in the central part of the island contrasts with the white sand beaches on its eastern perimeter. The seashore contains an outstanding selection of wildlife, including deer, pelicans, and loggerhead turtles.

Headquarters is on the mainland in St. Marys. Small visitor centers are at Sea Camp Dock and Dungeness Dock on the island. The ferry departs St. Marys at 9:00 A.M. and 11:45 A.M. daily except Tuesday and Wednesday (every day during peak season). No cars, bicycles, or pets are permitted. Return trips for the 45-minute ride are at 10:15 A.M. and 4:45 P.M. Reservations are strongly recommended, because the first departing and last returning runs are generally fully booked. Visitors willing to take their chances may arrive early and sign up on a standby list. For reservations call (912) 882–4336. If you take the 9:00 A.M. boat you will have about six hours on the island. The 11:45 A.M. boat will give you about four hours on the island.

A typical trip to the island includes a short walk to the ruins of the Dungeness Mansion (built by Thomas Carnegie in the late nineteenth century), a hike along the beach (swimming allowed but no lifeguards), and a walk back to the dock. It is best to take the early boat over to the island and the late boat back to the mainland if you wish to do anything other than breeze through sights on the south end of the island.

FACILITIES: Other than restrooms and drinking water, there are no public facilities on the island. Motels and restaurants are available near St. Marys. If you plan to spend the day on Cumberland Island, you should take your own lunch.

CAMPING: Sea Camp Beach (sixteen sites, two group camps) has restrooms, showers, and drinking water. Reservations are necessary. Four primitive backcountry campgrounds require a permit. All have well water that should be boiled prior to drinking.

FISHING: Surf fishing yields red bass, spotted trout, and bluefish. Cumberland Sound offers croaker, drum, trout, and red bass. No license is required for saltwater fishing.

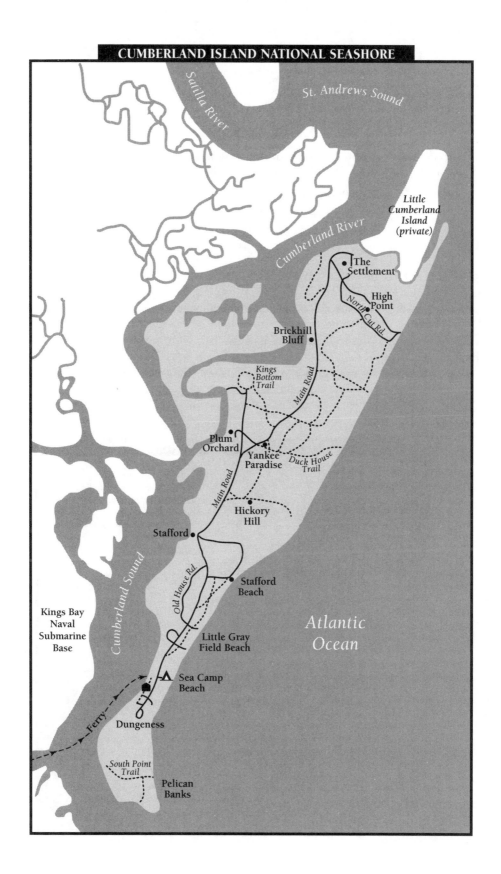

Satilla River

St. Andrews Sound

Cumberland River

Little
Cumberland
Island
(private)

The
Settlement

High
Point

North Cut Rd.

Brickhill
Bluff

Kings
Bottom
Trail

Main Road

Plum
Orchard

Yankee
Paradise

Duck House
Trail

Main Road

Hickory
Hill

Stafford

Old House Rd.

Stafford
Beach

Kings Bay
Naval
Submarine
Base

Cumberland Sound

Atlantic
Ocean

Little Gray
Field Beach

Sea Camp
Beach

Ferry

Dungeness

South Point
Trail

Pelican
Banks

FORT FREDERICA NATIONAL MONUMENT

Route 9, Box 286-C
St. Simons Island, GA 31522
(912) 638–3639

Fort Frederica National Monument was authorized in 1936 to preserve the remains of an eighteenth-century British fort and town built during the Anglo-Spanish struggle for control of what is now the southeastern United States. The park is located in southeastern Georgia, 12 miles northeast of Brunswick on St. Simons Island via the Brunswick–St. Simons toll causeway.

The settlement of Frederica was established in 1736 as an English answer to Spanish operations in the New World. In addition to building a fort overlooking the inland waterway, Frederica's citizens also laid out a town that soon included permanent homes and shops. A regiment of 650 British soldiers, sent to protect the town, was able to turn back a Spanish invasion force in 1742. The disbanding of the regiment in 1749, combined with a major fire in 1758, spelled the end for Frederica.

The park is open daily from 8:00 A.M. to 5:00 P.M., and a visitor center is open daily from 9:00 A.M. to 5:00 P.M. (extended in summer), containing museum exhibits and a twenty-five-minute film on the settlement. The remains of the town and fort are visible, and exhibits and

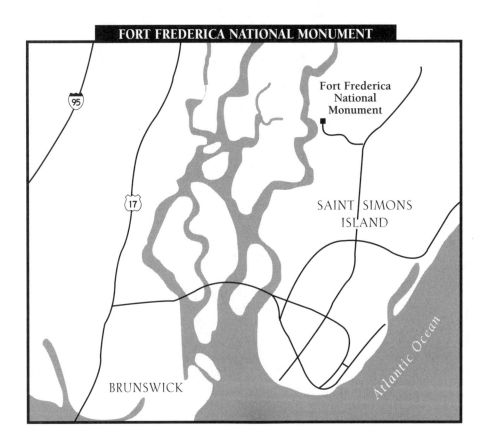

audio messages are located throughout the site. During summer months, park rangers offer conducted tours, talks, and demonstrations. The grounds have many live oak trees covered with Spanish moss, making a leisurely walk through the town site a pleasant experience.

A detached unit of the park, the Bloody Marsh Battle Site (open daily from 9:00 A.M. to 4:00 P.M.) marks the general area where outnumbered British troops ambushed and defeated a Spanish column in 1742. This battle halted an attempt to attack Frederica and proved to be a turning point in the Spanish invasion of Georgia. The site is 6 miles south of Frederica and is open daily.

FACILITIES: Food and lodging are available on St. Simons and in Brunswick and Jekyll. Modern restrooms, water, and a soft-drink machine are in the park's visitor center.

CAMPING: No camping is permitted within the monument grounds. Jekyll Island State Park offers camping facilities 13 miles southeast of Brunswick via State Highway 50.

FISHING: Fishing is permitted within the monument grounds. Inquire at the visitor center for local regulations.

FORT PULASKI NATIONAL MONUMENT
Box 30757
Savannah, GA 31410
(912) 786–5787

Fort Pulaski was proclaimed a national monument in 1924 to preserve a nineteenth-century fort that first demonstrated the ineffectiveness of old-style masonry fortifications when faced with rifled cannon. The 5,615-acre monument is located in southeastern Georgia, 17 miles east of Savannah via U.S. 80.

Construction on Fort Pulaski (named after Polish Count Casimir Pulaski, who was mortally wounded in Savannah during the American Revolution) began in 1829 as part of a coastal fortification system adopted after the War of 1812. The fort was completed in 1847 but never garrisoned by federal troops. On the eve of the Civil War, it was seized by several detachments of Georgia troops. Federal troops from Hilton Head Island were sent by ship to nearby Tybee Island, where they established artillery emplacements 1 mile from Pulaski. Bullet-shaped shells fired by the experimental rifled cannon were able to penetrate Fort Pulaski's walls, thus forcing the garrison to surrender in April of 1862, after a thirty-hour bombardment.

The monument is open daily except Christmas Day from 8:30 A.M. to 5:30 P.M., with extended hours in the summer. A visitor center with exhibits and tour information is near the fort entrance. The fort contains various exhibits on soldier life and artillery in the Civil War. Nature trails are available for hiking, and a memorial to John Wesley, who landed on this island in 1736, is located just north of the fort.

FACILITIES: No food or lodging is available at the monument. Restrooms and water are inside the fort and visitor center. A picnic area with tables, grills, restrooms, and water is available on a first-come basis.

CAMPING: No camping is permitted at the monument. Skidway Island State Park provides camping facilities a short distance southeast of Savannah.

FISHING: There is saltwater fishing from the shore of the island and a nearby pier. Boat ramp facilities are also available.

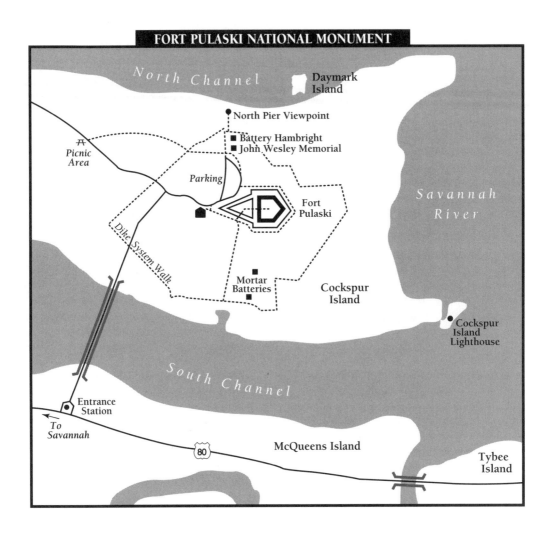

JIMMY CARTER NATIONAL HISTORIC SITE

Plains, GA 31780
(912) 824–3413

Jimmy Carter National Historic Site was authorized in 1987 to preserve some of the sites and structures associated with the life and presidency of Jimmy Carter and to interpret the history and culture of the small rural town that gave the nation the thirty-ninth president of the United States. The historic site is located in southwest Georgia, 10 miles west of Americus on U.S. Highway 280. Visitors interested in Civil War history should make a point to visit nearby Andersonville National Historic Site, 21 miles northeast of Plains.

More than any president in recent years, James Earl Carter, Jr., is closely identified with his hometown. Jimmy Carter was born in Plains, Georgia, on October 1, 1924. The eldest of four children, he grew up on a farm a short distance outside town. He graduated from Plains High School (closed in 1979) and attended Georgia Southwestern College (Americus, Georgia) and Georgia Institute of Technology before graduating from the U.S. Naval Academy in 1946. After his father's death, Carter resigned from the Navy and returned home to help run the family farm and the family seed and farm-supply store. He entered politics in 1963 as a state senator and was later elected governor of Georgia before being elected president of the United States in 1976. Carter was defeated in his 1980 presidential reelection bid by Ronald Reagan. The ex-president remains involved with the Carter Presidential Center in Atlanta and with several charitable organizations, including Habitat for Humanity, and he continues to spend a portion of his time in Plains. President Carter teaches Sunday School at Maranatha Baptist Church when he is in town. The public is welcome. The monthly schedule for this popular event can be obtained by calling the railroad depot.

The park is open daily from 9:00 A.M. to 5:00 P.M. The railroad depot in the downtown area serves as the historic site's visitor center and contains a small museum, an audiovisual presentation, and a book sales outlet. A guide brochure and rental cassette tape for touring by car are available at the depot. Tours are available from the Plain Peanut Store. The historic site consists of the railroad depot, which served as Carter's 1976 campaign headquarters; Plains High School; Carter's boyhood home; and the present Carter residence. All park buildings other than the railroad depot are currently closed to the public due to ongoing rehabilitation projects.

FACILITIES: Food, lodging, and other public facilities are available in Plains. Restrooms and drinking water are in the visitor center. A picnic area is in the town park.

CAMPING: A private campground with hookups is a short distance east of town on U.S. 280. Also see the camping section under Andersonville National Historic Site (Georgia).

KENNESAW MOUNTAIN NATIONAL BATTLEFIELD PARK

900 Kennesaw Mountain Drive
Kennesaw, GA 30152
(770) 427–4686

Kennesaw Mountain Battlefield Park comprises 2,884 acres and was authorized in 1917 to commemorate the site of two major Civil War engagements in 1864 during Sherman's march toward Atlanta. The battlefield is located in northwestern Georgia, 3 miles north of Marietta, a short distance off U.S. 41 and Interstate 75.

In May of 1864, General William Sherman launched an army of nearly 100,000 soldiers toward the Confederate rail and manufacturing center of Atlanta. In his way were 50,000 Southern troops in the vicinity of Kennesaw Mountain. After an initial battle at Kolb's Farm, two unsuccessful Union attacks on June 27 resulted in an extremely heavy casualty toll. Sherman then decided to flank the Confederate position, which made the Southerners abandon Kennesaw Mountain to protect their supply line to Atlanta.

The visitor center contains exhibits and a ten-minute slide program. Additional exhibits are located on the summit of Big Kennesaw Mountain, at Cheatham Hall, and near Kolb Farm. At Kolb Farm, the log house has been restored to its appearance during the Civil War but is not open to the public. A drive to the top of the mountain provides a panoramic view of the area. Hiking trails of 2, 5, 10, and 16 miles begin near the visitor center. The short trail is a self-guiding history-and-nature trail. A brochure for a walking-driving tour of historic Marietta is available in the park's visitor center.

FACILITIES: No lodging or food service is available in the park. Restrooms and drinking water are in the visitor center. Restaurants, motels, and a grocery store are a few miles outside the park entrance.

CAMPING: No camping is permitted in the park. A private campground is a few miles outside the park entrance, and a number of U.S. Army Corps of Engineers campgrounds are nearby on Lake Allatoona. One especially nice unit is Clark Creek South (tables, grills, hot showers, fishing, no hookups) about 15 miles north on Interstate 75; take exit 121 and then go 2 miles northeast.

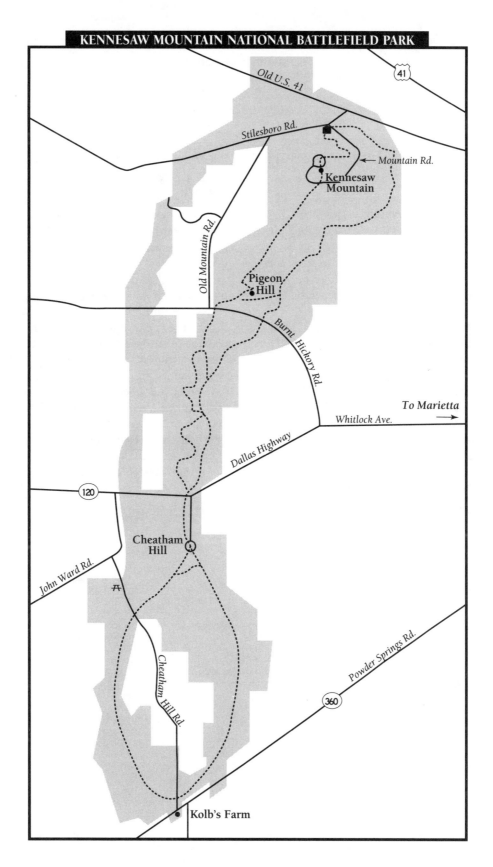

KENNESAW MOUNTAIN NATIONAL BATTLEFIELD PARK

Old U.S. 41

41

Stilesboro Rd.

Mountain Rd.

Kennesaw
Mountain

Old Mountain Rd.

Pigeon
Hill

Burnt Hickory Rd.

To Marietta

Whitlock Ave.

Dallas Highway

120

Cheatham
Hill

John Ward Rd.

Powder Springs Rd.

360

Cheatham Hill Rd.

Kolb's Farm

MARTIN LUTHER KING, JR., NATIONAL HISTORIC SITE

National Park Service
522 Auburn Avenue, N.E.
Atlanta, GA 30312
(404) 331–3920

Martin Luther King, Jr., National Historic Site comprises twenty-four acres and was established in 1980 to preserve a two-block neighborhood containing the birthplace, church, and grave of famous civil rights activist Dr. Martin Luther King, Jr. The site and preservation district contain a total of ninety-two acres. The park is in downtown Atlanta, along Auburn Avenue just off Interstate 75/85.

Martin Luther King, Jr., was born on January 15, 1929, in Atlanta, Georgia. His father, Martin Luther King, Sr., was pastor of nearby Ebenezer Baptist Church. Martin entered Atlanta's Morehouse College at age fifteen and became an ordained Baptist minister in 1947 when he was only seventeen years old. After moving to Montgomery, Alabama, as pastor to a Baptist church, King began leading the local black community in the nonviolent struggle for civil rights. This leadership was to continue throughout the South and resulted in passage of the Civil Rights Act of 1964 and the Voting Rights Act of 1965. Dr. King was awarded the Nobel Peace Prize in 1964. In 1968, at age thirty-nine, Martin Luther King, Jr. was shot and killed in Memphis, Tennessee.

The historic site encompasses a two-block area that includes Dr. King's home, church, and memorial grave site. The grave site is on property adjacent to Ebenezer Baptist Church, where Freedom Hall houses the Martin Luther King, Jr., Center for Non-Violent Social Change. Around the historic site, a preservation district includes residential and commercial sections of Sweet Auburn, the black community into which Dr. King was born and that had a significant impact on his life and on his struggle for civil rights.

FACILITIES: Food and lodging are available nearby in downtown Atlanta.

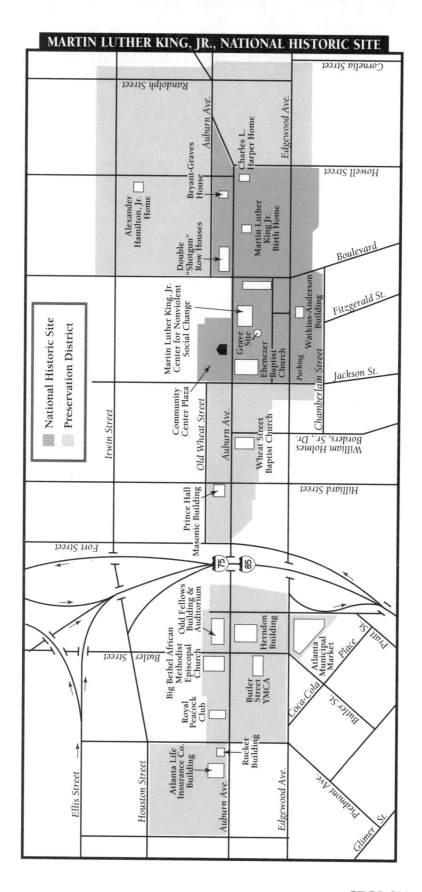

OCMULGEE NATIONAL MONUMENT

1207 Emery Highway
Macon, GA 31201
(912) 752–8257

Ocmulgee National Monument comprises 702 acres and was authorized in 1934 to preserve the remains of mounds and a settlement that exhibit the evolution of Indian culture in the southern United States. The monument is located in central Georgia, on the eastern edge of the city of Macon. Exit Interstate 75 at Interstate 16 and take U.S. 80 east. A small detached area of the park located south of Macon is currently open to the public by permit only.

Ocmulgee National Monument has a rich history of Indian culture. Nomadic ice-age hunters camped on the site more than 12,000 years ago. From the hunters and gatherers who lived here for thousands of years, a transition to gardening and then farming began between 1000 and 500 B.C. In A.D. 900, a large town with an economy based on corn agriculture was constructed within the present boundaries of the park. These people built large temple mounds and earth lodges. After 200 years, the village declined. Around A.D. 1350, a palisaded village with two mounds was built in the nearby Ocmulgee River swamps. It continued to exist until after the Spaniard Hernando De Soto's expedition entered the middle-Georgia area in A.D. 1540. The Mound Builders' culture was altered forever by the coming of European colonists. The Mound Builders' descendants, the Muskogee (Creek) Indians, were removed to Oklahoma during the Trail of Tears period.

The monument is open daily except Christmas Day and New Year's Day from 9:00 A.M. to 5:00 P.M. The visitor center contains an archaeological museum, and park personnel are on duty to answer questions. A short movie, "People of the Macon Plateau," is shown periodically each day. A ceremonial earthlodge, reconstructed on an original 1,000-year-old floor, is open on a self-guided basis. Ranger-programs are available by reservation. Mounds may be reached via a ½-mile-long paved road or walking trails. Opelofa Nature Trail winds along Walnut Creek, where swamp and forest ecology may be observed. The monument has more than 5 miles of walking trails.

FACILITIES: No food or lodging is available within the monument grounds. Most services can be found a short distance outside the entrance. Drinking water and modern restrooms are located at the visitor center, and a picnic area with tables and shade is by the main parking area.

CAMPING: No camping is permitted in the park. Indian Springs State Park (via U.S. 23) and High Falls State Park (via Interstate 75) are each approximately 35 miles northwest of Macon and offer camping, fishing, and swimming. Another campground is at Tobesofkee Lake, about 8 miles from the monument.

FISHING: A small pond near the Opelofa Nature Trail contains bluegill and crappie; bass and bluegill may be found in Walnut Creek. A park permit and a Georgia license are required. The permit may be obtained without charge at the visitor center.

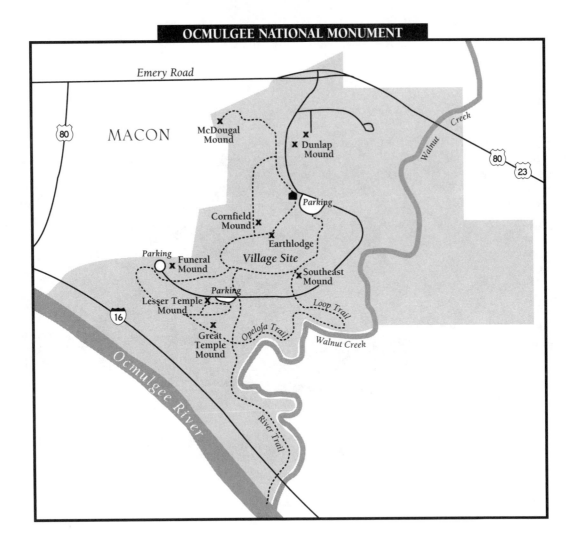

Monument to Marquette, Jolliet, and their Native American guides (Courtesy John M. Elliott, Forest Preserve District of Cook County)

ILLINOIS

CHICAGO PORTAGE NATIONAL HISTORIC SITE

c/o Cook County Forest Preserve
536 North Harlem Avenue
River Forest, IL 60305
(312) 261–8400, (708) 366–9420, (708) 771–1190
TDD, (800) 870–3666

Chicago Portage National Historic Site comprises ninety-one non-federal acres and was designated an affiliated area of the National Park Service in 1952 to help preserve a portage used by Native Americans and explorers as a link between the Great Lakes and the Mississippi River. The historic site is just west of the Chicago city limits, about ¼ mile south of U.S. 66 (Joliet Road) on Harlem Avenue.

The Chicago Portage was a short, low divide that served as an important route between the Great Lakes and the Mississippi River for generations of Indians and explorers. In 1673, Native Americans directed explorers Jolliet and Marquette up the Illinois and Des Plaines rivers to Portage Creek, where the travelers were required to portage their canoes to the south branch of the Chicago River. With completion of the Illinois and Michigan Canal in 1848, the Chicago River was connected with the Illinois River. The portage trail of these explorers, fur traders, and Native Americans that was a major factor in development of America's interior eventually became Route 66 and Joliet Road.

A monument and concourse area recognizing explorers Marquette and Jolliet and their Indian guides are just off Harlem Avenue at Chicago Portage Woods. Parking is available at the

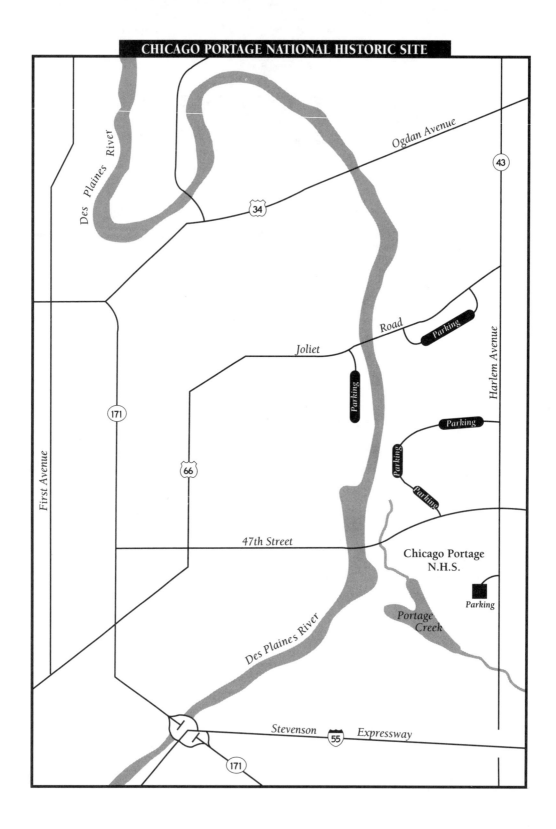

CHICAGO PORTAGE NATIONAL HISTORIC SITE

monument, where visitors can view a portion of Portage Creek. Ottawa Trail Woods, north of Forty-seventh Street, contains a ridge where visitors can walk beside the site of Laughton's Trading Post to Laughton's Ford. The Forest Preserve District in which the historic site is located offers recreational facilities including golf courses, bicycle trails, horseback riding trails, and nature centers.

FACILITIES: No food or lodging is available at the site, but both are located nearby. Picnic areas are north of Forty-seventh Street.

CAMPING: No camping is permitted.

FISHING: Fishing is available nearby at the Forest Preserve District. An Illinois license is required.

ILLINOIS AND MICHIGAN CANAL NATIONAL HERITAGE CORRIDOR

15709 South Independence Blvd.
Lockport, IL 60441
(815) 740–2047

Illinois and Michigan Canal National Heritage Corridor was authorized in 1984 to retain, enhance, and interpret the historic, natural, recreational, and economic resources of a land corridor that was instrumental in the opening of the West and the growth of Chicago. The corridor is located in northern Illinois along a narrow strip of land that begins in Chicago and follows the Des Plaines and Illinois rivers to the town of La Salle.

Land comprising the Illinois and Michigan Canal National Heritage Corridor has been used for centuries as a link between the East Coast and mid-America. The movement of Native Americans along this strip of land was recorded in 1673 by French explorers Jolliet and Marquette when they returned north after proving the Mississippi River flowed south to the Gulf of Mexico. Although trade over the portage route had substantially increased by the late 1700s, construction of a canal to connect Lake Michigan with the Illinois River did not begin until 1836. Financial difficulties delayed the canal's opening until 1848.

The canal was made 6 feet deep, 60 feet wide at water level, and 36 feet wide at the bottom along a main route 96 miles long. Fifteen locks lifted or lowered boats through the canal. Completion of the canal caused commerce to and from Chicago to increase until the city surpassed St. Louis as the Midwest's hub of commerce and population. Other towns along the canal also prospered. By the mid-1800s, rail transportation had captured most of the passengers and, to the dismay of the canal boat operators, much of the freight traffic that previously would have been shipped on the canal.

The National Heritage Corridor offers a multitude of things to see and do. Visitors can stroll through a small town, visit museums, tour a large scientific research laboratory, walk a trail following the canal towpath, and visit a restored lock-tender's house. There are eight visitor centers within the corridor: Isle a la Cache Museum in Romeoville, Illinois, Michigan Canal Visitor Center in Lockport, Will County Historical Society Museum in Lockport, Will-Joliet Bicenten-

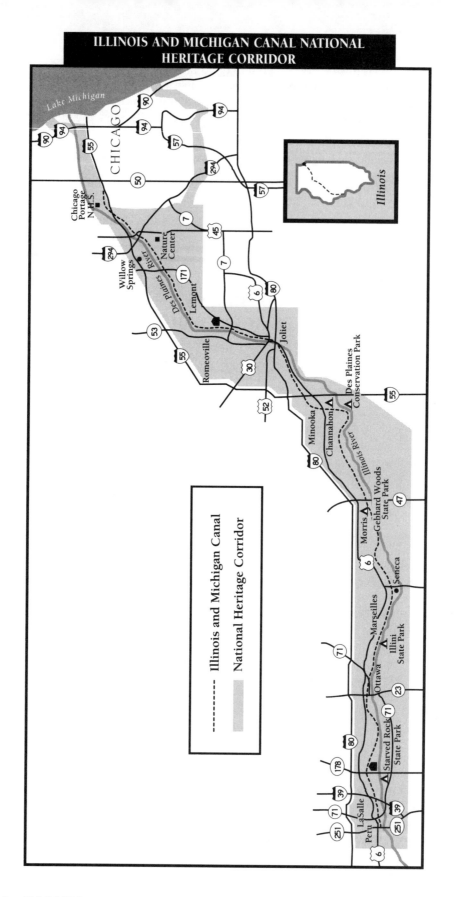

ILLINOIS AND MICHIGAN CANAL NATIONAL HERITAGE CORRIDOR

Illinois and Michigan Canal

National Heritage Corridor

nial Park in Joliet, Little Red Schoolhouse Nature Center in Willow Springs, Goose Lake Prairie State Natural Area in Morris, Illinois and Michigan Canal State Trail (Gebhard Wood Access) in Morris, and Illinois Waterway Visitor Center west of Ottawa.

FACILITIES: Food and lodging are available all along the corridor.

CAMPING: Public camping is available at Starved Rock State Park (133 spaces, full hookups, showers) southeast of La Salle, Illini State Park (ninety-five spaces, flush toilets) near Marseilles, and Des Plaines Conservation Area (twenty-four spaces, pit toilets) south of Channahon. Two campgrounds for backpackers and bicyclists are on the Illinois and Michigan Canal State Trail in Morris and in Channahon.

LINCOLN HOME NATIONAL HISTORIC SITE
413 South Eighth Street
Springfield, IL 62701
(217) 492–4150

This site, which contains approximately twelve acres, was established in 1972 to preserve the only home owned by Abraham Lincoln. The site is located between Seventh and Ninth streets in downtown Springfield, Illinois. A parking lot (fee) for the site is on Seventh Street.

Although Abraham Lincoln was born in Kentucky and spent his youth in Indiana, he was married and lived most of his adult life in Springfield, Illinois. Beginning in 1834, he represented Sangamon County in the Illinois General Assembly, and in 1847 he began serving his one term in the U.S. Congress. In between, he was married in 1842 and bought his first and only home for $1,500 in 1844. He and his family lived there until his election to the presidency in 1860.

The house was built in 1839 and has been restored to its 1860s appearance. Although the Lincolns sold most of their household goods in 1861, the home has since been furnished with some of the furniture actually used by the family. The historic site includes four blocks surrounding the house, and the exteriors of neighboring homes and buildings are being restored to their 1860s appearances. Free tickets for a tour of the home are distributed daily at the visitor center on a first-come basis. Bus groups are required to make reservations through the Springfield Convention and Visitors Bureau (800–545–7300).

Within walking distance of the site are the Old State Capitol (free admission), where Lincoln delivered his "House Divided" speech; the Lincoln–Herndon Law Offices (fee charged), where he practiced law; and the railway station where he delivered his farewell speech before leaving for Washington. Also in Springfield is the Lincoln Tomb in Oak Ridge Cemetery. Nearby is Lincoln's New Salem State Historic Site, where a reconstructed village marks the site of Lincoln's early years in Illinois. A guide to historic attractions in Springfield is available in the visitor center.

FACILITIES: No food or lodging is available at the site, but all types of services are provided within walking distance. Drinking water and modern restrooms are provided at the site.

CAMPING: No camping is permitted at the site. Lincoln's New Salem Historic Site, 20 miles northwest of Springfield near Petersburg on Highway 97, offers tables, grills, flush toilets, and showers.

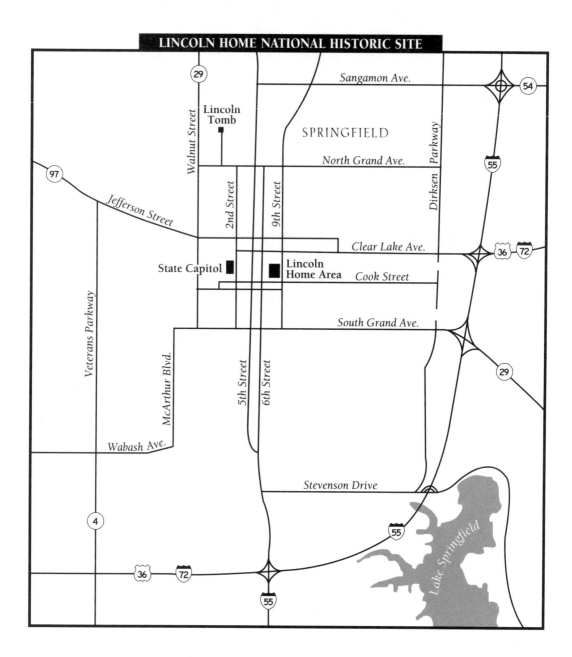

LINCOLN HOME NATIONAL HISTORIC SITE

SPRINGFIELD

Sangamon Ave.

Lincoln Tomb

North Grand Ave.

Walnut Street

Dirksen Parkway

Jefferson Street

2nd Street

9th Street

Clear Lake Ave.

State Capitol ■ ■ **Lincoln Home Area**   Cook Street

Veterans Parkway

McArthur Blvd.

5th Street

6th Street

South Grand Ave.

Wabash Ave.

Stevenson Drive

Lake Springfield

INDIANA

STATE TOURIST INFORMATION
(800) 289–6646

GEORGE ROGERS CLARK NATIONAL HISTORICAL PARK
401 South Second Street
Vincennes, IN 47591
(812) 882–1776

George Rogers Clark National Historical Park comprises twenty-six acres. It was authorized in 1966 to commemorate the 1779 seizure of Fort Sackville from the British by Lt. Col. George Rogers Clark. The memorial is located in southwestern Indiana, 53 miles south of Terre Haute, in the city of Vincennes. The park entrance is on Second Street, 4 blocks south of the downtown area.

In the spring and summer of 1778, George Rogers Clark and his small army from Virginia traveled down the Ohio River to attack British posts north of the Ohio. Capturing the villages of Kaskaskia and Cahokia, Clark subsequently led a 180-mile winter march across the flooded Illinois country to take British-held Fort Sackville in Vincennes. This victory, made possible with the aid of the region's French-speaking population, helped bring the Old Northwest under American control. In 1800, Vincennes was named the capital of the Indiana Territory. William Henry Harrison, who would become the ninth president of the United States, was appointed the territory's first governor.

The memorial, dedicated by President Franklin Roosevelt in 1936, stands on the site of old Fort Sackville. Nearby, St. Francis Xavier Church is a reminder of the early roots established by the French Catholic Church. The park also preserves approaches to Abraham Lincoln Memorial Bridge and the Buffalo Trace crossing of the Wabash River into Illinois. At the other end of

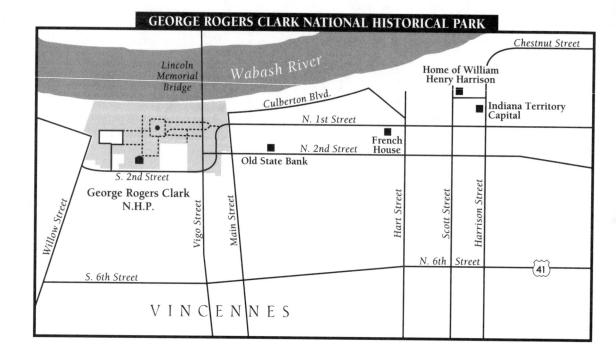

GEORGE ROGERS CLARK NATIONAL HISTORICAL PARK

town is the old territorial capitol building, an early newspaper printing office, and the home of Governor William Henry Harrison.

FACILITIES: Restrooms and drinking water are provided at the visitor center. Food and lodging are available nearby.

CAMPING: No camping is permitted in the park. Public camping is available at Ouabache Trails Park, located 3 miles north of Vincennes on the Wabash River.

Indiana Dunes National Lakeshore (opposite page)

INDIANA DUNES NATIONAL LAKESHORE

1100 North Mineral Springs Road
Porter, IN 46304
(219) 926–7561

Indiana Dunes was authorized by Congress in 1966. Today, it preserves over 13,000 acres of magnificent dunes, beaches, bogs, marshes, and prairie remnants. The park includes an 1830 restored homestead and a turn-of-the-century farm. The lakeshore is located in northwestern Indiana, approximately 40 miles southeast of Chicago via Interstate 80/94. It may be reached by the Chicago South Shore and South Bend Railroad.

In the Indiana Dunes area, visitors will stand on a flat bit of earth on which two things have been piled: sand and rocky glacial till. The piles of till, called moraines, tell the story of advancing glaciers that deposited this rocky earth in conveyor-belt fashion. The sand piles, called dunes, tell the story of a lake that shrank by stages after the glaciers disappeared. The glaciers pushed south, while the lake receded north.

The park's visitor center, located at U.S. 12 and Kemil Road in Porter County, Indiana, is open from 8:00 A.M. until 5:00 P.M. daily (8:00 A.M. to 6:00 P.M. in summer) except Thanksgiving, Christmas, and New Year's Day. The center offers information, an audiovisual program, nature walks, activity schedules, restrooms, and a bookstore. A visitor center serving the Bailly Homestead and Chellberg Farm, on North Mineral Springs Road, is open daily during summer and during weekends throughout the year.

Swimming beaches with parking and lifeguards are at West Beach (showers, bathrooms); Kemil Road (bathrooms); Central Avenue (bathrooms); and Mt. Baldy (no lifeguards, bathrooms). Twenty-four hiking trails throughout the park provide access to historical structures, dunes, woods, beaches, prairie, marshes, and the Little Calumet River. The Bailly area contains the Joseph Bailly homestead, a historic cemetery, and the restored Chellberg farm.

FACILITIES: No lodging is provided by the park service, but food concessions are at West Beach and Mount Baldy. Lodging and restaurants are available in nearby communities.

CAMPING: A campground (fifty conventional sites, twenty-five walk-in sites) with flush toilets and showers is at the national lakeshore at U.S. 12 and Broadway near Beverly Shores. A campground is also located in Indiana Dunes State Park, which is within the national lakeshore boundaries but is separately administered.

FISHING: Fishing is permitted within the national lakeshore. A current Indiana fishing license is required.

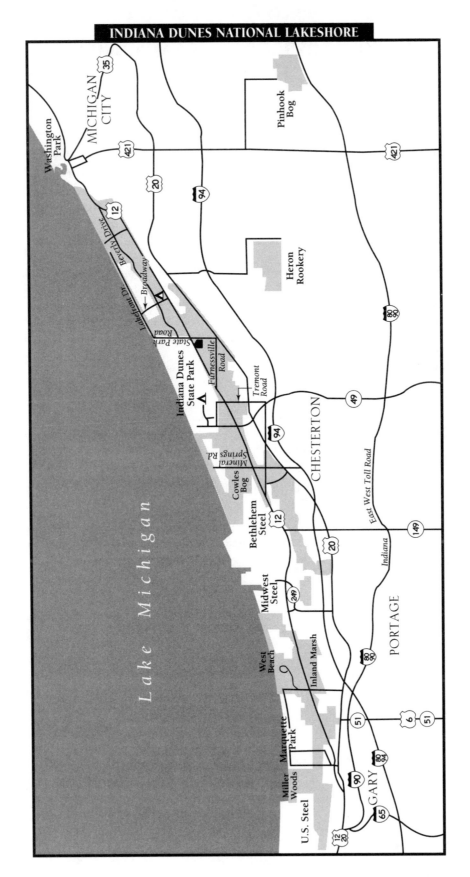

INDIANA DUNES NATIONAL LAKESHORE

Lake Michigan

MICHIGAN CITY

Washington Park

Pinhook Bog

Heron Rookery

Beverly Drive

Broadway

Lakefront Dr.

State Park Road

Indiana Dunes State Park

Furnessville Road

Tremont Road

Mineral Springs Rd.

Cowles Bog

CHESTERTON

Bethlehem Steel

East West Toll Road

Indiana

Midwest Steel

West Beach

Inland Marsh

PORTAGE

Marquette Park

Miller Woods

GARY

U.S. Steel

LINCOLN BOYHOOD NATIONAL MEMORIAL

P.O. Box 1816
Lincoln City, IN 47552
(812) 937–4541

Lincoln Boyhood National Memorial, comprising 200 wooded and landscaped acres, was authorized in 1962 to preserve the farm where Abraham Lincoln lived from 1816 to 1830. The memorial is in southern Indiana, 4 miles south of Dale on State Highway 162. Travelers on Interstate 64 can use exit 57, travel south on U.S. Highway 231, and follow the signs to Lincoln Park.

When Abraham Lincoln was seven years old, his family moved from Kentucky to Indiana and settled on 160 acres of wilderness land, where Abraham lived until he was twenty-one. This is where young Abraham helped his father, Thomas, clear the forest for a pioneer farm, and where his mother, Nancy, died when he was only nine. The growing youth split rails, plowed and planted, played, read, and learned to write. It was from here, in 1830, that Abraham Lincoln moved with his family to Illinois.

The memorial grounds are open daily year-round from dawn to dusk. The visitor center is open from 8:00 A.M. to 5:00 P.M. The memorial is closed Thanksgiving, Christmas, and New Year's days. Rangers are on duty to orient visitors to the memorial's features, including the visitor center; the grave of Nancy Hanks Lincoln, Abraham's mother; and the Lincoln Living Historical Farm, a working pioneer farm where costumed "pioneers" present family living and farming activities daily from mid-April through September. Most features of the park are wheelchair accessible. Admission is charged for individuals 17 or over.

FACILITIES: No food or lodging is available in the park. Restrooms and drinking fountains are in the visitor center.

CAMPING: Adjacent to Lincoln Boyhood National Memorial is the 1,747-acre Lincoln State Park, administered by the Indiana Department of Natural Resources. The state park offers camping, picnicking hiking, swimming, boating, and fishing. Fees are collected for entering the state park and for camping.

KENTUCKY

ABRAHAM LINCOLN BIRTHPLACE NATIONAL HISTORIC SITE

2995 Lincoln Farm Road
Hodgenville, KY 42748
(502) 358–3137

This 116-acre park was established in 1916 to commemorate the site of Abraham Lincoln's birth. It is located in north-central Kentucky, 3 miles south of Hodgenville on U.S. 31E/ Kentucky 61.

For $200, Thomas Lincoln bought the 300-acre Sinking Spring farm in 1808. Soon afterward, he moved his wife and one-year-old daughter into a one-room cabin where Abraham was born in February 1809. The Lincolns lived here about two and one-half years before a defective land title forced them to move 10 miles northeast to a farm on Knob Creek. For additional information on parks honoring Abraham Lincoln, see Lincoln Boyhood National Memorial (Indiana) and Lincoln Home National Historic Site (Illinois) in this book.

A visitor center, open daily except Christmas and Thanksgiving days contains an audiovisual program and exhibits depicting Abraham Lincoln's early life. Included is the original Bible of Thomas Lincoln. A short walk leads to the site of a giant oak that served as a marker for early surveys and to Sinking Spring, which provided cool water for the Lincolns. A memorial building protects the log cabin that is the traditional birthplace. Hiking trails are located in the park.

FACILITIES: No food or lodging is available at the site, but both are provided in Hodgenville. Restrooms and drinking water are in the visitor center. A picnic area is across Highway 31E from the visitor center.

CAMPING: No camping is permitted in the park. A state park with camping facilities is northeast via U.S. 31E at Bardstown.

CUMBERLAND GAP NATIONAL HISTORICAL PARK

P.O. Box 1848
Middlesboro, KY 40965
(606) 248–2817

Cumberland Gap National Historical Park, with more than 20,000 acres, was authorized in 1940 to memorialize the mountain pass on the Wilderness Road that served as a main entryway for settlers through the Alleghenies. The gap also was an important military objective in the Civil War. The park is located in southeastern Kentucky, with portions spilling over into Virginia and Tennessee. It can be reached by either U.S. 25E from Kentucky and Tennessee or U.S. 58 from Virginia.

From its discovery in 1750, Cumberland Gap proved to be a major focal point in early American history. The area was explored by Daniel Boone from 1769 until he helped mark the Wilderness Road in 1775. Soon after, settlers began to pour through the gap, setting the stage for Kentucky's statehood in 1792. The mountain pass was considered an important strategic location during the Civil War, and it changed hands a number of times.

The park's visitor center, near Middlesboro, Kentucky, is open daily except Thanksgiving, Christmas, and New Year's days, Martin Luther King's birthday, and Presidents' Day from 9:00 A.M. to 5:00 P.M. (8:00 A.M. to 6:00 P.M. in summer). Here visitors will find a museum, an orientation program, and an information desk. From this point, the 4-mile Pinnacle Road passes a small earthen Civil War fort on its way to a panoramic overlook and short-loop trail. Other interesting locations include Tri-State Peak, where a 2-mile round-trip trail leads to the meeting point of three states. East on U.S. 58, Hensley Settlement is a restored mountain community accessible by hiking. It contains three restored farmsteads with houses, barns, fields, a schoolhouse, and cemetery. The park contains about 55 miles of trails.

FACILITIES: No food or lodging is available in the park, but both are in Cumberland Gap and Tazewell, Tennessee, and Middlesboro. Restrooms and drinking water are in the visitor center.

CAMPING: Wilderness Road Campground (160 spaces, thirteen group sites) is open year-round and offers tables, grills, water, flush toilets, hot showers, and a dump station. Five backcountry campgrounds with primitive facilities are available by permit only.

See map on the following page.

Lincoln Home National Historic Site, Springfield, Illinois (opposite page)

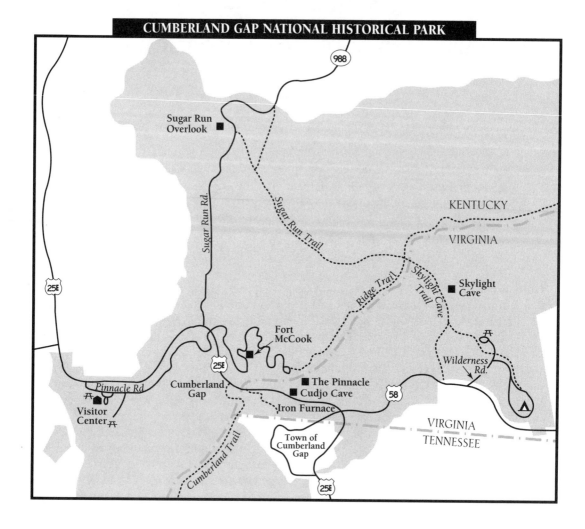

MAMMOTH CAVE NATIONAL PARK

Mammoth Cave, KY 42259
(502) 758–2328

This 53,000-acre park was established in 1941 to preserve the longest recorded cave system (more than 350 miles have been mapped) in the world, rugged hillsides, beautiful rivers, and the surface landforms associated with caves. The park is located in central Kentucky, approximately 90 miles south of Louisville via Interstate 65.

For thousands of years, Mammoth Cave's passageways and chambers have fascinated people who lived nearby or who passed through the area. Trips through the caves offer access to deep pits, high domes, and formations such as stalactites, stalagmites, and gypsum crystals. Varying types of guided tours (fee) are offered year-round, with tickets available in the visitor center. Wear comfortable shoes and a jacket (temperatures are mid-50s to low 60s) for these relatively strenuous walks. The center also contains an orientation film and a schedule of the various surface activities provided by park rangers. Tickets for an hour-and-ten-minute concessioner-operated cruise on the Green River also may be purchased here. The variety and frequency of cave tours and campfire programs are increased during the summer months. Cave tours sell out quickly during the summer, on holidays, and on weekends. Visitors are advised to reserve cave trips; call Destinet (800–967–2283).

A number of short walks and longer hiking trails are located throughout the park (some shown on map). A trail map is available at the visitor center.

FACILITIES: Mammoth Cave Hotel, a motel-type lodge, and cottages are available year-round. Reservations are strongly recommended for summer months. Write: Mammoth Cave Hotel, Mammoth Cave, KY 42259 (502–758–2225).

A dining room, coffee shop, craft center, and gift shop are located in the hotel. Laundry facility, post office, and groceries are available in a store near the campground. A service station also is located here.

CAMPING: An inviting, shaded campground (111 sites) near the visitor center is open March through November. It has flush toilets, picnic tables, and grills. A nearby store offers supplies and showers. At Houchin's Ferry a small campground (twelve sites, chemical toilets) is open year-round. Houchin's Ferry Campground is not suitable for large trailers or recreation vehicles. Dennison Ferry Campground (four sites, chemical toilet, no fresh water) is 7 miles from the visitor center, on the south bank of the Green River. No large trailers or RVs.

FISHING: Muskie, white perch, catfish, and bass live in Green and Nolin rivers. No license is required to fish at the park, but Kentucky regulations must be observed.

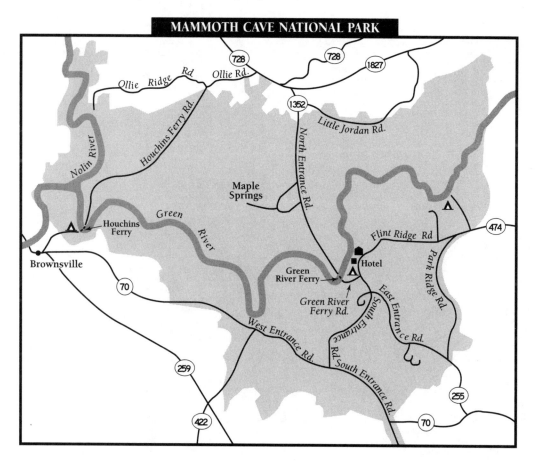

MAMMOTH CAVE NATIONAL PARK

MAINE

ACADIA NATIONAL PARK

P.O. Box 177
Bar Harbor, ME 04609
(207) 288–3338

Acadia National Park comprises nearly 39,000 acres and was established as a national monument in 1916 (changed to Acadia National Park in 1929) to preserve a rugged coastal area of mountains, forests, and offshore islands. The park is located approximately two-thirds of the way up the Maine coast, 48 miles southeast of Bangor via U.S. 1A and State Highway 3.

Acadia National Park is divided into three parts: Mount Desert Island, on which the main section of the park is located, includes the town of Bar Harbor, fishing villages, and small resort communities; the second section, Schoodic Peninsula, is the only part of Acadia on the mainland; Isle au Haut, the third section, may be reached only by boat.

On the way into the park, visitors should stop at the main visitor center (a short distance northwest of the town of Bar Harbor) to pick up a park map and schedule of activities. The center also offers a fifteen-minute film and pictures of the park. Most visitors in a hurry stop at the visitor center, drive the 20-mile scenic loop road, and travel up Cadillac Mountain Summit Road to the highest point on the East Coast. This point provides magnificent vistas of the surrounding coastline. For those able to spend more time, the park offers a historical museum on Little Cranberry Island (reached by ferry) and a museum, nature center, and wildflower garden

Acadia National Park (opposite page)

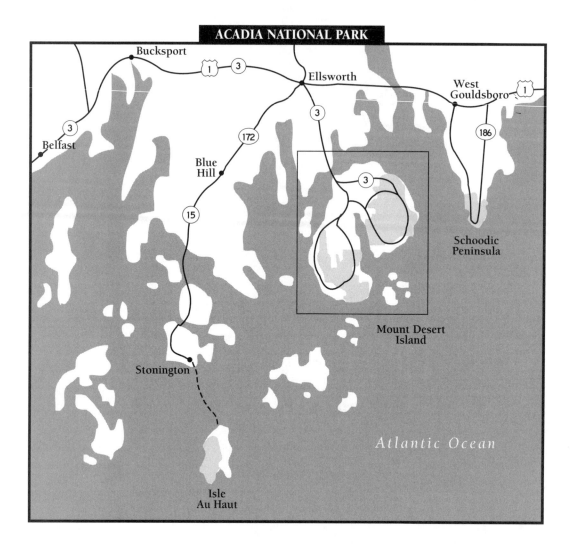

ACADIA NATIONAL PARK

at Sieur de Monts Spring. Scheduled ranger-guided walks, hikes, boat trips, and amphitheater programs with descriptions and telephone numbers for making reservations are listed in the schedule of activities. Try one of these to better understand the park's environment, wildlife, and inhabitants. Swimming with lifeguards on duty can be found at Echo Lake and at Sand Beach. Numerous hiking trails lead throughout the park, and 45 miles of smooth graveled carriage roads circle Jordan Pond and Eagle Lake and wind around Sargent and Penobscot mountains. Ranger-guided walks of the tidal pools are particularly rewarding. Bicycles may be rented in Bar Harbor and Southwest Harbor. Carriage rides are available at Wildwood Stables near Seal Harbor.

Winter activities at Acadia National Park include cross-country skiing, ice fishing, and limited ice skating and ice boating. No downhill ski facilities are available. Forty-three miles of designated park routes are available for over-snow vehicles.

FACILITIES: No lodging is available within the park, but hotels, motels, inns, and bed-and-breakfast establishments are located throughout the island; many of these are in the town of Bar Harbor. A concessioner offers meals and souvenirs at the south end of Jordan Pond and snacks at Cadillac Mountain and Thunder Hole.

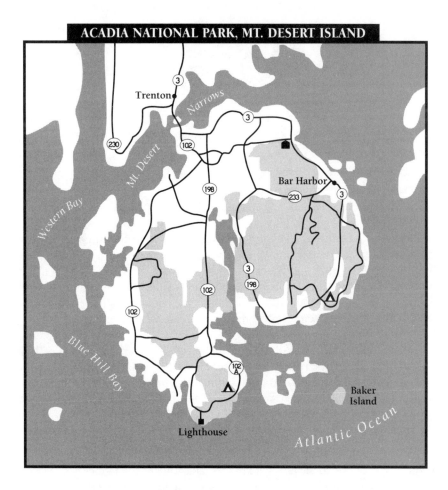

CAMPING: Blackwoods (325 spaces) and Seawall (218 spaces of which 104 are walk-in only at reduced cost) campgrounds offer tables, grills, flush toilets, and dump stations. A private facility offering pay showers is near each of the campgrounds. Blackwoods accepts reservations and is the only campground open year-round. Reserve through Destinet (800–365–2267). Blackwoods Campground is more centrally located, maybe a little nicer, and generally is filled first.

FISHING: Brook trout, lake trout, Atlantic salmon, pickerel, perch, and bass may be caught in the many lakes, with a Maine license. Shore fishing (no license required) produces a variety of saltwater fish. Fishing is generally fair to poor.

APPALACHIAN NATIONAL SCENIC TRAIL

P.O. Box 807
Harpers Ferry, WV 25425
(304) 535–6331

Established in 1968, the 2,000-plus-mile Appalachian National Scenic Trail follows the Appalachian Mountains through fourteen states connecting Mount Katahdin, Maine, with Springer Mountain, Georgia. The trail is accessible at numerous locations between its two end points.

To view the ridges, streams, and lakes along the entire length of the Appalachian Trail, a backpacker must be willing to devote four to six months' time in an effort to accumulate approximately five million steps, either all at once or bit by bit over the years. If the goal is something less than hiking the entire length, it is possible to enjoy hikes of a few hours, a few days, or a few weeks. Those who hike through the trail at one time usually begin at Springer Mountain in late March or early April to avoid the still relatively severe weather prevalent in the mountains of the Northeast.

The National Trails System Act of 1968, which established the Appalachian Trail, encouraged individual states to participate in its protection. The Appalachian Trail Conference (ATC) coordinates the efforts of thirty-one trail clubs in maintaining stewardship over the assigned regions. A list of guidebooks and maps of the trail may be obtained by writing Appalachian Trail Conference, P.O. Box 807, Harpers Ferry, WV 25424 (304–535–6331). Additional information is available from ATC or one of the member clubs.

FACILITIES: Although most of the Appalachian Trail passes through wilderness, it occasionally comes close to developed areas, where hikers take advantage of grocery stores, restaurants, motels, hostels, showers, and the like. Guidebooks available from the ATC provide a detailed listing of facilities. Many hikers send supplies ahead to post offices along the way.

CAMPING: About 200 trailside shelters are available on a first-come basis. These shelters are generally spaced one moderate day's hiking distance apart and are to be used one night only. There are also many campgrounds and designated campsites along the trail.

FISHING: Fishing is available at various locations along the trail. An appropriate state license is required.

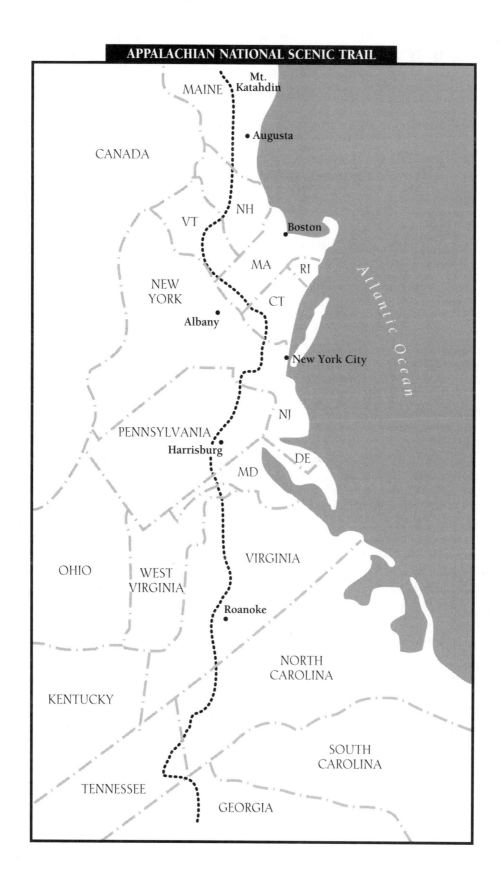

ROOSEVELT CAMPOBELLO INTERNATIONAL PARK

P.O. Box 97
Lubec, ME 04652
(506) 752–2922

Roosevelt Campobello International Park is a 2,800-acre park established in 1964 as a joint memorial by Canada and the United States, funded by both countries and administered by a joint United States–Canadian commission. The park includes the summer home of President Franklin D. Roosevelt. The park is located on Campobello Island in the Canadian province of New Brunswick and is reached via Franklin D. Roosevelt Memorial Bridge from Lubec, Maine. There is no admission charge.

In 1883 Franklin Roosevelt's father purchased four acres and a partially completed home on Campobello Island. The house was completed two years later, and subsequently the Roosevelt family spent most summers here. After Franklin and Eleanor were married, a cottage near the main home was purchased by Sara Roosevelt, the president's mother, in 1910, and later given to them. They and their children were also to spend summers on the island until Franklin was stricken with poliomyelitis here in 1921. Following this, his visits were infrequent.

The park and reception center are open daily for twenty weeks beginning on the Saturday prior to Memorial Day. Visiting hours are from 9:00 A.M. to 5:00 P.M. (the Roosevelt cottage closes at 4:50). Here, information is available, and two films and some exhibits help interpret the significance of the park. A short walk from the reception center allows visitors to tour the Roosevelt cottage, which contains original furnishings and some personal belongings of the family. Tours of the home are self-guiding, although guides are stationed throughout the cottage to provide information and answer questions.

Eight and a half miles of walking trails wander through the park's natural area, and three park drives have been developed for automobiles. A map and descriptions of the trails may be obtained at the reception center. Visitors may also want to stop just across the FDR Bridge at the New Brunswick information station to obtain maps and information on other sights on the island and in the province.

FACILITIES: Drinking water and modern restrooms are in the reception center. Tourist facilities including restaurants, motels, and gift shops are available in the villages of Welshpool and Wilson's Beach on the island or at Lubec on the mainland.

CAMPING: No camping is permitted within the Roosevelt Campobello International Park, but only 2 miles away, Herring Cove Provincial Park provides camping facilities (eighty spaces) with tables, grills, flush toilets, showers, electrical hookups, and a dump station (506–752–2396). As is typical of provincial parks in New Brunswick, an enclosed picnic shelter has two wood-burning stoves complete with wood to burn. The provincial park accepts American money and will convert it to Canadian currency at the prevailing exchange rate.

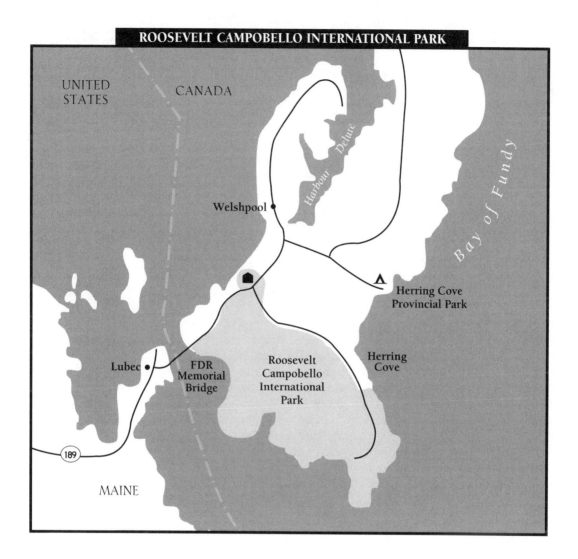

ROOSEVELT CAMPOBELLO INTERNATIONAL PARK

UNITED STATES

CANADA

Welshpool

Harbour Deluc

Bay of Fundy

Herring Cove
Provincial Park

Lubec

FDR
Memorial
Bridge

Roosevelt
Campobello
International
Park

Herring
Cove

189

MAINE

SAINT CROIX ISLAND INTERNATIONAL HISTORIC SITE

c/o Acadia National Park
P.O. Box 177
Bar Harbor, ME 04609
(207) 288–3338

Saint Croix Island International Historic Site comprises thirty-five acres and was authorized in 1949 to commemorate the attempted French settlement here, which led to the founding of New France. The island is located off the mainland of eastern Maine, with the site entrance 8 miles south of Calais via U.S. 1. There is currently no ferry service to the island.

With a commission from a fur-trade monopoly to explore for minerals, settle the land, and spread Christianity, Lieutenant General Pierre de Gau Sieur de Monts set sail from France for North America in 1604. After some exploration of the mainland, he sailed into the Bay of Fundy and up the St. Croix River in the early summer. De Monts found an island with a location that would provide control of the river and named it Saint Croix (above the island two long coves meet with the river to form a cross). The men set about constructing fortifications and shelters, and in August the two large ships returned to France, leaving seventy-nine men to spend the winter. The poorly prepared group fared badly, and by the time supply ships arrived the next June, thirty-five men were dead. After further exploration, a decision was made to move the settlement across the Bay of Fundy to Port Royal, near the present town of Annapolis Royal, Nova Scotia, and Saint Croix Island was abandoned.

With the exception of a Coast Guard navigation light, there are no federal facilities on the island. The park is administered by the superintendent of Acadia National Park. A reconstruction of the village founded after Saint Croix was abandoned can be seen at Port Royal National Historic Park in Nova Scotia.

FACILITIES: No facilities of any kind are on the island. Food service and lodging are available in Calais.

CAMPING: No camping is permitted within the historic site's grounds.

FISHING: Fishing is permitted; a Maine license is required.

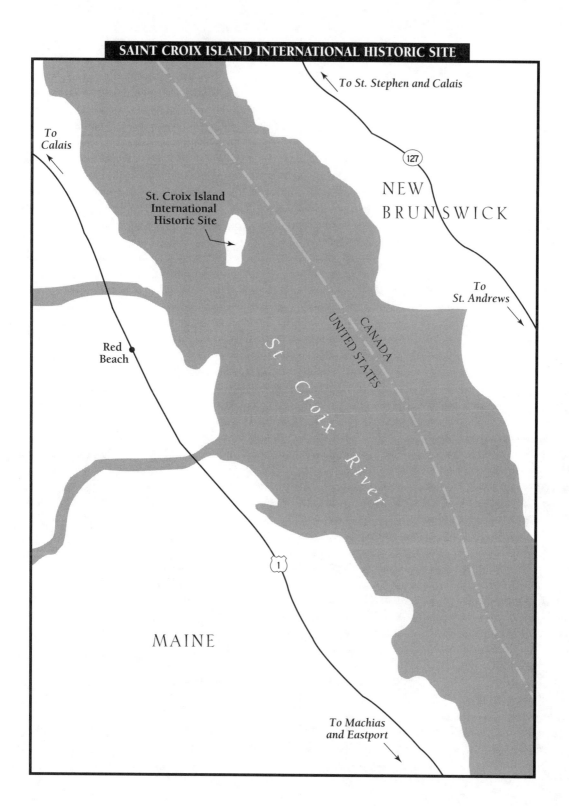

SAINT CROIX ISLAND INTERNATIONAL HISTORIC SITE

To St. Stephen and Calais

To Calais

127

NEW BRUNSWICK

St. Croix Island International Historic Site

To St. Andrews

CANADA
UNITED STATES

Red Beach

St. Croix River

1

MAINE

To Machias and Eastport

MARYLAND

ANTIETAM NATIONAL BATTLEFIELD
Box 158
Sharpsburg, MD 21782
(301) 432–5124

Antietam National Battlefield consists of 3,200 acres and was established in 1890 to commemorate the battlefield where General Robert E. Lee's first invasion of the North was ended in 1862. The battlefield is located in western Maryland, 12 miles south of Hagerstown via State Highway 65. It is approximately 70 miles northwest of Washington, D.C.

During September of 1862, Robert E. Lee's 40,000 Confederate troops were being pursued by a Union force of 87,000 led by George B. McClellan. Lee's army took its position on the high ground to the west of Antietam Creek, and on September 17 the battle began. The bloodiest day in American military history left 12,410 Federals and 10,700 Confederates killed, wounded, captured, or missing. Although the battle, which took place over a 12-square-mile area, was tactically a draw, Lee's advance was halted, and President Lincoln was given an opportunity to issue the forerunner of the Emancipation Proclamation.

The visitor center, located north of Sharpsburg on Maryland Highway 65, is open daily 8:30 A.M. to 5:00 P.M. (8:00 A.M. to 6:00 P.M. in summer) except Thanksgiving Day, Christmas Day, and New Year's Day. Here visitors will find exhibits and a twenty-six-minute-long motion

Fort McHenry National Monument and Historic Shrine (opposite page)

picture covering the battle story. From this point, an 8½-mile self-guiding tour highlights the main points of interest with wayside exhibits (text numbers are keyed to the map). The auto tour takes from forty-five minutes to one-and-one-half hours. Rental taped tours are available. Interpretive markers are at Turner's, Fox's, and Crampton's gaps on South Mountain and at Shepherdstown Ford.

1. Dunker Church, a scene of repeated clashes, has been reconstructed.

2. North Woods, where General Hooker launched the initial attack but was stopped by Jackson's troops in the cornfield.

3. From East Woods, General Mansfield was fatally wounded as corps attacked from the northeast.

4. Miller's thirty-acre cornfield changed hands several times in two-and-one-half hours.

5. In West Woods, Stonewall Jackson's divisions cut down more than 2,200 Federals in twenty minutes.

6. Mumma Farm, which was burned by Confederates to prevent use by Union sharp-shooters.

7. Roulette Farm, where Union troops crossed the fields on their way to meet Confederates posted in the Sunken Road.

8. Three hours of battle in Bloody Lane resulted in 5,000 casualties.

9. At Burnside Bridge, a few hundred Georgia riflemen held off four Union divisions for four hours.

10. Location of the final attack. After taking the bridge, Burnside's troops pressing toward Sharpsburg were stopped by Hill's Confederates arriving from Harpers Ferry.

11. Antietam National Cemetery contains the remains of 4,776 Federal troops.

FACILITIES: Food and lodging are available nearby in Sharpsburg, a town of about 900 residents. Water and restrooms are in the visitor center.

CAMPING: Camping in the park is limited to organized groups, and reservations are required. A walk-in tent campground is located on the C&O Canal, 5 miles south on Harpers Ferry Road. Greenbrier State Park, 15 miles northeast via Highway 34 and alternates 40, 66, and 40, offers 200 sites with flush toilets, showers, laundry facilities, and a forty-two-acre lake for fishing, boating, and swimming.

FISHING: Fishing is permitted in Antietam Creek; a Maryland license is required. Fishing is prohibited from Burnside Bridge.

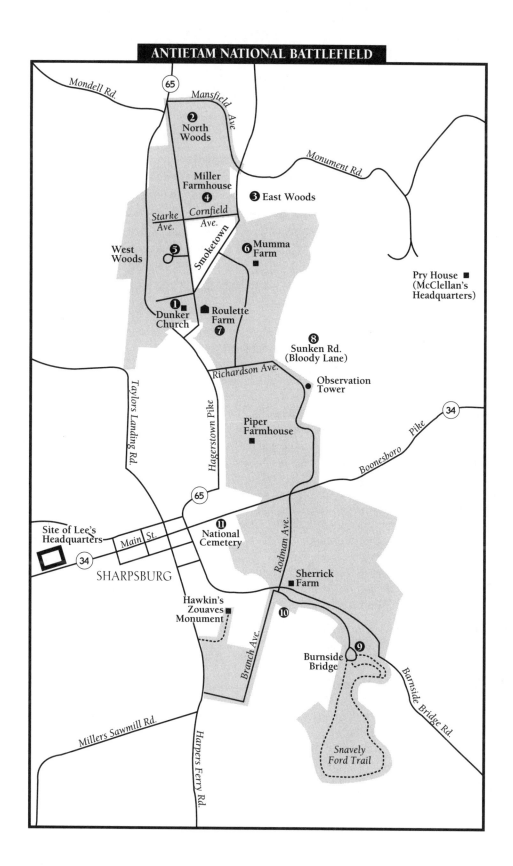

Mondell Rd.

65

Mansfield Ave

❷ North Woods

Monument Rd.

Miller Farmhouse

❹ Cornfield

❸ East Woods

Starke Ave.

Cornfield Ave.

West Woods

Smoketown

❺

❻ Mumma Farm

Pry House ■ (McClellan's Headquarters)

❶ Dunker Church

Roulette Farm

❼

❽ Sunken Rd. (Bloody Lane)

Observation Tower

Richardson Ave.

Taylors Landing Rd.

Hagerstown Pike

Piper Farmhouse

Boonesboro Pike

34

65

Site of Lee's Headquarters

Main St.

❶❶ National Cemetery

Rodman Ave.

34

SHARPSBURG

Sherrick Farm

Hawkin's Zouaves Monument

Branch Ave.

❿

❾ Burnside Bridge

Barnside Bridge Rd.

Millers Sawmill Rd.

Harpers Ferry Rd.

Snavely Ford Trail

ASSATEAGUE ISLAND NATIONAL SEASHORE

7206 National Seashore Lane
Berlin, MD 21811
(410) 641–1441

Assateague Island National Seashore was authorized as part of the National Park Service in 1965 to preserve nearly 50,000 acres of water area and sandy beach along a 37-mile barrier island. The park is located on the Atlantic coast of southern Maryland and northern Virginia. Visitor access to Assateague Island is at the extreme northern end near Ocean City, Maryland, or the extreme southern end near Chincoteague, Virginia. Between these two developed areas are 25 miles of roadless beach and marsh including a 12-mile strip of wild beach in Chincoteague National Wildlife Refuge that is accessible by foot only.

Assateague is a barrier island formed by sand rising from the ocean floor and shaped by wind and waves. The island's mild surf and moderate temperatures make this an ideal place for outdoor water-related activities, including swimming, fishing, canoeing, and beachcombing. The island's most famous residents are ponies which, according to legend, came ashore 200 years ago from a wrecked Spanish galleon. Park historians, however, believe the horses were placed there by farmers to avoid taxation and fencing requirements on the mainland.

The seashore's Barrier island Visitor Center at the north end contains exhibits, publications, and information about the island. A paved road extends through Assateague State Park and into the national seashore, but only properly equipped over-sand vehicles are allowed on the 13-mile beach route that begins at the end of Bayside Drive. A permit is required. The shallow saltwater marshes in Chincoteague Bay provide excellent canoeing, and a canoe launch is at the end of Ferry Landing Road (rentals available). A protected beach and bathhouse are near the park entrance. Three 1/2-mile nature trails interpret three lesser known life zones of a barrier island: marsh, forest, and dunes.

At the park's south end, a 3-mile paved road leads through the national wildlife refuge to the beach. Beyond Toms Cove Beach, a 5-mile route is available to over-sand vehicles only (permit required). The Refuge Visitor Center provides information and literature on the wildlife refuge; a National Park Service visitor center is at the beach.

FACILITIES: No lodging is available in the seashore area. During summer months, bathhouses, a bait-and-tackle shop, and food service are in Assateague State Park. Motels, restaurants, and stores are in the towns of Chincoteague, Virginia, and Ocean City, Maryland.

CAMPING: The only developed camping facilities are in the northern section. Assateague State Park has tables, hot showers, and flush toilets. Immediately south, the National Park Service operates the more primitive campgrounds of Bayside and Oceanside with tables, a sanitary station, portable toilets, and cold water. Three oceanside backpack campsites, four bayside canoe-in campsites, and a group camp are available. Write for specific information or call the campground office (410–641–3030).

FISHING: Surf fishing is permitted along most of the shoreline. No license is required. Clamming and crabbing are permitted throughout the bay behind Assateague Island.

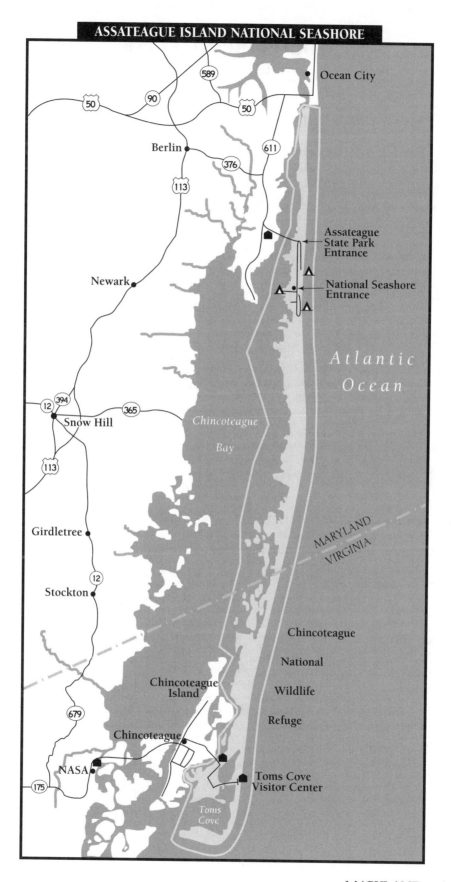

Ocean City

589

90

50

50

Berlin

611

376

113

Assateague
State Park
Entrance

National Seashore
Entrance

Newark

*Atlantic
Ocean*

394

12

365

*Chincoteague
Bay*

Snow Hill

113

MARYLAND

VIRGINIA

Girdletree

12

Stockton

Chincoteague

National

Wildlife

Refuge

Chincoteague
Island

679

Chincoteague

NASA

175

Toms Cove
Visitor Center

*Toms
Cove*

CATOCTIN MOUNTAIN PARK

6602 Foxville Road
Thurmont, MD 21788
(301) 663–9330

Catoctin Mountain Park provides numerous outdoor recreational possibilities on nearly 5,800 acres of forested land along an eastern ridge of the Appalachian Mountains. The park is 65 miles northwest of Washington, D.C., with the main entrance on Maryland Highway 77, 3 miles west of Thurmont and U.S. 15.

The land of Catoctin Mountain Park was purchased by the federal government in 1936 after decades of misuse by settlers, who had virtually ruined it. Forests had been cleared to obtain wood for making charcoal, trees were stripped of bark for tanning, and poor farming practices depleted and eroded the soil. In 1954, a portion of the land was given to Maryland and became Cunningham State Park. The state park adjoins Catoctin Mountain Park.

The park's visitor center, just off State Highway 77, provides information, a schedule of interpretive programs, and a small museum. The park contains picnic areas, a 6-mile horse trail, and 25 miles of foot trails. Hog Rock, Browns Farm Environmental Study Area, Cunningham Falls, and Deerfield Nature trails are self-guiding and nature-oriented; leaflets are available at the trailheads. Blue Blazes, Whiskey Still, Charcoal, Sawmill, and Spicebush trails have descriptive signs along the way. During winter months, trails are used for cross-country skiing and snowshoeing. Portions of park roads are also closed for winter recreation.

Many of the recreational activities mentioned are also available in Cunningham Falls State Park. In addition, the state park contains a man-made lake that provides opportunities for swimming, fishing, and boating. The park office in the William Houck area is open year-round.

FACILITIES: Rustic cabins are available for rent at Camp Misty Mount, about a mile from the visitor center. Modern restrooms and showers are centrally located. For reservations call (301) 271–3140. Seasonal picnic areas with restrooms, tables, and fireplaces are at Owens Creek, Chestnut, Manor, and William Houck. Food can be obtained in the William Houck area of Cunningham Falls State Park.

CAMPING: Owens Creek Campground (fifty-one sites, 22-foot trailer limit) is heavily wooded and offers tables, grills, water, and modern restrooms from mid-April to mid-November. Two campgrounds (148 sites) with similar facilities but also including showers are in Cunningham State Park. The state park campsites generally have less shade than those in Owens Creek. All the campgrounds generally are filled on weekends but have openings on week nights.

FISHING: Trout live in Big Hunting Creek (fly fishing, catch-and-release only), and wild brook and brown trout are caught in Little Owens Creek. Additional fishing is available in the state park. A Maryland license is required in either place.

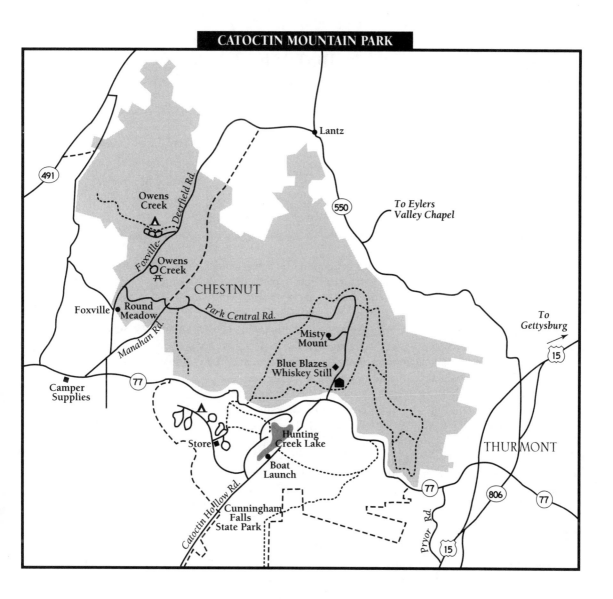

491

Lantz

Owens
Creek

Deerfield Rd.

550

*To Eylers
Valley Chapel*

Foxville

Owens
Creek

CHESTNUT

Park Central Rd.

Foxville • Round
Meadow

Manahan Rd.

Misty
Mount

Blue Blazes
Whiskey Still ◆

*To
Gettysburg*

15

77

Camper
Supplies ■

Store

Hunting
Creek Lake

Boat
Launch

Catoctin Hollow Rd.

Cunningham
Falls
State Park

77

THURMONT

Pryor Rd.

806

77

15

CHESAPEAKE & OHIO CANAL
NATIONAL HISTORICAL PARK
P.O. Box 4
Sharpsburg, MD 21782
(301) 739–4200

Chesapeake & Ohio Canal National Historical Park comprises 20,781 acres and was established in 1938 to preserve a strip of land along the route of a historic 185-mile-long nineteenth-century canal. The canal follows the Potomac River between Washington, D.C., and Cumberland, Maryland.

Construction on the C&O Canal commenced in 1828 in an effort to provide economical water transportation between the industrialized East Coast and the resources of the Midwest. Designed to follow the Potomac and trans-Allegheny trade route to the Ohio River, the canal was used as each section was completed. The cost of building the completed 184.5 miles of canal was $22 million. It included seventy-four lift locks, eleven aqueducts, seven dams, a 3,117-foot tunnel, and a variety of bridges, culverts, section houses, and lock houses. The canal was never a financial success and was severely damaged by two major floods. The entire project became obsolete with the completion of the faster and less expensive Baltimore & Ohio Railroad, and by 1924 the C&O Canal had been abandoned.

The park's main visitor center is at the Great Falls Tavern (301–299–3613). The center contains exhibits and information on conducted walks and other programs. Information may also be obtained at Georgetown (202–472–4376), Antietam Creek, Four Locks, Hancock, Cumberland, and at park headquarters near Sharpsburg. The canal towpath, which served as a walking surface for mules that pulled the boats, remains unobstructed along the entire length of the canal. Although it can become quite slippery during wet weather, the towpath generally makes a good path for hiking and bicycling. Boating is popular between Georgetown and Violettes Lock near Seneca, and canoes may be rented at Swains Lock and at Fletcher's Boat House.

FACILITIES: No food or lodging is available in the park. Camping supplies, ice, food, and soft drinks may be purchased at most stores along the various access roads.

CAMPING: Hiker-biker overnight campsites for tent camping are spaced approximately every 5 miles from Horsepen Branch to Evitts Creek. All have toilets, picnic tables, grills, and, in most cases, water. Only one campsite, Antietam Creek, has adjacent parking. Drive-in camping areas at McCoys Ferry, Fifteen Mile Creek, and Spring Gap provide primitive facilities.

FISHING: Bass, sunfish, and a number of other species live in Big Pool near Fort Frederick, Little Pool at Hancock, and Battie Mixon Pond at Oldtown. Fishing is also permitted in the Potomac River. A state fishing license is required.

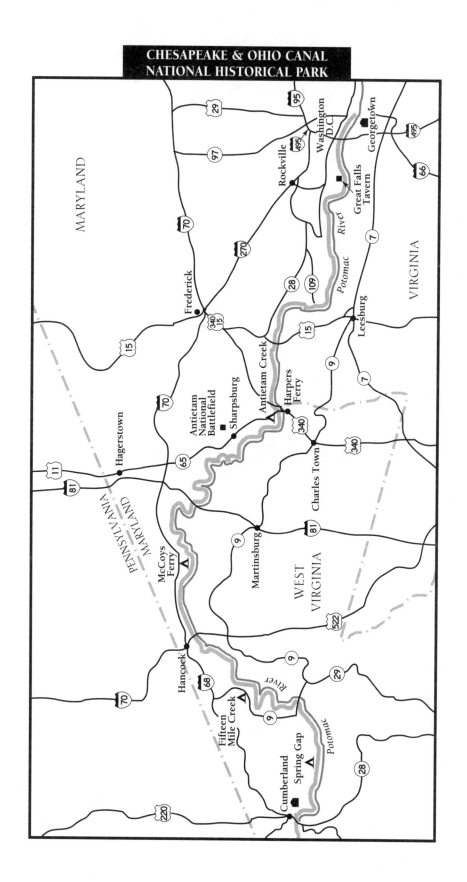

CLARA BARTON NATIONAL HISTORIC SITE

5801 Oxford Road
Glen Echo, MD 20812
(301) 492–6245

Clara Barton National Historic Site comprises about one acre and was established in 1975 to preserve the home of the founder of the American Red Cross. The house is located in Glen Echo, Maryland, a short distance northwest of the District of Columbia off MacArthur Boulevard via Massachusetts Avenue and Goldsboro Road or the Clara Barton Parkway.

Clara Barton first learned of the International Red Cross during a trip to Europe in 1869. After helping civilian victims of the Franco-Prussian War, she returned to the United States intent on expanding the organization to this country. Years of effort finally resulted in establishing the first chapter of the American Red Cross in 1881. As president of the American organization from its inception until 1904, Clara Barton was instrumental in having the American Red Cross engage in both peacetime and wartime aid.

The home was built in 1891 and given to Clara Barton by real estate developers who hoped to use her name and the name of the American Red Cross to promote their venture. The home was initially used as a Red Cross warehouse before being modified for living quarters and

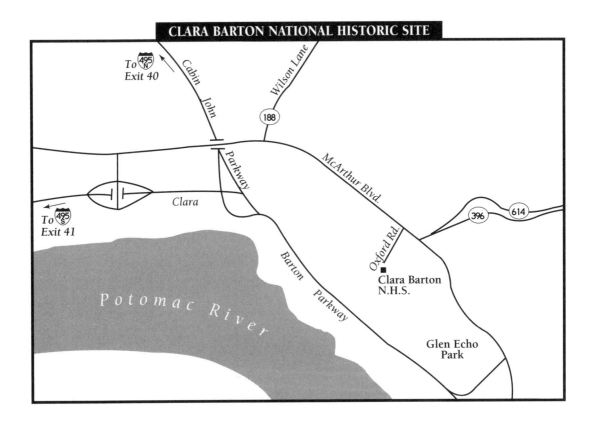

offices in 1897. Prior to acquisition by the National Park Service in 1975, the home passed through a number of owners. The house is currently open daily from 10:00 A.M. to 5:00 P.M. for thirty- to forty-minute guided tours that begin at half past the hour. It is closed Thanksgiving Day, Christmas Day, and New Year's Day.

FACILITIES: A small restroom is available in the house. Concessions may be found next door in Glen Echo Park from May through September, and full services are available nearby in Glen Echo.

FORT McHENRY NATIONAL MONUMENT AND HISTORIC SHRINE
Baltimore, MD 21230
(410) 962–4290

Fort McHenry National Monument and Historic Shrine comprises forty-three acres and was authorized in 1925 to commemorate the site of a battle during the War of 1812 where Francis Scott Key was inspired to write "The Star-Spangled Banner." The fort is located 3 miles southeast of Baltimore's inner harbor via Light Street, Key Highway, Lawrence Street, and East Fort Avenue. It is also readily accessible from Interstate 95 (northbound or southbound), taking exit 55, Key Highway, Lawrence Street, and East Fort Avenue.

Fort McHenry was constructed in the 1790s to protect Baltimore against attack from either England or France, which were then engaged in a major war. In 1814, following Napoleon's defeat England was able to devote more effort to problems in the United States. After arriving in America, a British force attacked Washington. While negotiations for peace were being discussed, the British sailed up Chesapeake Bay to attack Baltimore. Anchored 2 miles below Fort McHenry, sixteen British warships bombarded the fort for twenty-five hours. At dawn on September 14, while the American flag was still waving over Fort McHenry, Francis Scott Key began writing the poem that was soon put to music and in 1931 became the national anthem of the United States.

The fort is open daily except Christmas Day and New Year's Day from 8:00 A.M. to 5.00 P.M. with extended summer hours. Before visiting, call the park to verify days and hours of operation. A visitor center near the star-shaped structure offers exhibits and a sixteen-minute film. Guided activities are available during summer months. Wayside exhibits are located along the walk.

FACILITIES: No food or lodging is available in the park. A concessioner sells souvenirs, postcards, and film; restrooms and water are in the visitor center.

CAMPING: No camping is permitted on the monument grounds. The nearest public campsite is in Patapsco Valley State Park, west of Baltimore.

See map on the following page.

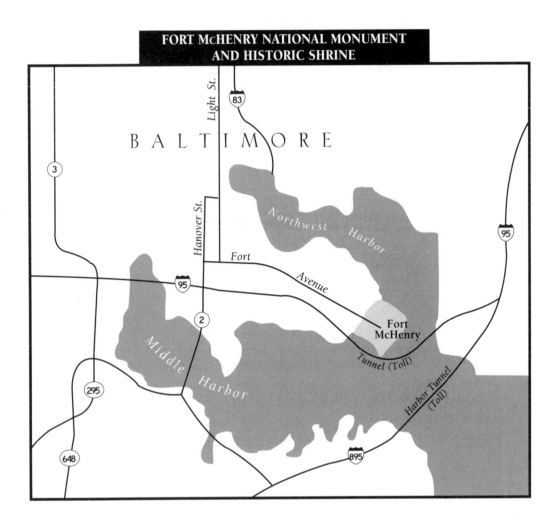

FORT McHENRY NATIONAL MONUMENT AND HISTORIC SHRINE

BALTIMORE

Light St.

Hanover St.

Northwest Harbor

Fort Avenue

Fort McHenry

Tunnel (Toll)

Harbor Tunnel (Toll)

Middle Harbor

83

3

95

2

95

295

648

895

FORT WASHINGTON PARK

c/o National Capital Parks–East
1900 Anacostia Drive, S.E.
Washington, DC 20020
(301) 763–4600

Fort Washington Park comprises 341 acres and preserves an outstanding example of an early-nineteenth-century coastal fortification. The park also includes recreational facilities. Fort Washington Park is located 8 miles south of the District of Columbia on the Maryland side of the Potomac River opposite Mount Vernon. It is reached from Interstate 495 (exit 3A South) by turning south onto Indian Head Highway (Highway 210) and then right onto Fort Washington Road. (See the map of the George Washington Memorial Parkway in the Virginia section for an approximate location.)

Construction of the first Fort Washington was completed in 1809 as part of America's effort to defend the ports and harbors of the new nation. In 1814 the fort was destroyed by American troops to prevent capture during the British invasion of the capital. Work on the present fort commenced almost immediately after the departure of British military forces, but because of delays and a greater feeling of security in the United States, it was not completed until 1824. The fort's masonry structure was later made obsolete by the introduction of rifled artillery. In the late 1890s, concrete gun batteries with breech-loading artillery were constructed on the military reservation around the original fort. The site was in use by the United States Army until the end of World War II. Fort Washington has the honor of being the only permanent fortification ever constructed to protect our nation's capital.

The park is open daily except Christmas and New Year's days from 8:30 A.M. to dark. The fort and visitor center are open from 9:00 A.M. to 5:00 P.M. Fort Washington Park has hiking trails, a picnic area, tennis court, basketball court, and open park land for other recreational activities.

FACILITIES: No food service or lodging is available in the park. Picnic sites are available. Groceries may be purchased about 3 miles away.

CAMPING: No camping is permitted in the park. Cedarville State Park offers camping facilities 25 miles east near the town of Cedarville. The nearest National Park Service campground is at Greenbelt Park near Washington, D.C.

FISHING: Fishing off the banks of the Potomac River offers the possibility of catching carp and catfish. A Maryland license is required.

GREENBELT PARK

6565 Greenbelt Road
Greenbelt, MD 20770
(301) 344–3948

Greenbelt Park was made a part of the National Park Service in 1950 to preserve 1,175 acres of wooded land. It provides easily accessible camping facilities for Washington, D.C. visitors, and nature study and outdoor recreation to urban dwellers. The park is located 12 miles northeast of Washington, D.C., via the Baltimore–Washington Parkway. Exit at Greenbelt Road (Maryland Highway 193). From Interstate 495, use exit 23.

The Greenbelt Park area is in the process of recovering from 150 years of agricultural abuse. After clearing trees and depleting the land, farmers left the area in the early 1900s and nature began healing its wounds. Now numerous varieties of plants and wildlife again have made their home here.

The park contains 12 miles of well-marked trails including Azalea (1.2 miles), Blueberry (1.2 miles), and Dogwood (1.4 miles). A 6-mile loop trail, also used as a bridle trail, circles the western half of the park. Three developed picnic areas with tables, fireplaces, and restrooms are in the park's northern section. Restrooms and picnic areas are wheelchair-accessible.

Greenbelt Park provides a convenient place to camp for Washington, D.C., sightseers. Because downtown parking is generally limited, it is recommended that visitors drive to and park at either the New Carrollton or Greenbelt Metro stations.

FACILITIES: No lodging or food service is available in the park. Motels, restaurants, grocery stores, and service stations are nearby on Greenbelt Road and off Interstate 495 at exit 20.

CAMPING: A 174-site campground provides tables, grills, showers, and flush toilets. Trailers are limited to 30 feet and a fourteen-day limit is imposed.

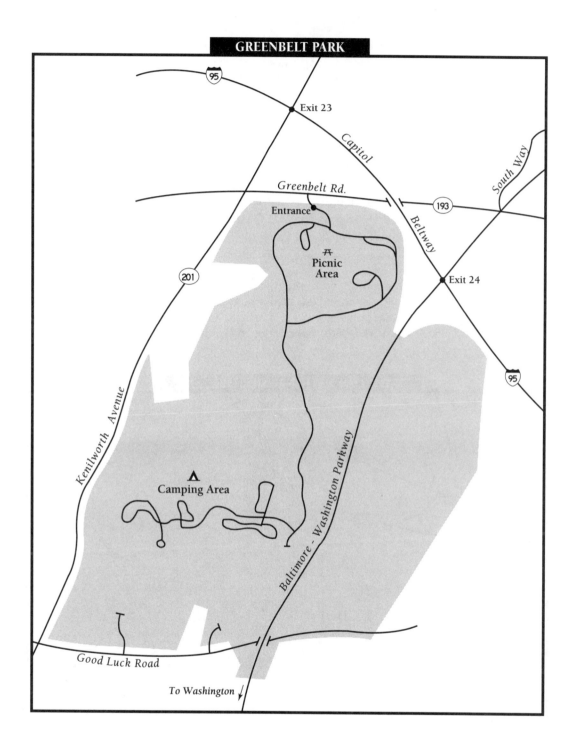

GREENBELT PARK

95

Exit 23

Capitol

South Way

Greenbelt Rd.

193

Entrance

Beltway

Picnic Area

201

Exit 24

95

Kenilworth Avenue

Camping Area

Baltimore - Washington Parkway

Good Luck Road

To Washington

HAMPTON NATIONAL HISTORIC SITE

535 Hampton Lane
Towson, MD 21286
(410) 962–0688

Hampton National Historic Site comprises sixty-three acres and was designated part of the National Park Service in 1948 to preserve a fine example of the lavish Georgian mansions built in America during the latter part of the eighteenth century. The park is located a short distance north of Baltimore via York Road (Maryland Highway 45) and Dulaney Valley Road (Maryland Highway 146). Turn east on Hampton Lane immediately after crossing Interstate 695 (exit 27B).

Construction on Hampton commenced during the spring of 1783 and continued for seven years. It was to become one of the largest and most ornate homes built during the post-Revolutionary period. The mansion was built by merchant and agriculturalist Charles Ridgely, who also owned a large ironworks that supplied shot and cannons to patriot forces during the

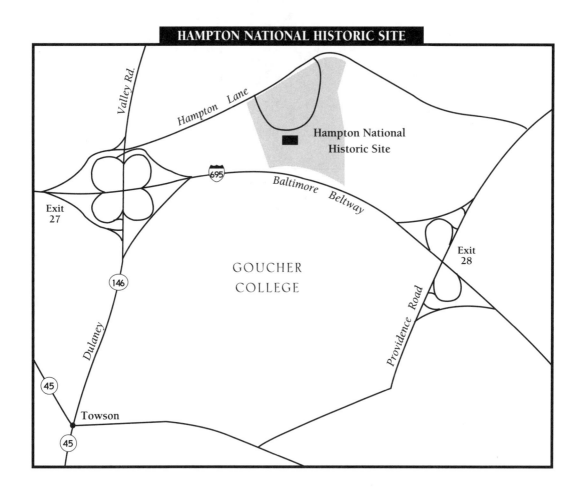

Revolution. Succeeding generations of the Ridgely family continued to occupy Hampton, once the centerpiece of a 25,000-acre estate.

Hampton has been restored to its nineteenth-century appearance. The mansion is open for tours every day from 9:00 A.M. to 4:00 P.M. It is closed on New Year's Day, Thanksgiving, and Christmas. The formal gardens and grounds of Hampton, including many native and exotic specimen trees, contribute to the grandeur of the estate. Twenty-seven outbuildings including slave quarters and stables may also be viewed.

FACILITIES: Lodging is not available at the site but can be obtained in nearby Towson. A gift shop and a tearoom that serves luncheons are in the house. Restrooms and drinking water are provided.

CAMPING: No camping is permitted at the site. Patapsco State Park, near Interstate 695 on Baltimore's west side, offers camping facilities.

MONOCACY NATIONAL BATTLEFIELD

c/o Antietam National Battlefield
Box 158
Sharpsburg, MD 21782
(301) 432–5124

Monocacy National Battlefield was authorized in 1934 to commemorate the site of an 1864 Civil War battle in which Union forces, although defeated, delayed the Confederates long enough to mount a successful defense of Washington, D.C. The park is located in Maryland, 4 miles south of Frederick where Interstate 270 intersects the Monocacy River. The center of the battlefield may be reached by exiting off Route 270 to State Highway 355 south.

With Grant's Federal forces stymied in their move toward Richmond and the other Union army in West Virginia, Robert E. Lee ordered Confederate General Jubal Early to march up the Shenandoah Valley and attack Washington. Near Frederick, a small Union force under the command of General Lew Wallace was able to delay the attack and provide time for reinforcements to arrive, thus discouraging further Confederate advances.

Most of the battlefield remains in private ownership. As a result, there is no development at the site other than four state monuments that have been erected. The National Park Service is, however, planning the park's future and acquiring land. Management of the area has been placed under personnel at Antietam National Battlefield Site. Plans include interpretive overlooks along a trail system through the battlefield. A visitor orientation center, picnic areas, additional trails, and canoe access points will also be added.

Facilities: No facilities are available at the battlefield.

See map on the following page.

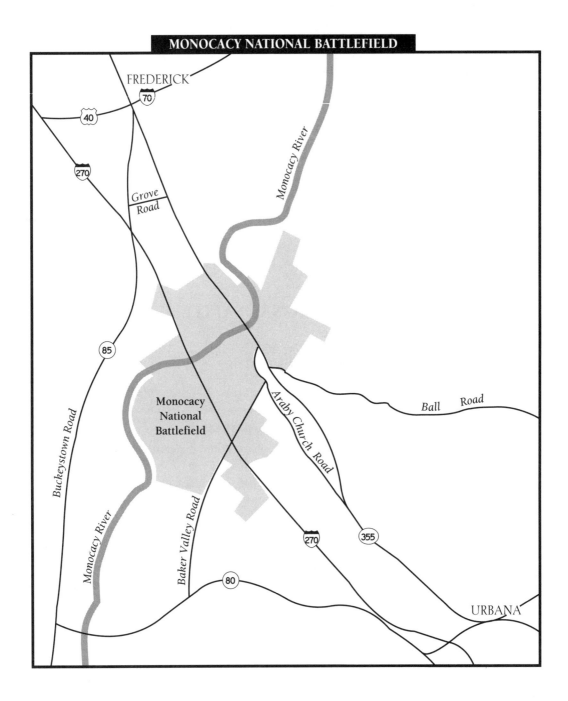

PISCATAWAY PARK

c/o National Capital Parks–East
1900 Anacostia Drive, S.E.
Washington, DC 20020
(301) 763–4600

Piscataway Park was authorized in 1961 and preserves over 4,200 acres of scenic and historical land along the shoreline of the Potomac River across from Mount Vernon. The park is located 19 miles south of the District of Columbia via Indian Head Highway (Maryland Highway 210). Ten miles south of Interstate 495, turn right onto Bryan Point Road at the Accokeek traffic light. The park is 4 miles west on the Potomac River. Marshall Hall is accessible from Highway 210 onto Highway 223.

Piscataway Park, named for the Piscataway Indians who inhabited this area from the fourteenth to the eighteenth century, consists of cultivated fields, tidal swamps and marshes, and wood thickets. Foot access along the Potomac is available from the ends of Bryan Point and Wharf roads, where boat launching is also possible. At low tide, most of the shore is accessible for hiking. At the end of Bryan Point Road, National Colonial Farm, an agricultural-historical project of Accokeek Foundation, provides an exhibit and demonstration of agricultural methods, crops, and livestock of a modest tidewater farm of the mid-eighteenth century.

FACILITIES: Restrooms and drinking water are available at the National Colonial Farm and Marshall Hall. Picnic facilities are in Saylor Memorial Grove.

CAMPING: No camping is permitted in the park.

FISHING: Fishing from the bank is permitted with a Maryland license. Carp, catfish, and perch are possible catches. A fishing pier is available.

THOMAS STONE NATIONAL HISTORIC SITE

6655 Rose Hill Road
Port Tobacco, MD 20677
(301) 934–6027

Thomas Stone National Historic Site was authorized in 1978 to restore and preserve Habre de Venture, the Georgian mansion that was the home of Thomas Stone, a signer of the Declaration of Independence and a delegate to the Continental Congress. The site is in southern Maryland, about 25 miles south of Washington, D.C., and 5 miles west of La Plata. It is 1 mile north of Maryland Highway 6 on the Rose Hill Road.

Thomas Stone was born in 1743 near Port Tobacco, Maryland. He completed his law education around 1765 and was elected to the Continental Congress in 1775. Although opposed to war, Stone voted for and signed the Declaration of Independence. He subsequently served three terms in the state Senate but declined his selection as a representative to the Constitutional Convention. Stone died October 5, 1787, after a lifetime of public service, and is buried alongside his wife, Margaret, on the Habre de Venture plantation.

Stone bought the plantation in 1770, two years after he married Margaret Brown. Many people believe that Stone purchased the 442-acre plantation with 400 pounds sterling from his wife's dowry. The tobacco plantation, which increased in size to 1,300 acres by the time of Stone's death, was owned by the Stone family until 1936.

The site is open daily (except Wednesday through Sunday during winter months), with guided tours on Sundays. The National Park plans to eventually restore the site to its appearance around 1900. Interpretation of the site centers on the life of Thomas Stone and on changes that have occurred at Habre de Venture.

FACILITIES: Restrooms and drinking water are available at the site. Food and lodging are in La Plata, 5 miles east.

CAMPING: There are a limited number of campgrounds in the area. Information on camping is available at the visitor contact station.

MASSACHUSETTS

STATE TOURIST INFORMATION
(800) 227–6277

ADAMS NATIONAL HISTORIC SITE
P.O. Box 531
Quincy, MA 02269
(617) 770–1175

Adams National Historic Site was designated as part of the National Park Service in 1946 to commemorate the distinguished men and women of the Adams family who dedicated their lives to the development and service of the United States. The thirteen-acre park is comprised of four units: the birthplaces of John Adams and John Quincy Adams; the "Old House," home to four generations of the Adams family; the United First Parish Church; and the park's visitor center; all located in Quincy Massachusetts, 8 miles southeast of Boston. The visitor center is at 1250 Hancock Street in the Presidents Place Galleria.

The John Adams and the John Quincy Adams birthplaces are the oldest still-standing presidential birthplaces in the United States. In 1735, John Adams was born in the saltbox-style house located only 75 feet from where his son John Quincy Adams would be born in 1767. In the John Quincy Adams birthplace, young John and his bride Abigail started their family and the future president launched his career in politics and law. John Adams maintained his law office in the house and it was here that he, Samuel Adams, and James Bowdoin wrote the Massachusetts Constitution. This document, still in use, greatly influenced development of the United States Constitution.

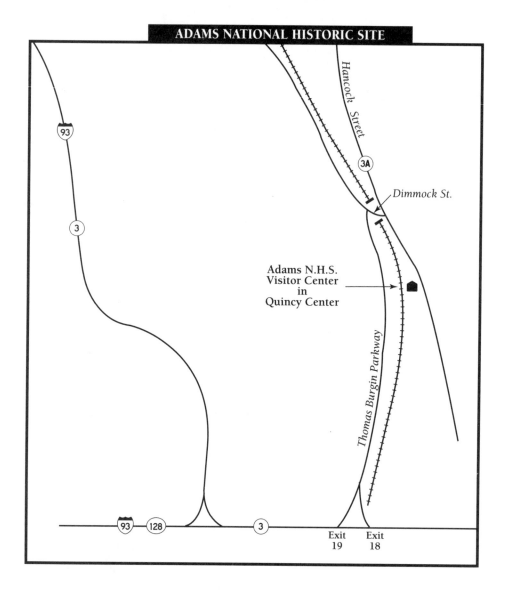

The Old House, built in 1731 by a wealthy West Indian sugar planter, was to become the resident of four generations of the Adams family from 1787 to 1927. It was home to presidents John Adams and John Quincy Adams; first ladies Abigail and Louisa Catherine Adams; Civil War Minister to Great Britain Charles Francis Adams; and literary historians Henry and Brooks Adams. The Adams family's legacy of service to their nation is reflected as much by the 78,000 artifacts inside the Old House as by its historic landscape. Following a tour, visitors may stroll the Old House grounds, which include a historic orchard and an eighteenth-century-style formal garden, containing thousands of annual and perennial flowers. The 1873 Carriage House is also available for self-guided tours.

The United First Parish Church was constructed in 1828. This national landmark structure, designed by Alexander Parish, was partially financed through a generous land donation from John Adams. The crypt beneath the sanctuary of the church is the final resting place of presidents John Adams and John Quincy Adams, and first ladies Abigail and Louisa Catherine Adams.

Adams National Historic Site is open seven days a week from 9:00 A.M. to 5:00 P.M., April 19 to November 10. Guided tours of the site are offered approximately every forty-five minutes. Visitors must register for tours (fee charged) at the visitor center. The tour includes travel via a trolley to the historic homes. Tour space is limited, and is filled on a first-come basis. Advance reservations (617–770–1175) are required for groups of eight or more.

FACILITIES: No facilities are available at the site. Food and lodging are available in Quincy.

CAMPING: No camping is permitted at the site. Wompatuck State Park offers nice wooded campsites (400 sites) with tables, flush toilets, electrical hookups, and showers, 11 miles southeast of the site in Hingham. Wompatuck State Park is reached via highways 3, 3A, and 228. The park can be difficult to find but is seldom filled.

BLACKSTONE RIVER VALLEY NATIONAL HERITAGE CORRIDOR

1 Depot Square
Woonsocket, RI 02895
(401) 762–0440

Blackstone River Valley National Heritage Corridor was established in 1986 to interpret the history and coordinate development along a 250,000-acre river valley that gave birth to the American Industrial Revolution. The corridor surrounds 46 miles of river and canals that run from Worcester, Massachusetts, to Providence, Rhode Island.

The American Industrial Revolution took seed and blossomed in the Blackstone River Valley of New England. The river initially attracted settlers in search of a source of food and drinking water. Later the river attracted craftsmen and industrialists who constructed diversionary dams to provide power for small machinery, textile mills, iron forges, and gristmills. Falls along the Blackstone prevented the river from being widely used for transportation until canals were constructed to circumvent these obstructions. Visitors can walk along sections of the canal and towpath in state parks in Lincoln, Rhode Island, and Uxbridge, Massachusetts. Railroads made water transportation along the canals obsolete by the mid-1800s.

The Blackstone River Valley continues to provide a link to its agricultural and industrial roots. Hilltop villages where settlers lived before the industrial development and mill villages that provided housing to the thousands of workers remain as a testament to the history of this valley. Farmlands characterized by open fields, stone walls, and orchards are uphill from the river.

No federal lands or facilities are within the heritage corridor. The National Park Service works with state and local governments and historic and environmental organizations to protect the valley's heritage and to plan for its future. Information centers are at: Roger Williams National Memorial, 282 North Main Street, Providence, RI 02903; River Bend Farm Visitor Center, Blackstone River and Canal Heritage State Park, 287 Oak Street, Uxbridge, MA (508–278–7604); Broad Meadow Brook Wildlife Sanctuary, Massachusetts Audubon, 414 Massasoit Road, Worcester, MA 01604.

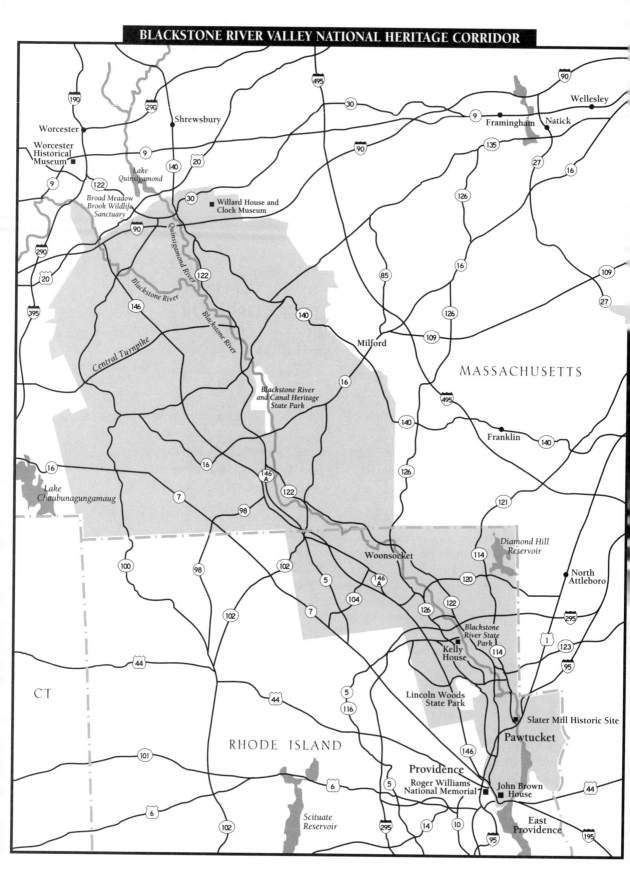

FACILITIES: A wide variety of restaurants and accommodations are in the Blackstone River Valley.

CAMPING: Several private campgrounds are in the national heritage corridor. Camping facilities and directions can be obtained at an information center or chamber of commerce.

FISHING: Fishing is permitted in the Blackstone River with a valid state license.

BOSTON AFRICAN AMERICAN NATIONAL HISTORIC SITE

46 Joy Street
Boston, MA 02114
(617) 742–5415

Boston African American National Historic Site was established in 1980 to preserve and commemorate original buildings that housed the nineteenth-century free Afro-American community on Beacon Hill. The site is located in downtown Boston in the Beacon Hill area just north of Boston Common.

The first Africans arrived in Boston in 1638 as slaves. Additional slaves continued to be brought to Boston, but at the same time, a significant free black population became a part of the city. By the late 1700s, a federal census listed no slaves in the entire state of Massachusetts.

Boston African American National Historic Site comprises the area of the city where African-Americans pressed for civil rights, pursued the political process, and forced an end to school segregation. The site is best seen by following the Black Heritage Trail, which is identified by signs and winds through the Beacon Hill area. A fairly brisk walk along the trail requires about an hour and includes a couple of steep hills. Included on the walking tour are twelve private residences not open to the public, two public buildings, and a memorial. Among the buildings are the oldest black church building still standing in the United States, a school built in 1834 by a white businessman for the education of black children, and one of the city's first schools with an integrated student body.

The site's headquarters is at 46 Joy Street. Brochures on the Black Heritage Trail may be obtained here or at the visitor center of Boston National Historical Park at 15 State Street. During summer months living-history programs and films on Afro-American history are presented.

FACILITIES: No food or lodging are provided by the National Park Service, but both are available nearby. Restrooms and drinking water are at the visitor center at 15 State Street and at the main visitor center of Boston National Historical Park.

CAMPING: No camping is available at the site. (See the camping section under Boston National Historical Park.)

Charles Street Station

Cambridge St.

Bowdoin Street Station

Charles St.

Phillips St.

Grove St.

Anderson St.

Garden St.

Irving St.

Russel St.

Hancock St.

Bowdoin St.

Revere St.

Myrtle St.

Pinckney St.

West Cedar St.

Cedar Lane Way

Louisburg Square

BEACON HILL

Mount Vernon St.

Chestnut St.

Joy St.

STATE HOUSE

Beacon St.

BOSTON COMMON

Park St.

PUBLIC GARDEN

■ Boston African American N.H.S.
••• Black Heritage Trail
Ⓣ Rapid Transit Station

Park Street Station

Tremont St.

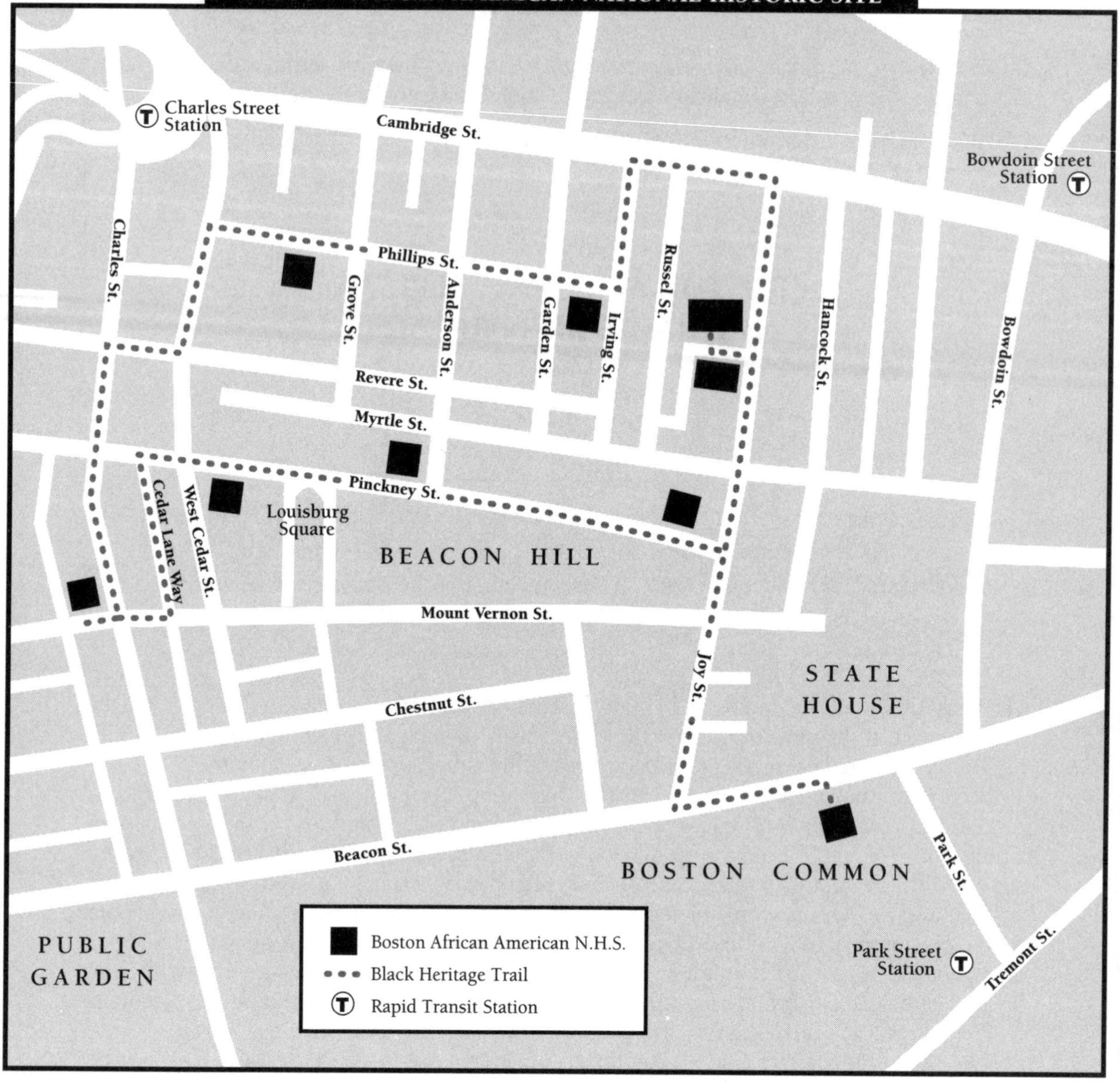

BOSTON NATIONAL HISTORICAL PARK

Charlestown Navy Yard
Boston, MA 02129
(617) 242–5642 and 242–5601

Boston National Historical Park was established in 1974 to preserve a number of Boston's oldest and most important historic structures. Most, such as Faneuil Hall, have associations with the American Revolution. The park also includes the Charlestown Navy Yard, the location of the U.S.S. *Constitution* and the only American navy yard preserved as a historic site.

The original settlers of present-day Boston fled from England in an attempt to escape religious persecution, but their descendants played an active role in the history of the British Empire. When England imposed taxes on the colonists to help pay for their defense, resistance to the mother country became open. When town meetings protesting the taxes were held in Faneuil Hall, and at Old State House, John Hancock and Samuel Adams denounced the tax laws. In 1773, a town meeting in the Old South Meeting House resulted in a march to the waterfront, where cargoes of tea were dumped into the harbor. In 1775, lanterns were hung in the steeple of Old North Church to warn the Charlestown militia of the movement of British troops toward Concord, if Paul Revere was unable to deliver the same message in person. Two months after the conflict at Lexington and Concord, British troops landed near the present Charlestown Navy Yard and drove American soldiers from Charlestown in the Battle of Bunker Hill. In 1776, after the British had occupied Boston for twenty-one months, Washington's troops dragged artillery to Dorchester Heights and forced the enemy to evacuate the city.

Boston National Historical Park is a group of federal, private, and municipal sites that have related themes. Many of the sites provide interpretive services such as exhibits and talks; some also have guided tours. A visitor's first stop should be the National Park Service Visitor Center at 15 State Street across from the Old State House. Here visitors will find park personnel to answer questions and a slide program on sites along the Freedom Trail. From mid-April through late November, rangers lead frequent one-and-one-half-hour walks along the downtown section of the trail. The Freedom Trail begins at Boston Common, winds through the historic district and the Charlestown Navy Yard, and ends in Charlestown at the Bunker Hill Monument. The Navy Yard is where the U.S.S. *Constitution* is berthed and another visitor center is located. Visitors may take guided tours of the *Constitution* and the U.S.S. *Cassin Young,* a World War II destroyer. The entire trail, which is marked by a red line on the sidewalk, is $2\frac{1}{2}$ miles long. Sixteen historic sites are along the route.

Unless you are staying in a downtown hotel, it is best to park outside the city and take the rapid-transit system into the downtown area. The Greater Boston Convention and Visitors Bureau, Inc., maintains an information booth on Boston Common. The booth is near the Park Street exit of the T (rapid transit system). Freedom Trail maps are available at the information booth and at the visitor center.

FACILITIES: All visitor services are available along the route. A special treat is selecting something to eat among the great variety of food vendors in Faneuil Hall Marketplace. Restrooms and drinking water are at the visitor center and the Charlestown Navy Yard.

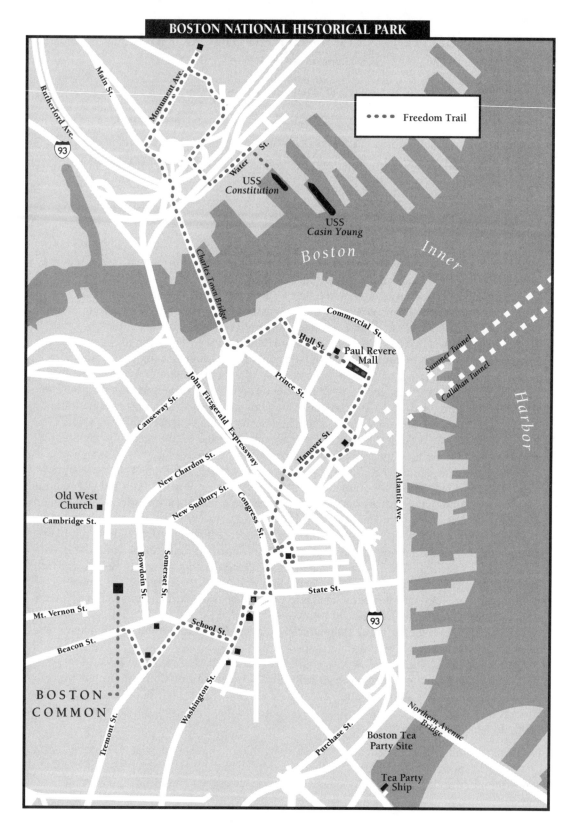

• • • • Freedom Trail

USS
Constitution

USS
Casin Young

Boston   Inner

Commercial St.

Hull St.

Paul Revere
Mall

Summer Tunnel

Callahan Tunnel

Harbor

Main St.

Rutherford Ave.

Monument Ave.

Water St.

Charles Town Bridge

John Fitzgerald Expressway

Causeway St.

Prince St.

New Chardon St.

New Sudbury St.

Hanover St.

Congress St.

Atlantic Ave.

Old West
Church

Cambridge St.

Bowdoin St.

Somerset St.

Mt. Vernon St.

School St.

State St.

Beacon St.

Washington St.

**BOSTON
COMMON**

Tremont St.

Purchase St.

Northern Avenue Bridge

Boston Tea
Party Site

Tea Party
Ship

Old North Church in Boston National Historic Park (opposite page)

CAMPING: No camping is permitted in the park areas. The nearest public camping for those wishing to visit downtown Boston is at Wompatuck State Park, south of the city in Hingham (617–749–7160). Here campers will find 400 shaded spaces with water, tables, grills, flush toilets, a dump station, and showers. Some sites have electricity. From Highway 3, take exit 15 and Highway 228 4½ miles north to Free Street. Turn right on Free Street and drive slightly less than a mile to the park. No reservations are accepted. Boston's rapid-transit system has a stop in Braintree, about 9 miles away from the park.

FISHING: Fishing is available at a number of spots in the city, including from the bridge crossing to the Charlestown Navy Yard.

CAPE COD NATIONAL SEASHORE

99 Marconi Site Road
Wellfleet, MA 02667
(508) 349–3785

Cape Cod National Seashore was authorized in 1961 to protect nearly 45,000 acres (27,000 acres of land area) of ocean beaches, dunes, woodlands, freshwater ponds, and marshes. The park is on the Cape Cod Peninsula in southeastern Massachusetts and is reached by auto via U.S. 6 or by air service or ferryboat from Boston to Provincetown.

On this peninsula, where the Pilgrims first glimpsed the New World, visitors will find numerous outdoor activities. Visitor centers in Eastham and Provincetown contain exhibits, audio-visual programs, and information services to help introduce the area's natural and historical features. The visitor centers are open from spring until early winter. Call ahead for seasonal closure dates and hours. In mid-winter, visitor information is available at park headquarters in Wellfleet.

Self-guiding trails are located at Beech Forest, Pilgrim Heights, Pamet Cranberry Bog, Great Island, the Marconi Station Site, Fort Hill, and Salt Pond Visitor Center. Three bike paths with bike rentals are nearby. Lifeguards are present for swimming at Coast Guard, Nauset Light, Marconi, Head of the Meadow, Race Point, and Herring Cove beaches. Over-sand vehicles require a permit and must use designated sand routes in Province Lands Area only. Guided walks, talks, and evening programs take place daily during summer and on a reduced schedule in spring and fall seasons.

FACILITIES: No food or lodging is provided by the National Park Service, although a concessioner sells refreshments at Herring Cove Beach. Drinking water and modern restrooms are located at both visitor centers and at the beaches. Motels, restaurants, groceries, and gas stations are in towns adjoining the park. Information and reservations for accommodations can be obtained by writing the Cape Cod Chamber of Commerce, Hyannis, MA 02601.

CAMPING: No camping is provided by the National Park Service, although several private campgrounds are located in the area. The nearest public camping is at Nickerson State Park in Brewster. The campground has a dump station, water, flush toilets, and showers but no

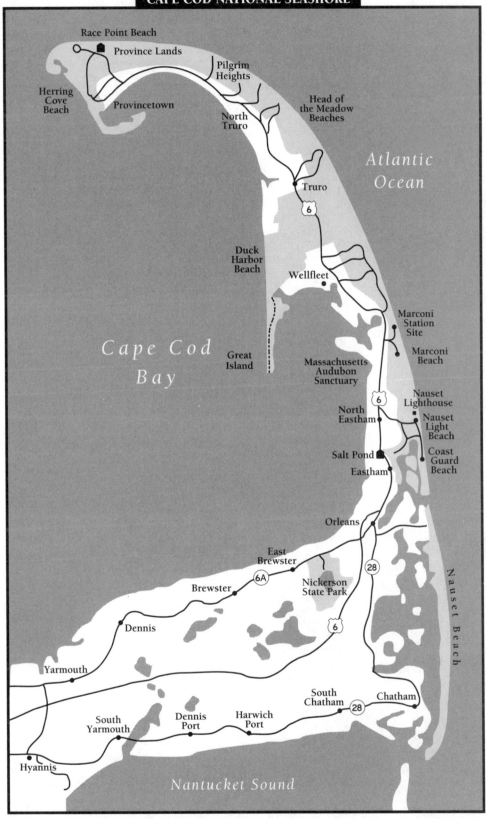

hookups. A limited number of reservations are accepted, and it fills up early during summer. Shawme Crowell State Forest, near Sandwich on Route 130, has the same facilities and fills up later in the day.

FISHING: Rainbow and brook trout and warm-water sport fish live in a number of freshwater ponds (license required). No license is required for surf fishing.

FREDERICK LAW OLMSTED NATIONAL HISTORIC SITE

99 Warren Street
Brookline, MA 02146
(617) 566–1689

Frederick Law Olmsted National Historic Site was authorized in 1979 to preserve and interpret the home and office of Olmsted, the great conservationist and founder of the profession of landscape architecture in America. The site is located 5 miles west of downtown Boston in the suburb of Brookline via Highway 9. Turn south off Highway 9 on Warren Street and drive to the intersection of Warren and Dudley. Parking is limited.

Frederick Law Olmsted (1822–1903) was born in Hartford, Connecticut, and began his career in landscape architecture with the design of New York's Central Park. It was the first of thousands of public and private landscapes throughout America attributed to the genius of Olmsted, his sons, and successors. In Brookline in 1883, Olmsted established a full-scale professional office that expanded and perpetuated his landscape design ideals, philosophy, and influence over the course of the next century. The Olmsted Archives is one of the most heavily researched museum collections in the National Park Service and contains design and planning documents detailing such treasured American landscapes as the U.S. Capitol Grounds, the White House, the Jefferson Memorial, the United States Military Academy at West Point, Great Smoky Mountains National Park, Niagara Falls Reservation, Yosemite Valley, and park systems in Boston, Chicago, Louisville, and Seattle.

Fairsted, the name given to the Olmsted home and office, serves as both a historic house museum and a center for the study and preservation of American landscapes. The scope and magnitude of Olmsted's design work is presented to visitors through exhibits, films, and tours of the historic office and grounds. The Olmsted Archives assists researchers with documentation, while the Olmsted Center for Landscape Preservation shares technical expertise in historic landscape preservation and maintenance. Visitor hours are Friday, Saturday, and Sunday from 10:00 A.M. to 4:30 P.M. Groups and researchers are accommodated at other times by appointment.

FACILITIES: Full facilities are available in nearby Brookline.

CAMPING: No camping is permitted at the site. (See camping section under Boston National Historical Park.)

See map on the following page.

Nauset Lighthouse at Cape Cod National Seashore (opposite page)

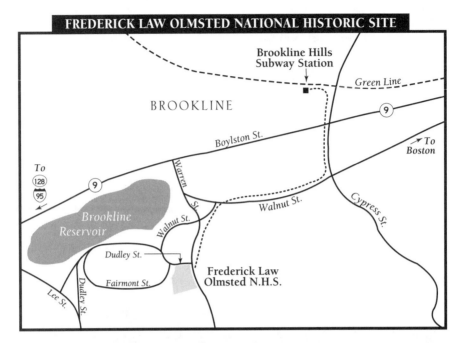

FREDERICK LAW OLMSTED NATIONAL HISTORIC SITE

BROOKLINE

Brookline Hills
Subway Station

Green Line

Boylston St.

To
Boston

To
128
95

Warren St.

Brookline
Reservoir

Walnut St.

Walnut St.

Cypress St.

Dudley St.

Lee St.

Dudley St.

Fairmont St.

Frederick Law
Olmsted N.H.S.

Photographic archives in the historic Olmsted office, where photographs representing thousands of landscape design projects nationwide are stored. (Courtesy J. David Bohl)

JOHN FITZGERALD KENNEDY NATIONAL HISTORIC SITE

83 Beals Street
Brookline, MA 02146
(617) 566–7937

John Fitzgerald Kennedy National Historic Site was authorized as part of the National Park Service in 1967 to preserve the house that was the birthplace and early boyhood home of the thirty-fifth president of the United States. The site is located a short distance west of Boston in the suburb of Brookline at 83 Beals Street. Limited street parking is available and the site is easily reached by public transportation.

This house was purchased by Joseph P. Kennedy in 1914 just prior to his marriage to Rose Fitzgerald. During their residence here, four of their children—Joseph Jr. (1915), John (1917), Rosemary (1918), and Kathleen (1920)—were born. In 1921, the house was sold to a friend, and the Kennedys moved to a larger home on the corner of Abbottsford and Naples Road (#1 on map). John F. Kennedy lived in this second house from age four to ten. The birthplace home was repurchased by the Kennedys in 1966, and the restoration and refurnishing to its 1917 appearance was supervised by Rose Kennedy.

The historic site is open Wednesday through Sunday (10:00 A.M. to 4:30 P.M.) from mid-May through mid-October. Park ranger-guided tours of the home are offered periodically throughout the day. Exhibits and a video presentation are available in the small visitor center. The site's interior is not wheelchair-accessible. In addition to this home and the second house purchased by Joseph P. Kennedy, the area also contains St. Aidan's Catholic Church, where the Kennedy children were baptized (#2 on map); Edward Devotion School, where John and Joseph, Jr., began their formal education (#3 on map); and the site of Dexter School, where the boys soon transferred (#4 on map). The historic house in front of the school building is open to the public on Tuesdays and Thursdays from 2:30 P.M. to 5:00 P.M. The house on Naples Road is privately owned, and the owner's privacy and property must be respected. Visitors are asked to view the home only from the sidewalk or from across the street. Neighborhood walking tours are offered by park rangers throughout the summer.

FACILITIES: No facilities are available at the site, but food and lodging may be found nearby.

CAMPING: No camping is permitted at the site. (See the camping section under Boston National Historical Park.)

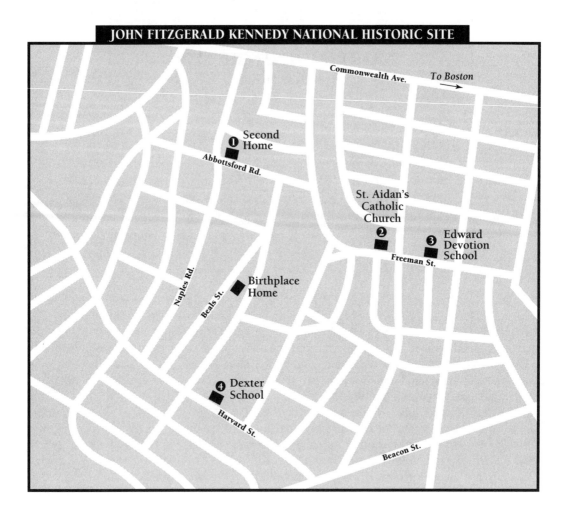

JOHN FITZGERALD KENNEDY NATIONAL HISTORIC SITE

Commonwealth Ave.   To Boston

① Second Home

Abbottsford Rd.

St. Aidan's Catholic Church

② ③ Edward Devotion School

Freeman St.

Naples Rd.

Beals St.

◆ Birthplace Home

④ Dexter School

Harvard St.

Beacon St.

John F. Kennedy National Historic Site (opposite page)

LONGFELLOW NATIONAL HISTORIC SITE

105 Brattle Street
Cambridge, MA 02138
(617) 876–4491

Longfellow National Historic Site comprises two acres and was authorized in 1972 to preserve the home where poet Henry Wadsworth Longfellow lived from 1837 to 1882. The house is located at 105 Brattle Street in Cambridge, Massachusetts, a suburb of Boston.

Henry Wadsworth Longfellow was born in Portland, Maine, in 1807. In 1835, he accepted a position at Harvard after being graduated from Bowdoin College and studying in Europe for three years. The house into which he was to move two years later was built in 1759 for a wealthy Tory who fled prior to the Revolution. Later, during the siege of Boston, George Washington used the home as his headquarters. It was here that Longfellow wrote his most famous poetry, including *Evangeline, Hiawatha,* and *The Courtship of Miles Standish.*

The house is open for one-half-hour conducted tours (fee charged) daily from 10:00 A.M. to 4:30 P.M. except Thanksgiving Day, Christmas Day, and New Year's Day. Visiting the site is sometimes a problem because of a lack of parking. There are several pay parking lots and garages in Harvard Square. Another solution is to park in Boston under the Boston Common and take the Red Line subway to Harvard Square. From here, a .6-mile walk up Brattle Street takes you past two colonial mansions. Returning to Harvard Square by way of Mason Street you pass the site of Washington Elm, under whose branches George Washington accepted command of the Continental Army.

An interesting side trip is a guided tour of Harvard University. The tours leave twice daily during summer months from an information center a short distance from the Harvard Square rapid-transit stop.

FACILITIES: Drinking water and modern restrooms are in the visitor center, and food and lodging can be found nearby. Downtown Cambridge near the rapid-transit stop is filled with restaurants.

CAMPING: No camping is permitted on the site. (See the camping section under Boston National Historical Park.)

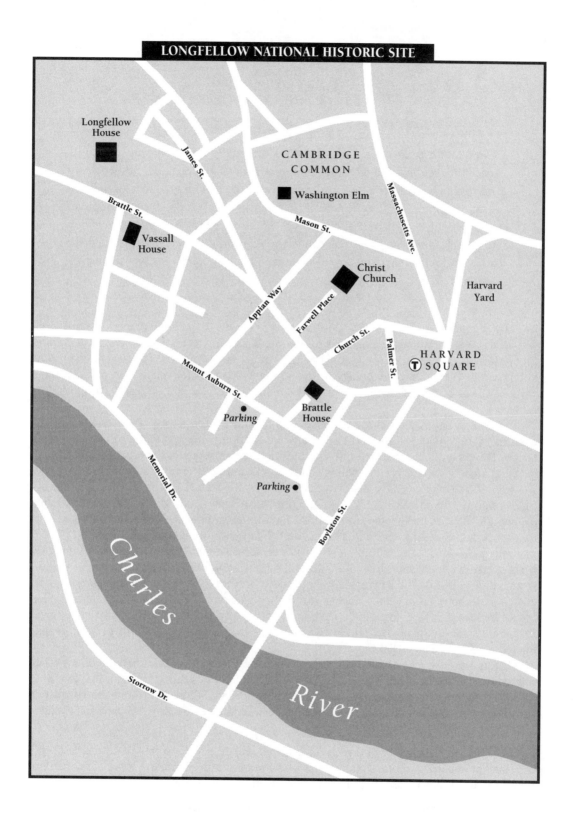

LONGFELLOW NATIONAL HISTORIC SITE

Longfellow House

CAMBRIDGE COMMON

Washington Elm

James St.

Massachusetts Ave.

Brattle St.

Mason St.

Vassall House

Appian Way

Christ Church

Farwell Place

Harvard Yard

Church St.

Palmer St.

HARVARD T SQUARE

Mount Auburn St.

Parking

Brattle House

Memorial Dr.

Parking

Boylston St.

Charles

Storrow Dr.

River

LOWELL NATIONAL HISTORICAL PARK

67 Kirk Street
Lowell, MA 01852
(508) 970–5000

Lowell National Historical Park, with sites located throughout the city of Lowell, was authorized in 1978 to commemorate America's first planned industrial city. The park offers visitors a look at the country's past, including tours of a mill and a canal system. The historical park is in northeastern Massachusetts, approximately 30 miles northwest of Boston via U.S. 3. Take U.S. 3 or Interstate 495 to the Lowell connector. Exit the connector at Thorndike Street and follow the brown-and-white signs to Lowell National and State Parks visitor parking on Dutton Street.

The city of Lowell, America's first great industrial town, was named for Francis Cabot Lowell, who as a young man brought England's textile manufacturing technology to the United States. From a tiny rural hamlet, Lowell launched the United States into the industrial age by combining capital, labor, and technology to mass-produce cotton cloth. It is this past combined with the town's revival following decades of economic decline that is on display in the historical park.

The park's visitor center at the corner of Market and Dutton streets (246 Market Street) is open daily from 8:30 A.M. to 5:00 P.M. A large free-parking area is directly behind the visitor center. The center is in a restored mill complex on the site of one of the town's original textile facilities. Here, visitors can view exhibits and an outstanding twenty-minute multi-image slide show that help to interpret the history of Lowell. Lowell National Historical Park includes historic cotton textile mills, worker housing, 5.6 miles of canals, and industrial history exhibits. Among the latter is the Boott Cotton Mills Museum featuring a re-created weave room with ninety operating power looms and exhibits on the American Industrial Revolution.

Visitors may make reservations at the visitor center for guided tours of the area. Among the tours offered are a mill and canal tour (two-and-one-half hours) by trolley, canal barge, and foot that includes a ride on the Pawtucket Canal and the Merrimack River; a waterpower tour (one-and-one-half hours) to the Guard Locks and Francis gate on the Pawtucket Canal; and Exploring Lowell tours to less frequently seen areas of the city. The mill and canal tour is given frequently and is probably the one to choose if time is limited. Another tour for visitors with limited time is the Pawtucket Canal tour.

Visitors may also take part in a variety of festivals, regattas, and markets taking place throughout the summer months, including the Lowell Folk Festival, the largest free folk festival in the nation. The Working People Exhibit is at 40 French Street. Visitors should plan on spending at least half a day and could easily take an entire day visiting the park facilities and taking two or more tours.

FACILITIES: In the vicinity of the visitor center there are a wide variety of ethnic, fast-food, and fine dining restaurants. Lodging may be found nearby. Drinking water and modern restrooms are at the visitor center and the Boott Cotton Mills Museum.

CAMPING: No camping is permitted in the park. Harold Parker State Forest (134 sites) offers a campground with tables, grills, water, flush toilets, showers, swimming, and fishing. The forest is approximately 13 miles east of Lowell. From Highway 38, drive 7¾ miles north on Interstate 495 and 5½ miles southeast on Highway 114.

FISHING: Fishing for bass, perch, and catfish is available in the Merrimack River. A good location is directly below the Pawtucket Dam. Fishing is not permitted in the canals.

MINUTE MAN NATIONAL HISTORICAL PARK

174 Liberty Street
Concord, MA 01742
(617) 369–6993

Minute Man National Historical Park comprises 945 acres and was designated a part of the National Park Service in 1959 to commemorate the scene of the fighting on April 19, 1775, that opened the American Revolution. The park is located northwest of Boston along Battle Road (State Highway 2A) between the towns of Lexington and Concord.

Upon hearing that colonists were stockpiling arms and ammunition in Concord, British Commander Thomas Gage sent 700 soldiers from Boston to confiscate the supplies. Patriots from Boston, including Paul Revere, heard of the plan and rode ahead to warn colonists along the way. After a short battle at Lexington Green the morning of April 19, British troops marched to Concord, where they destroyed military stores and engaged in additional fighting. As the British returned toward Boston, Americans took up positions along the route and continued to exchange fire. Later, the day's most extensive battle occurred as British forces moved out of Lexington. This action, combined with a great deal of inaccurate reporting, sparked the struggle that was to end in America's independence.

Battle Road Visitor Center is open daily from 9:00 A.M. to 5:30 P.M. Here visitors will find exhibits, interpretive talks, and a twenty-two-minute movie. Interpretive talks are also given at the North Bridge Visitor Center on Liberty Street in Concord, which provides exhibits, a twelve-minute audiovisual program, and a bookstore. The North Bridge Visitor Center is open from 9:00 A.M. to 5:30 P.M. during the season, with reduced hours in the winter.

Interesting places in the area include the following: The Wayside, home of Nathaniel Hawthorne and Margaret Sidney (thirty-minute tour, fee); the Ralph Waldo Emerson Home (thirty-minute tour, fee); Orchard House, where Louisa May Alcott wrote *Little Women* (forty-five-minute tour, fee); Concord Museum, with seventeen rooms of period furniture (fee charged); Old Manse, home of Emerson's grandfather (fee charged); and Walden Pond, path to site of Thoreau's cabin (parking fee). In Lexington, tours of Buckman Tavern, Munroe Tavern, and the Hancock-Clark House are sponsored by the Lexington Historical Society (fee charged). Visitors can easily spend from half a day to a full day touring the park and historic sites along the road.

FACILITIES: No food or lodging is available in the park, but both can be found nearby in Lexington or Concord. Restrooms and water are provided at Battle Road Visitor Center and North Bridge Visitor Center.

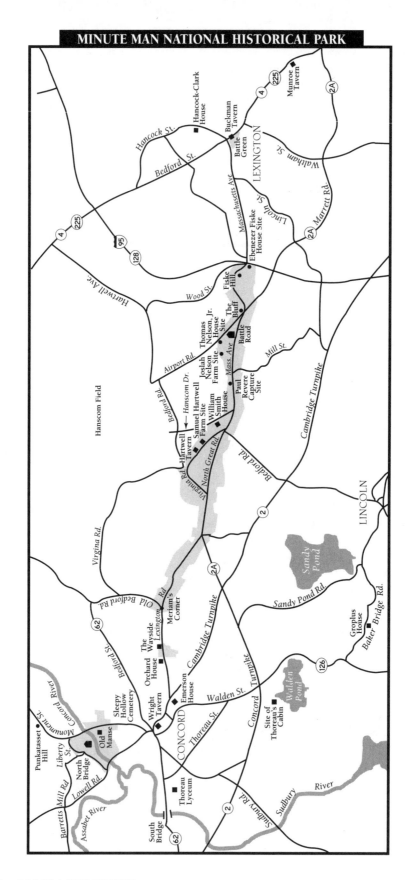

CAMPING: No camping is permitted in the park. Harold Parker State Forest, 28 miles northeast of the historical park, provides 134 sites with water, tables, grills, flush toilets, showers, swimming, and fishing. From the Battle Road Visitor Center, drive ¾ mile east to Interstate 95, go 18½ miles north to U.S. 1, 1¾ miles north on 1 to Highway 114, and 6½ miles northwest on 114 to the park entrance.

SALEM MARITIME NATIONAL HISTORIC SITE
174 Derby Street
Salem, MA 01970
(508) 740–1650

This portion of the Salem waterfront was designated a national historic site in 1938 to preserve part of one of the famous port cities of early America. The nine-acre site is located on the northern Massachusetts coastline in the city of Salem. From Route 1A, turn east onto Derby Street.

Salem's maritime fame dated from the early 1700s when the town was known as home to the New World's most able sea captains. During the American Revolution, Salem's ships captured nearly 450 vessels, most of which were brought into port. Following the war, the city became a center for trade as its ships sailed to all corners of the earth in search of new markets for America's raw materials and products. Later, as ships increased in size and Americans moved westward, Salem's shallow harbor resulted in a diversion of trade to the deep-water ports of Boston and New York.

The historic site includes three wharves and a number of restored buildings clustered on the waterfront. Derby Wharf, the longest and oldest of the wharves, was built in 1762 and was once covered with fourteen warehouses. The Derby Wharf Trail leads to a small lighthouse built in 1871. Across from the wharves, the National Park Service has restored three homes, a warehouse, a scale house, a store, and the Custom House, which represented the U.S. government in issuing permits and collecting taxes.

A small orientation center is located on Central Wharf. The National Park Service offers guided tours and programs throughout summer months. The West India Goods Store is operated by Eastern National Park and Monument Association; goods in the store are sold to the public.

The city of Salem includes a number of tourist attractions in addition to the historic site. Among the museums and numerous restored homes are the House of the Seven Gables, the Salem Witch Museum, and the Peabody Essex Museum of Salem. The National Park Visitor Center on New Liberty and Essex streets in downtown Salem provides information on Salem and Essex County, and a twenty-seven-minute film on the 400-year history of the area.

FACILITIES: No lodging or food service is available at the site, although both can be found nearby. Restrooms and drinking water are behind the Central Wharf orientation center. There is no parking at the site. Visitors park in a facility across the street from the downtown visitor center.

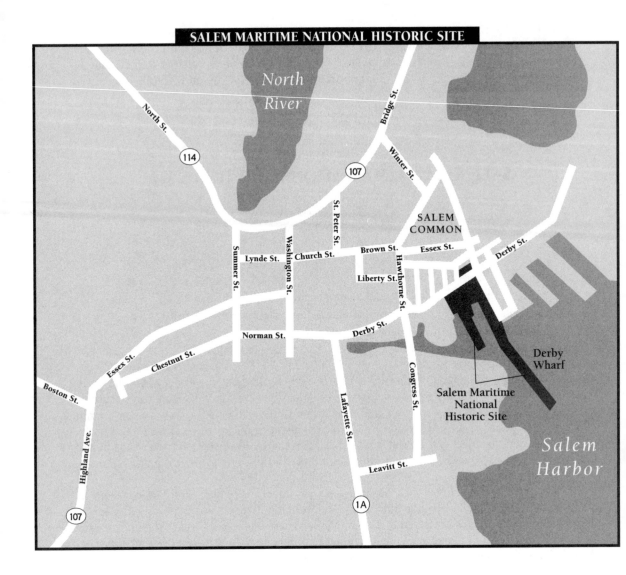

CAMPING: No camping is permitted at the site. Approximately 10 miles northwest via Highway 114, Harold Parker State Forest offers camping with flush toilets, showers, boating, swimming, and fishing but no hookups. No reservations are accepted.

FISHING: Fishing is permitted along the wharf.

SAUGUS IRON WORKS NATIONAL HISTORIC SITE

244 Central Street
Saugus, MA 01906
(617) 233–0050

Saugus Iron Works National Historic Site comprises eight and one-half acres and was reconstructed to its mid-1600s appearance by the American Iron and Steel Institute in the 1950s. In 1969, the area was incorporated into the National Park Service. The site is located 10 miles northeast of Boston via U.S. 1. Exit at Main Street; the site is near the intersection of Main and Central streets.

New England's need for manufactured items resulted in construction of North America's first integrated iron works at Saugus in 1646. The abundance of iron ore, streams for water power, and hardwood forests for buildings, machinery, and making charcoal prompted a group of English investors to import skilled workmen and raise capital for the project. The indirect process of producing liquid iron, which was poured into long bars and then forged into wrought iron, was used here. The works also included a rolling and slitting mill that flattened and slit some of the wrought-iron bars. Although the mill was eventually closed because of mismanagement and an inability to earn a profit, the iron works helped lay the foundation for the iron and steel industry in the United States.

Park personnel are stationed at a small entrance station to help answer visitor questions. Conducted walks begin here for a tour of the reconstructed furnace, forge, ironhouse, rolling mill, and Iron Works House. This latter building is the only original structure still standing. A museum is near the entrance station. During summer months, living-history programs take place at the site. A nature trail is also available.

FACILITIES: No food or lodging is available at the site, although both can be found outside. A drinking fountain and restrooms are adjacent to the museum. There is a picnic area.

CAMPING: No camping is permitted at the site. Harold Parker State Forest, approximately 13 miles northwest via U.S. 1 and State Highway 114, offers shaded sites with flush toilets, showers, swimming, boating, and fishing. No hookups are available, and reservations are not accepted.

SPRINGFIELD ARMORY NATIONAL HISTORIC SITE

One Armory Square
Springfield, MA 01105
(413) 734–8551

Springfield Armory National Historic Site was authorized in 1974 to preserve the history of the first National Armory. Armory technology and products profoundly affected the lives of soldiers and civilians alike. From Interstate 91 take Broad Street Exit (exit 4 northbound, exit 5 southbound) and follow the city's attractions sign system to the Armory. Free parking is available at museum.

The Arsenal at Springfield was established in 1777 to manufacture cartridges and gun carriages for the American Revolution. In 1794 President George Washington authorized the conversion of the arsenal to the first National Armory. For nearly 200 years the armory researched, developed, and manufactured military arms from the M1795 flintlock to the M-1 and M-14. Armory arms were essential in all major conflicts in U.S. history.

Visitors come from around the world to see the armory's last remaining operation, the museum. "Armory Industry" presents the story of important people and processes. Visitors become familiar with the "American System of Manufactures," and inventions such as the Blanchard Eccentric Lathe. The lathe and other armory inventions dramatically advanced the mass production of consumer products such as keys, shoes, baseball bats, and furniture. Important people include Women Ordnance Workers (WOWS) and inventors such as Erskine Allin, David Lyle, and John Garand. WOW's kept the armory operating and made improvements to the manufacturing process during World War II. The inventors developed the Trapdoor Springfield Rifle, Life Saving Gun, and the M-1 Rifle.

"Armory Arms" presents the story of U.S. shoulder arms, edged weapons, and pistols. Displayed are examples from our nation's largest collection of experimental and standard U.S. military arms and distinctive collections. Of special interest are Jefferson Davis's personal rifle, the collection of developmental M-1s from patent model to production model, a Texas Ranger Colt Walker, and the "Organ of Muskets" made famous by the Longfellow poem, *The Arsenal at Springfield.*

In addition, the site offers a self-guided walking tour, special exhibits, historical film, special events, and public or school programs.

FACILITIES: Open year-around, the buildings are wheelchair-accessible. Food and lodging are available nearby. Restrooms and drinking water are in the museum.

CAMPING: No camping is allowed on-site. The nearest campground is at Granville State Forest, 20 miles west of Springfield on State Highway 57.

MICHIGAN

STATE TOURIST INFORMATION
(800) 543–2937

FATHER MARQUETTE NATIONAL MEMORIAL
Straits State Park
St. Ignace, MI 49781
(906) 643–8620

Father Marquette National Memorial, an affiliated fifty-two-acre area of the National Park Service, was authorized in 1975 to pay tribute to a French priest and explorer who contributed greatly to the settlement of this region of the country. The memorial is located in the southern tip of Michigan's Upper Peninsula, in Straits State Park, near the town of St. Ignace.

Jacques Marquette arrived in Quebec in 1666 as a newly ordained French priest. Over the next decade, he founded the towns of Sault Ste. Marie and St. Ignace, Michigan; discovered and mapped the upper stretches of the Mississippi River; and founded a mission at an Indian village in Illinois. In 1675, on the shore of Michigan's Lower Peninsula, Father Marquette died of disease at the age of thirty-seven.

The memorial is open 9:00 A.M. to 8:00 P.M. from Memorial Day to mid-September. The park comprises a memorial, an amphitheater, and a museum. The museum contains exhibits, a copy of Father Marquette's journal, and a sixteen-minute film on an important time in the priest's life.

FACILITIES: Food and lodging are available in St. Ignace. Restrooms and drinking water are in the museum.

CAMPING: Developed campsites (275 sites) with flush toilets, showers, and electric hookups are available in Straits State Park.

ISLE ROYALE NATIONAL PARK

800 East Lakeshore Drive
Houghton, MI 49931
(906) 482–0984

Isle Royale National Park was legislated by Congress in 1931 to preserve a 134,000-acre roadless island of pristine forests, lakes, and shores. The park, located in northwestern Lake Superior 20 miles from the Canadian mainland, is 45 miles long and 9 miles wide. It is accessible only by boat or floatplane. Passenger ferries to the island are available at Houghton (National Park Service boat) or Copper Harbor, Michigan, and Grand Portage, Minnesota. A floatplane flies a regular schedule from Houghton. Reservations are required.

Isle Royale (named by French trappers) is the centerpiece of a park that is 70 percent under water. The island was created by volcanic lava flows and shaped by glaciers and water. Only 10,000 years ago, the last glacier smoothed the island before pausing on its southwestern end. The interior portion of Isle Royale contains more than thirty lakes and is covered by hardwood and conifer trees. The shore areas and lake borders are generally mixed evergreen forests. More than 200 varieties of birds have been spotted here. Wildlife includes the beaver, moose, red fox, red squirrel, snowshoe hare, and timber wolf.

The island has been inhabited off and on for 4,000 years. Prehistoric Indians mined copper here beginning around 2000 B.C., although the most active years were from A.D. 800 to 1600. Beginning in the 1840s, white miners began to exploit the native copper, an industry that continued intermittently for fifty years.

The park is open to visitors April 16 to October 31, with full services offered mid-June to August 31. Rain is frequent, and evenings generally are cool. A variety of interpretive programs are available, including conducted walks and evening slide programs. There are 165 miles of hiking trails in the park, including some that are self-guiding. Boat tours and rental boats are at Rock Harbor Lodge. For current transportation schedules and rates, write the park superintendent.

FACILITIES: Rock Harbor Lodge has sixty motel-type units and twenty housekeeping cabins. Meals, campstore, public showers, and a laundry also are available here. At Windigo, visitors will find a campstore selling snack food. For reservations and information, write National Park Concessions, Inc., Box 405, Houghton, MI 49931 (906–337–4993). In winter, write National Park Concessions, Inc., Mammoth Cave, KY 42259 (502–773–2191).

CAMPING: Thirty-six campgrounds are on the island. Generally, there are no tables or grills, and only Rock Harbor and Washington Creek have treated drinking water. A camping registration permit is required.

FISHING: Northern pike inhabit twenty-eight inland lakes and Lake Superior. Lake trout are found in Lake Superior and Siskiwit Lake. Other waters contain rainbow and brook trout, perch, walleye, and whitefish. A Michigan license is required for Lake Superior waters but not for the island's inland lakes or streams. The best fishing is in spring and fall.

ISLE ROYALE NATIONAL PARK

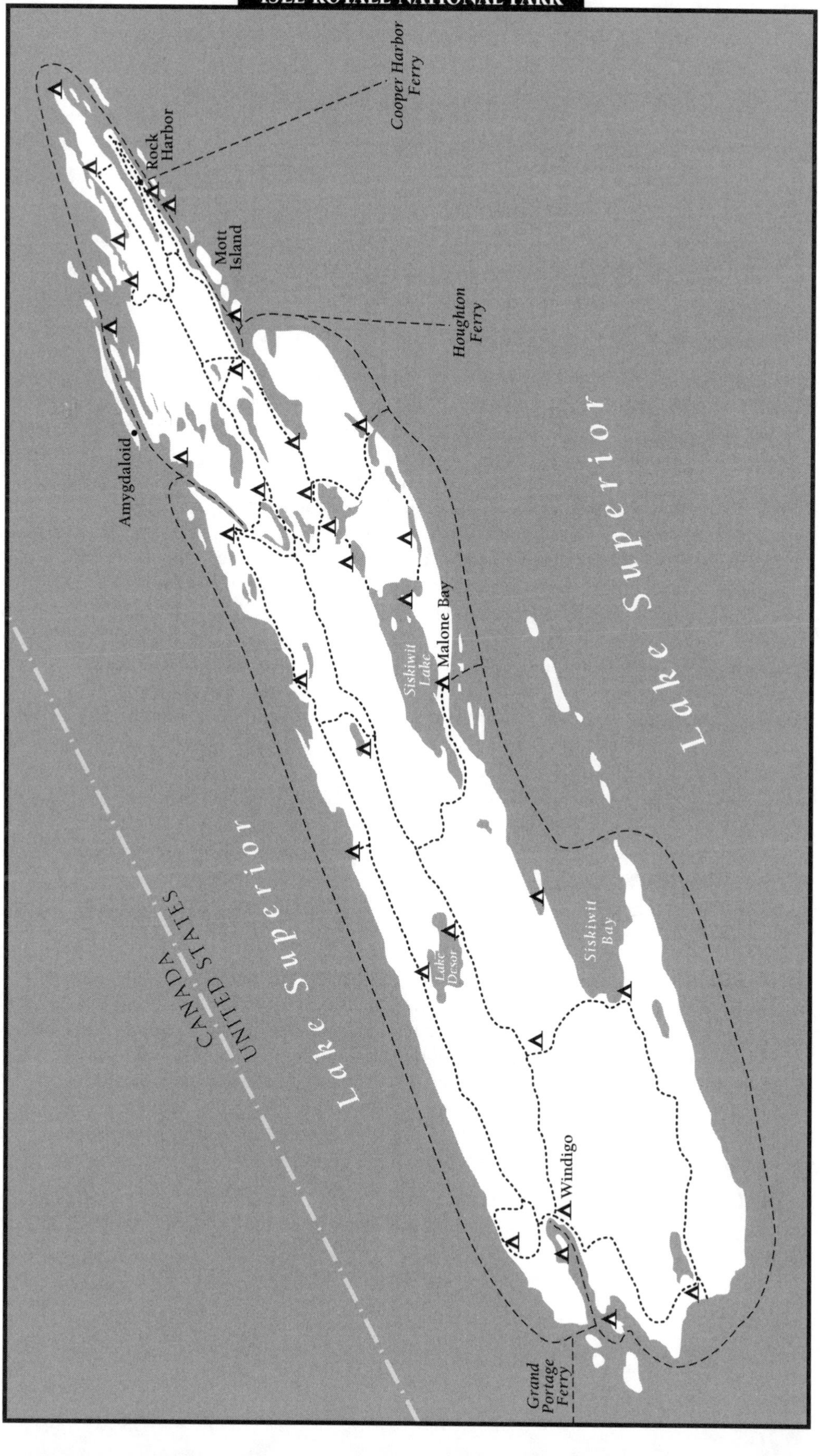
Cooper Harbor Ferry
Rock Harbor
Mott Island
Houghton Ferry
Amygdaloid
Malone Bay
Siskiwit Lake
Lake Superior
CANADA
UNITED STATES
Lake Superior
Siskiwit Bay
Lake Desor
Windigo
Grand Portage Ferry

PICTURED ROCKS NATIONAL LAKESHORE

P.O. Box 40
Munising, MI 49862
(906) 387–3700

Pictured Rocks National Lakeshore, authorized in 1966, comprises more than 70,000 acres of multicolored cliffs, broad beaches, sand dunes, waterfalls, ponds, and forests. The park is located along the south shore of Lake Superior in Michigan's Upper Peninsula, between the communities of Munising and Grand Marais.

The Pictured Rocks National Lakeshore offers a variety of sights. Along a 15-mile section at the western end of the park, multicolored sandstone cliffs rise as much as 200 feet above lake level. The Pictured Rocks cliffs are accessible by automobile at Miner's Castle, by hiking along Lakeshore Trail, and by boat from Lake Superior. Privately operated scenic cruises sail out of Munising from June 1 to October 10. Twelvemile Beach lies east of the Pictured Rocks cliffs and offers a broad sand-and-pebble beach for sunbathing, beachcombing, and hiking. Lake Superior is generally too cold for all but the hardiest of swimmers. At the park's eastern terminus are the Grand Sable Banks, an exposed glacial deposit rising to 275 feet above the lake at a 35-degree angle. Perched atop the banks are the 85-foot-high Grand Sable Dunes.

Inland you will find a densely covered hardwood forest surrounding lakes, ponds, streams, waterfalls, and bogs. On the west side of the park, Munising Falls drops 50 feet over a sandstone bluff into a natural amphitheater. The Sable, Chapel, and Miner's falls are popular sites to visit.

Nature walks and campfire programs are conducted during the summer. Schedules are posted at ranger stations and camping areas. The Munising Falls Visitor Center, located near Munising on Sand Point Road, is unstaffed and open daily from mid-May to October. The Grand Sable Visitor Center, located just west of Grand Marais on County Road H-58, and the Grand Marais Maritime Museum are open seasonally.

Popular winter activities include skiing on two groomed and tracked cross-country ski trail systems, snowshoeing, snowmobiling, ice fishing, and winter camping.

FACILITIES: Motels, restaurants, groceries, and camping supplies are available in Munising and Grand Marais.

CAMPING: Vehicle-accessible campgrounds are located at Hurricane River (twenty-two spaces), Little Beaver Lake (eight spaces), and Twelvemile Beach (thirty-seven spaces). Each campground has picnic tables, fire grills, tent pads, water, and vault toilets. Handicapped-accessible campsites are available at each of the campgrounds. Numerous other campgrounds are available in the nearby Hiawatha National Forest and Lake Superior State Forest.

Backcountry camping also is popular along the 42-mile-long Lakeshore Trail, a segment of the North Country National Scenic Trail. Campers are required to use the designated backcountry campgrounds, and a permit is required.

FISHING: Lake Superior offers lake trout, whitefish, and coho salmon, while inland lakes have sunfish, perch, bass, pike, and trout. Brook and rainbow trout are found in the streams and rivers. A Michigan license is required.

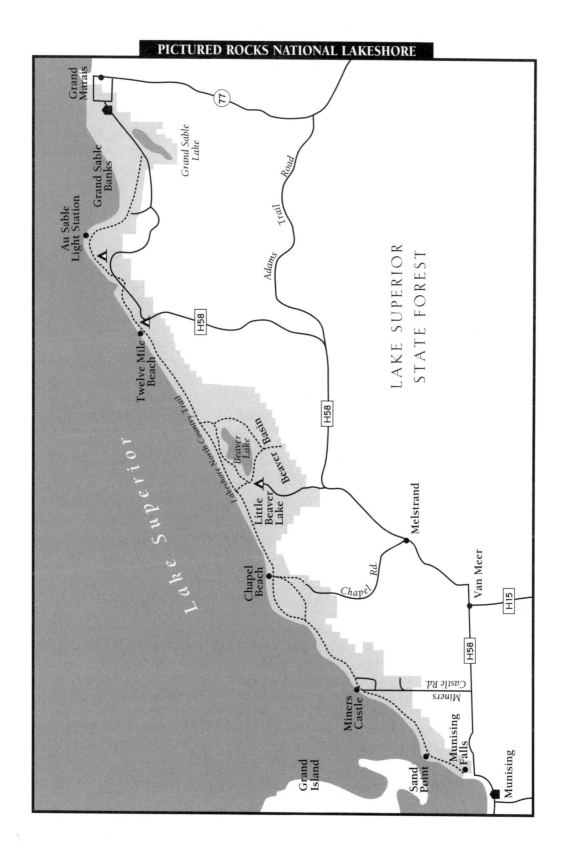

SLEEPING BEAR DUNES NATIONAL LAKESHORE

9922 Front Street
Empire, MI 49630
(616) 326–5134

Sleeping Bear Dunes National Lakeshore, authorized in 1970, comprises more than 71,000 acres of beaches, sand dunes, forests, and lakes. The park is located west of Traverse City, along the northwestern shoreline of Michigan's lower peninsula.

Eleven thousand years ago, glacial ice began to melt, and the great quantities of rock, sand, and silt that it carried were deposited or washed away by meltwater to create the present-day landscape. The dunes of the Sleeping Bear Plateau formed as winds coming across Lake Michigan blew sand up the bluffs at the lake edge and across the plateau. The Valley of the Giants on South Manitou Island contains Atlantic white cedar trees that may be 500 years old.

The park visitor center, on Highway M-72 at the east edge of the village of Empire, is open every day except Christmas and Thanksgiving. Visitors will find exhibits, a schedule of programs including summer guided walks, maps, a slide program, and book sales. The Maritime Museum near Glen Haven is open in summer and features exhibits on Great Lakes maritime history housed in a restored Coast Guard station. Near Glen Haven, visitors can stop at the Dune Climb and clamber to the top of the Sleeping Bear Plateau. Also nearby is the Pierce Stocking Scenic Drive that offers outstanding views of the dunes, valleys, and Lake Michigan. Several small lakes in the park offer fishing and boating. Canoes may be rented for the Platte and Crystal rivers. In season, passenger ferries originating at Leland carry campers and day visitors to North and South Manitou islands.

FACILITIES: Handicapped-accessible restrooms are at the Empire visitor center. Meals and lodging are available in Empire, Glen Arbor, Frankfort, and Traverse City.

CAMPING: On the mainland, D.H. Day Campground (88 sites) offers tables, grills, tent pads, vault toilets, water, and a sanitary dump station. The newly refurbished Platte River Campground (180 sites) offers tables, tent pads, grills, water, flush toilets, hot showers, and electrical hookups. There are also two primitive backcountry campgrounds. On South Manitou Islands are three primitive walk-in campgrounds, and North Manitou Island offers backcountry camping.

FISHING: Fishing is good, with possibilities for bass, bluegill, trout, northern pike, and salmon. A Michigan license is required.

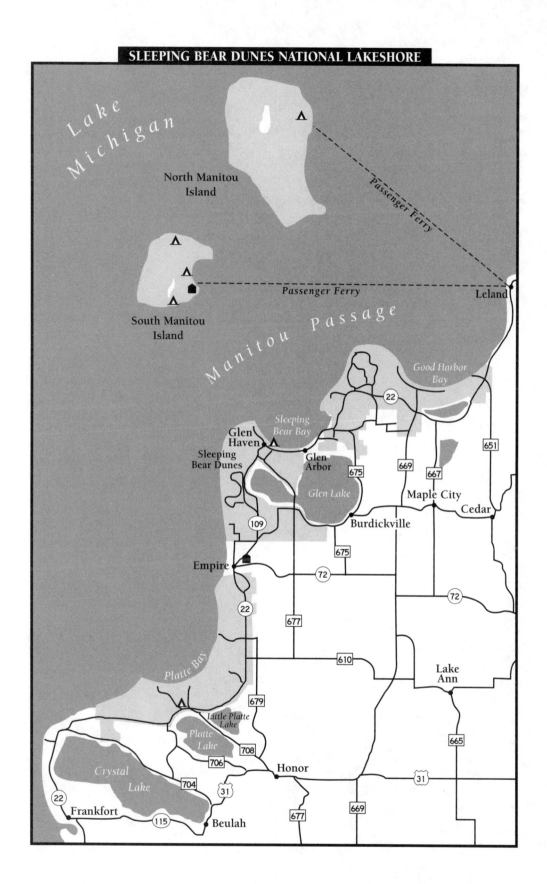

Lake Michigan

North Manitou Island

Passenger Ferry

Passenger Ferry

South Manitou Island

Leland

Manitou Passage

Good Harbor Bay

22

Sleeping Bear Bay

Glen Haven

Sleeping Bear Dunes

Glen Arbor

675

669

667

651

Glen Lake

Maple City

Cedar

109

Burdickville

675

Empire

72

72

22

677

610

Lake Ann

679

665

Little Platte Lake

Platte Lake

708

706

Crystal Lake

704

Honor

31

22

Frankfort

115

Beulah

677

669

31

MICHIGAN / 137

MISSISSIPPI

STATE TOURIST INFORMATION
(800) 927–6378

BRICES CROSS ROADS NATIONAL BATTLEFIELD SITE
c/o Natchez Trace Parkway
Rural Route #1, NT-143
Tupelo, MS 38801
(601) 680–4025

Brices Cross Roads, situated on one acre, was established in 1929 to commemorate the site of a brilliant victory for Confederate forces during an 1864 Civil War battle. The park is located in northeastern Mississippi, 6 miles west of Baldwyn on State Highway 370. The hundred-plus Confederate soldiers who died during the battle are buried in the adjacent Bethany Church cemetery.

As Sherman's Union forces fought through northern Georgia, Confederate commanders decided to attack what they believed was the enemy's most vulnerable element—a single-track railroad acting as the Union supply line between Nashville and Chattanooga.

Beginning in Tupelo, Mississippi, the Confederate General Nathan Forrest set out on June 1, 1864, to strike at the Union line in middle Tennessee. Alerted to Forrest's objective, Sherman sent General Samuel Sturgis and 8,100 Union troops to head off the attack. Forrest withdrew to Tupelo and concentrated 3,500 troops along the railroad between Guntown, Baldwyn, and Booneville. The two forces met on the Baldwyn Road, approximately 1 mile east of Brices on June 10. During the daylong battle, Forrest's Confederate troops routed the opposition across

Natchez Trace Parkway (opposite page)

the bridge over Tishomingo Creek and were able to capture most of the Union artillery and more than 1,500 Union troops. The engagement was considered a brilliant tactical victory for Forrest.

FACILITIES: No facilities or park personnel are at Brices, but visitors may view most of the area where the battle took place. Park folders are available at the site. A visitor center at Tupelo on the Natchez Trace Parkway serves as headquarters for this park.

CAMPING: No camping is permitted in the park, but J. P. Coleman State Park (east of Corinth) and Tombigbee and Trace state parks (near Tupelo) offer camping facilities.

GULF ISLANDS NATIONAL SEASHORE

Mississippi District
3500 Park Road
Ocean Springs, MS 39564
(601) 875–9057

Gulf Islands National Seashore, authorized in 1971, is comprised of nearly 96,000 mostly underwater acres in Mississippi and Florida. The seashore comprises both mainland units and offshore islands and keys with white sand beaches, historic structures, and ruins. The Mississippi section consists of one mainland unit at Davis Bayou that is reached via Park Road off U.S. 90 and a series of islands accessible only by boat. The Florida section of the park is discussed in the Florida chapter of this book.

The site's white sand has been washed down streams and rivers from the north over a period of centuries. The islands are still evolving as they continue to build up on the western sides and erode on the eastern ends. One of the few stabilizing factors available is the protective covering of vegetation. The clean gulf waters and white sandy beaches plus old historic forts make Gulf Islands National Seashore one of the most heavily visited areas of the National Park Service. Although much of the visitation occurs during summer in designated swim beaches such as Langdon Beach on Santa Rosa Island in Florida and West Ship Island in Mississippi, miles of deserted beaches are open to exploration.

Europeans first arrived here in the early 1500s, and soon a struggle commenced to settle the area of present-day Mississippi. French Canadian explorer, Pierre Le Moyne d'Iberville was the first recorded white person to land on Ship Island (1699). In 1821 the United States purchased the last of West Florida, so that France and Spain were excluded from further development in the region. Beginning the next year and continuing through World War II, the United States developed and updated fortifications along the coast.

A visitor center is located at Davis Bayou on the mainland. Here visitors will find exhibits, an audiovisual presentation, and publications. Davis Bayou also has picnic shelters, a ball field, a self-guiding nature trail, and boat ramps. There is no sandy swimming beach in this area. A concessioner-operated boat offers daily passenger access to West Ship Island from Gulfport from March through Labor Day. Write Pan Isles, Inc., P.O. Box 1467, Gulfport, MS 39502. Guided tours of Fort Massachusetts on West Ship Island are offered during summer months.

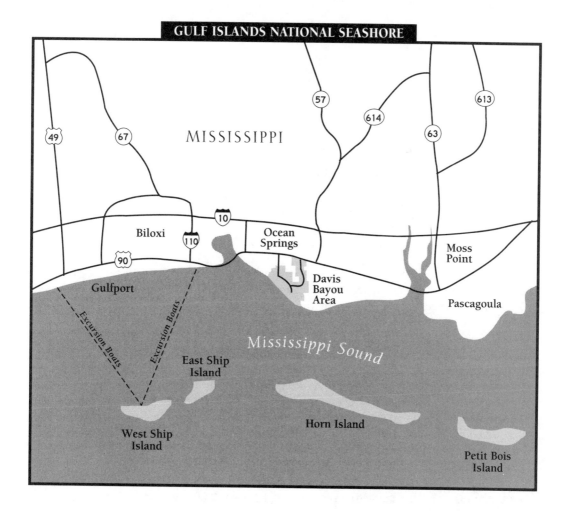

FACILITIES: No lodging is available in the park. Limited food service is offered on tour boats and on West Ship Island. Restrooms and drinking water are available in the visitor center and the picnic grounds at Davis Bayou and at Fort Massachusetts on West Ship Island. West Ship Island also provides a bathhouse and lifeguards during the busy season for swimmers using the beach area.

CAMPING: Davis Bayou offers camping (fifty-one spaces) with water, grills, tables, flush toilets, showers, hookups, and a dump station. Primitive camping is permitted on East Ship, Horn, and Petit Bois Islands.

FISHING: Surf fishing—with possibilities for pompano, ling, mackerel, and sea trout—is permitted along the beach where there are no swimmers. A license is required for saltwater fishing in both Florida and Mississippi.

NATCHEZ NATIONAL HISTORICAL PARK

P.O. Box 1208
Natchez, MS 39121
(601) 446–5790

Natchez National Historical Park is comprised of nearly eighty-two acres and was authorized in 1988 to interpret the history of Natchez from its European settlement as a French trading post through the years before the Civil War when the city was a commercial, cultural, and social center of the South's cotton belt. The historical park's three units are within 4 miles of one another in the city of Natchez in southwestern Mississippi.

Natchez's location on a bend in the Mississippi River resulted in the city experiencing a rich and turbulent history. The French settled the area and established a trading post here in the early 1700s. It was successively occupied by the British, Spaniards, and Americans. The rich agricultural land of the lower Mississippi Valley and the strategic river location caused the city to become the center for the South's "King Cotton." To a large extent, the economic vitality of the cotton economy depended on the cheap labor supplied by slaves.

The historical park consists of three units, only one of which is fully operational. The visitor center, open Monday through Friday from 8:00 A.M. to 4:00 P.M., is at 504 South Canal Street, near the site of the old fort.

Melrose Estate is the main operating unit of the historical park. This antebellum home was constructed in the late 1840s for a wealthy lawyer and cotton planter. The estate passed through several owners until the National Park Service purchased it in 1990. The site consists of the mansion, several outbuildings, a formal garden, carriage house, stable, cottage, and slavery exhibit. The grounds are open daily from 8:30 A.M. to 5:00 P.M. Admission is free. Guided tour of the mansion (fee charged) are conducted between 9:00 A.M. and 4:00 P.M.

The William Johnson House Complex at 210 State Street was in the process of restoration in early 1997. Johnson was a free African-American who chronicled life in antebellum Natchez. The home will include an exhibit on African-American history in Natchez. The upper floors will recreate the Johnson family living quarters and tell the story of his life.

Property comprising the site of Fort Rosalie, the French palisade built to protect the French trading post, is currently being purchased by the National Park Service. A recent acquisition serves as park headquarters.

FACILITIES: Restrooms and drinking water are at park headquarters and at the Melrose Estate. Food and lodging are nearby.

CAMPING: No camping is permitted in the historical park. Natchez State Park, 13 miles northeast of town on U.S. Highway 61 offers twenty-eight sites with water, flush toilets, tables, and grills.

FISHING: A large pond on the Melrose Estate may be fished from the banks only.

NATCHEZ TRACE PARKWAY

Rural Route #1, NT-143
Tupelo, MS 38801
(601) 680–4025

Natchez Trace Parkway was established as part of the National Park Service in 1938. It contains over 49,000 acres along a route that generally follows the old Indian trace (trail) between Natchez and Nashville. To date, 416 of the estimated 445 miles are completed.

The Natchez Trace was originally no more than an Indian footpath connecting Natchez with the Choctaw villages near present-day Jackson and the Chickasaw villages in the northeastern portion of the state. After the American Revolution the trail was made into a crude road by traders who floated products down the Mississippi River and returned to Nashville along the path. After the United States created the Mississippi Territory with Natchez as its capital, money was appropriated to improve the road so that mail service could be extended into the area. From 1800 to 1820, the trace was the region's most heavily traveled road, but the later appearance of steamboats on the Mississippi caused it to diminish in importance.

The park's headquarters is located in Tupelo. Here, in the visitor center, a film explaining the trace's history is available. At various points along the parkway, visitors can find self-guiding nature trails, exhibits, interpretive markers, and picnic tables. Some points of interest, with numbers keyed to those found on the map (in sequence from south to north), follow.

1. Old Trace exhibit shelter.

2. Emerald Mound (A.D. 1600) is one of the largest ceremonial Indian mounds in the United States.

3. Loess Bluff Nature Area displays a deep deposit of topsoil blown into the area during the ice age.

4. Restored Mount Locust Inn.

5. Bullen Creek Nature Trail wanders through a mixed hardwood-pine forest.

6. A section of the Old Natchez Trace is identified.

7. Copper ornaments and other artifacts were found in the hilltop graves of Mangum Mound.

8. Grindstone Ford marked the beginning of wild territory to early-day travelers heading north.

9. Rocky Springs Site includes a campground, picnic area, nature trail to historic spring and town site, and a section of the Old Trace.

10. Ross Barnett Reservoir (not a part of the parkway) has picnicking, marina, and boat landing.

11. Ridgeland Crafts Center features demonstrations and sales of Mississippi crafts.

12. The Indian burial mounds were built more than 500 years ago.

13. Nature trail through a typical Southern swamp.

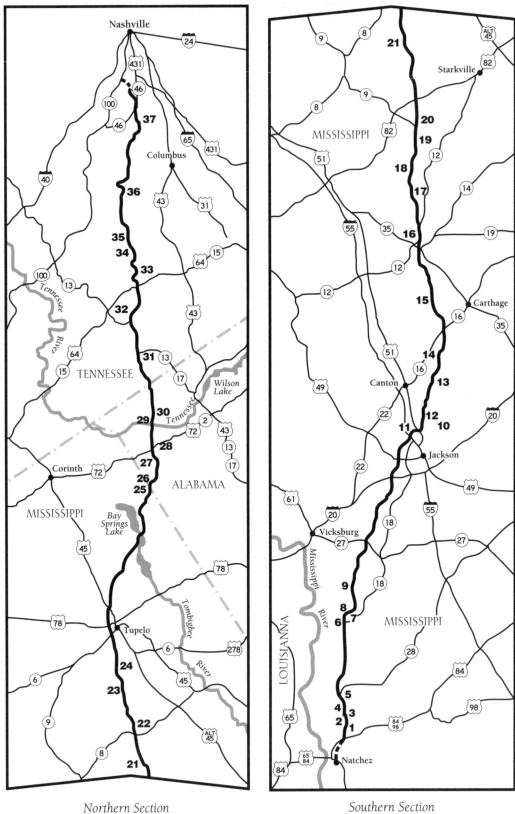

Northern Section

Southern Section

14. Nature trail featuring native Southern plants.

15. Nature trail along an abandoned beaver dam (includes exhibit shelter).

16. Nature trail along a creek and up a hillside.

17. Nature trail through cypress swamp that is changing into a mixed hardwood forest.

18. Old Trace is visible as it winds through the woods.

19. Jeff Busby Site contains gas station, campground, picnic area, and nature trail.

20. Original Natchez Trace leads into woods along present roadway.

21. Section of original trace crosses parkway.

22. Village site of prehistoric and historic Indians. Includes exhibit shelter (with recording) near still-visible burial mounds.

23. Davis Lake Forest Service Area has camping, picnicking, swimming, and boating.

24. Site of old Chickasaw village. Includes exhibit shelter and nature trail.

25. Trail to cave site.

26. Early Indian temple mound.

27. A steep ¼-mile trail leads to the highest point on the parkway in Alabama.

28. Exhibit shelter telling story of Chickasaw chief who owned an inn near this site.

29. Colbert Ferry has restrooms, picnicking, fishing, swimming, and boat-launching facilities.

30. Nature trail along creek to a flowing spring.

31. Three sections of the Old Trace are visible.

32. Nature trail through forest, with identified plants.

33. A 2½-mile one-way loop drive over a section of the Old Natchez Trace.

34. Exhibit shelter illustrates mining.

35. Meriwether Lewis Site contains a campground, picnic area, hiking trail, and the grave of this famous explorer.

36. A tobacco farm and barn and Old Trace Drive are located here.

37. An 1818 house near the Duck River.

FACILITIES: There are no overnight facilities along the parkway, but motels and restaurants may be found in nearby towns. The only service station is at Jeff Busby. Drinking water and restrooms are available at the visitor center, the campgrounds, and a number of picnic areas along the way.

CAMPING: Park Service campgrounds with tables, grills, water, and flush toilets are at Jeff Busby (eighteen sites, campstore), Meriwether Lewis (thirty-two sites), and Rocky Springs (twenty-two sites). All three are open year-round. Additional camping is available at Davis Lake and Tishomingo and Trace state parks.

FISHING: Fishing is available at various points along and near the parkway. Appropriate state licenses are required.

TUPELO NATIONAL BATTLEFIELD

c/o Natchez Trace Parkway
Rural Route #1, NT-143
Tupelo, MS 38801
(601) 680–4025

Tupelo National Battlefield, situated on one acre, was established in 1929 to commemorate the site of an important battle between Union forces and Confederate troops sent to cut General William Sherman's supply line. The park is located in northeastern Mississippi within the city limits of Tupelo. It is on Mississippi Route 6, 1 mile west of U.S. 45 and 1.2 miles east of the Natchez Trace Parkway.

As General William Sherman battled through Georgia during the summer of 1864, one of his primary concerns was protection of the railroad bringing supplies from Louisville to his army. As a result, Grant assigned a large number of Union troops to the task of destroying a Confederate force that was trying to interrupt this supply line. On July 14, 1864, the two armies met in Harrisburg (now within the Tupelo city limits), and Confederate troops were badly mauled, sustaining heavy losses. Short of rations and ammunition, the Federals began their return to their base in La Grange, Tennessee, the following day. Although Union troops were unable to destroy the Confederate force, they did keep the railroad supply line from being damaged.

The park's visitor center is incorporated with the Tupelo visitor center of the Natchez Trace Parkway. Here visitors will find park interpreters to answer questions and provide information about the battle. Park folders are available at the battlefield.

FACILITIES: Both lodging and food service are available in the town of Tupelo.

CAMPING: No camping is permitted at the site, but Tombigbee State Park offers camping facilities nearby.

VICKSBURG NATIONAL MILITARY PARK

3201 Clay Street
Vicksburg, MS 39180
(601) 636–0583

The park, which contains 1,741 acres, was established in 1899 to preserve the site of a decisive Civil War battle that gave the Union control of the Mississippi River and split the Confederacy into two parts. The park is in western Mississippi in Vicksburg. Exit Interstate 20 at U.S. 80 (West Clay Street, exit 4-B).

From the outbreak of the Civil War, Union authorities realized that control of the Mississippi River would permit movement of troops and supplies into the Deep South. In addition, it would divide the Confederacy by isolating Arkansas, Texas, and most of Louisiana. By the late summer of 1862, Union forces had captured most of the Confederate strongholds along the river, leaving Vicksburg and Port Hudson as the only major obstacles to Union domination of the Mississippi.

Ulysses S. Grant and his Federal forces first attacked Vicksburg on May 19, 1863. Unable to capture the city in two assaults, Grant began a long siege using field guns, gunboats, and trench warfare. By the end of June, Confederate forces began to despair of relief. With munitions and food in short supply, they finally surrendered on July 4. The surrender at Port Hudson five days later gave the Union complete control of the river.

A visitor center contains exhibits and information to help interpret the park. From here, a 16-mile tour leads past many of the historic sites associated with the battle. Included are Shirley House, the only surviving wartime structure in the park; Vicksburg National Cemetery, where 17,000 Union soldiers are buried; and restored Federal approach trenches. Also included within the park is the U.S.S. *Cairo* Museum and Gunboat. The museum displays artifacts recovered from the U.S.S. *Cairo*. Sailors' personal gear, cookware, and weaponry are among the many artifacts on display. The restored gunboat is open for visitors to walk aboard.

FACILITIES: No food and lodging are available in the park, but both are found nearby. Drinking water and restrooms are provided in both the visitor center and *Cairo* Museum.

CAMPING: No camping is permitted in the park. The National Park Service operates the Rocky Springs Campground (twenty-two sites, tables, grills, flush toilets) on the Natchez Trace Parkway, 27 miles south of Vicksburg via Highway 27 and the Parkway.

See map on the next page.

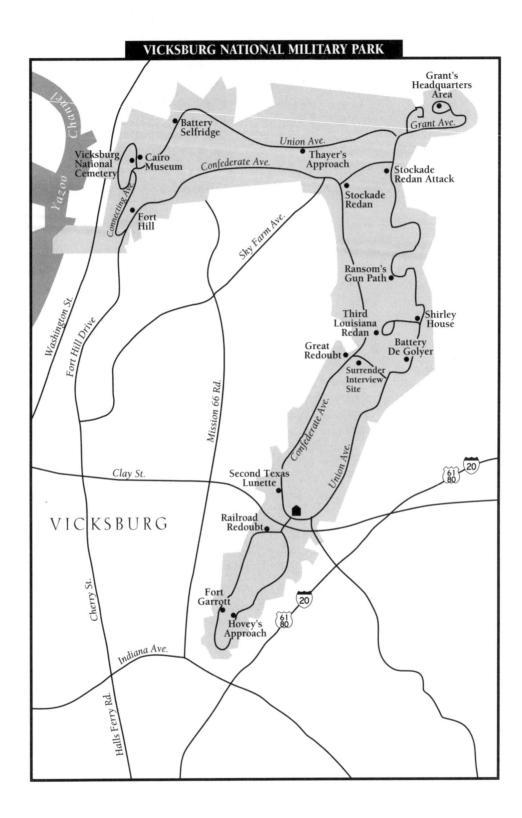

Grant's
Headquarters
Area

Battery
Selfridge

Union Ave.

Grant Ave.

Vicksburg
National
Cemetery

Cairo
Museum

Confederate Ave.

Thayer's
Approach

Stockade
Redan Attack

Connecting Ave.

Stockade
Redan

Fort
Hill

Sky Farm Ave.

Ransom's
Gun Path

Washington St.

Fort Hill Drive

Third
Louisiana
Redan

Shirley
House

Battery
De Golyer

Great
Redoubt

Surrender
Interview
Site

Mission 66 Rd.

Confederate Ave.

Union Ave.

Clay St.

Second Texas
Lunette

61
80

20

VICKSBURG

Railroad
Redoubt

Cherry St.

Fort
Garrott

20

61
80

Hovey's
Approach

Indiana Ave.

Halls Ferry Rd.

NEW HAMPSHIRE

STATE TOURIST INFORMATION
(603) 271–2343

SAINT-GAUDENS NATIONAL HISTORIC SITE
Rural Route #3, Box 73
Cornish, NH 03745
(603) 675–2175

Saint-Gaudens National Historic Site comprises 150 acres and was authorized in 1964 as a memorial to one of America's greatest sculptors, Augustus Saint-Gaudens. It contains his work, home, gardens, and studios. The site is located on the western New Hampshire border, 2 miles north of Windsor, Vermont, on State Highway 12A. From Interstate 89, take exit 20. From Interstate 91, use exit 8 if northbound or exit 9 if southbound.

Augustus Saint-Gaudens (1848–1907) moved with his family to New York soon after his birth in Dublin, Ireland. After leaving to study in Paris and Rome, he returned to America and soon received critical acclaim for his work. In addition to large sculptures, he redesigned the $10 and $20 gold pieces in 1907. In 1885, Saint-Gaudens moved to this New Hampshire home that once served as an inn, and it was here that his most productive years were spent. The Cornish community eventually attracted many other artists, including poets, painters, playwrights, and musicians.

The park is open daily from 8:00 A.M. until dark from late May through October. Buildings are open from 9:00 A.M. to 4:30 P.M. daily. A fee is charged for entrance. Brochures for a self-guiding tour of the furnished home, gardens, and studios are available. Saint-Gaudens's works in bronze, plaster, and marble are on display throughout the site. A 2½-mile trail that loops down to a pond in the Blow-Me-Down Natural Area and a ¼-mile Blow-Me-Down Ravine Trail are popular attractions.

From early July to late August, concerts are held at the site on Sunday afternoons at 2:00 P.M. The Saint-Gaudens memorial trustees also sponsor exhibitions by contemporary painters and sculptors. Visitors should make a point to drive a few miles south on Highway 12A to see the longest covered bridge in the United States, which crosses the Connecticut River to Windsor, Vermont.

FACILITIES: No food or lodging is available at the site. Restrooms are near the parking area. Food can be found in Windsor, Vermont, 2 miles south.

CAMPING: No camping is permitted at the site. Vermont's Ascutney State Park, 5 miles southwest of Windsor and a short distance off U.S. 5, offers sites with tables, grills, flush toilets, a dump station, and pay showers.

FISHING: Fishing is available in Blow-Me-Down Pond at the historic site as well as in the nearby Connecticut River.

Saint-Gaudens' Home and Studio (Courtesy Saint-Gaudens National Historic Site)

NEW JERSEY

STATE TOURIST INFORMATION
(800) 537–7397

EDISON NATIONAL HISTORIC SITE
Main Street and Lakeside Avenue
West Orange, NJ 07052
(201) 736–0550

Edison National Historic Site comprises twenty-one acres and was established in 1955 to preserve Thomas A. Edison's home along with the laboratory where he worked from 1887 until his death in 1931. The site is located at Main Street and Lakeside Avenue in West Orange, New Jersey, 2 miles north of the Garden State Parkway and ½-mile east of Interstate 280.

Born in Ohio in 1847, Thomas A. Edison had developed his first patented invention by 1868. Edison's first laboratory was built in 1876 in Menlo Park, New Jersey, and it was there that he developed the incandescent light. Ten years later, Edison moved to West Orange, and constructed a new and much larger laboratory. Here he developed the phonograph, the motion picture camera, the fluorescent lamp, and a nickel-iron alkaline storage battery. In his lifetime, Thomas A. Edison was granted 1,093 U.S. patents.

The laboratory area preserves the original main laboratory building and four smaller red brick structures that were used for experiments in the fields of chemistry, physics, and metallurgy. Guided tours (one hour) of the laboratory are conducted daily from 10:30 A.M. to 3:30 P.M. The library, machine shop, and chemistry lab remain as they were during Edison's life. The Lab Museum visitor center is open daily from 9:00 A.M. to 5:00 P.M. except Thanksgiving Day,

Christmas Day, and New Year's Day. The twenty-nine-room Edison home, Glenmont, is open for conducted tours Wednesday through Sunday from 11:00 A.M. to 4:00 P.M. Reservations are required for all groups.

FACILITIES: Food service and lodging can be found near the site.

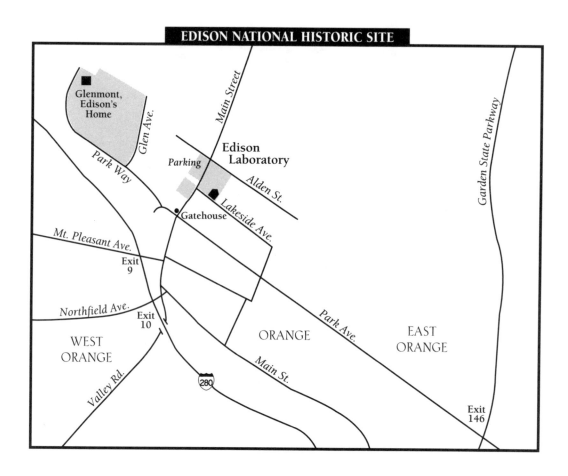

MORRISTOWN NATIONAL HISTORICAL PARK

Washington Place
Morristown, NJ 07960
(201) 539–2085

Morristown National Historical Park includes 1,685 acres and was authorized in 1933 to commemorate the site where the Continental Army under George Washington spent two winters during the American Revolution. The park is located in north-central New Jersey, in four separate sections in or near the town of Morristown.

In January 1777, George Washington moved the Continental Army into winter quarters at Morristown, where the easily defensible location saw his men through the winter in spite of a smallpox epidemic and shortages of food and clothing. As weather improved and the roads dried, the army left and did not return for two years. After wintering at Valley Forge the following year, Washington again selected Morristown in December 1779 as the location to spend the winter. The unusually severe weather and shortages during this second winter nearly destroyed the morale of both officers and enlisted men in what proved to be one of the Continental Army's severest trials. In spite of these hardships, Washington moved the troops to battle in the spring.

Washington's restored headquarters building and the adjacent museum (fee charged) contain information and exhibits interpreting the army's stay in Morristown. Both buildings are open daily from 9:00 A.M. to 5:00 P.M. The Jockey Hollow Visitor Center and nearby Wick House that served as Major General St. Clair's headquarters are also open from 9:00 A.M. to 5:00 P.M. A self-guiding nature trail is in the encampment area. All buildings are closed on Thanksgiving Day, Christmas Day, and New Year's Day. At Fort Nonsense, soldiers fortified a ridge in May 1777, although no traces of the earthworks remain. Wayside exhibits at Fort Nonsense interpret the site.

FACILITIES: No food or lodging is available within park boundaries, although both can be found nearby. Restrooms and drinking water are at the visitor center, museum, and Washington's headquarters.

CAMPING: No camping is permitted in the park. A public campground is approximately 20 miles northwest of Morristown National Historical Park at Allamachy Mountain State Park, 2 miles north of Hackettstown.

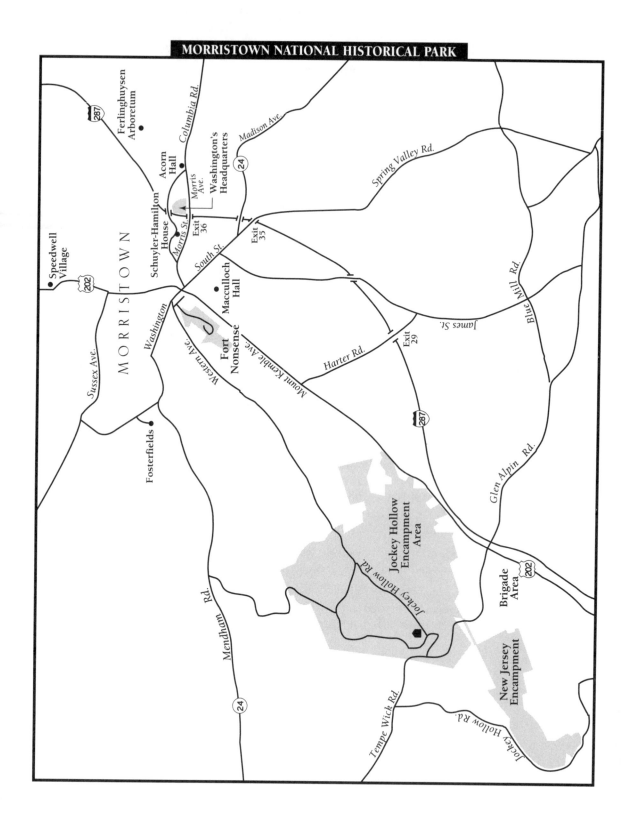

PINELANDS NATIONAL RESERVE

P.O. Box 7
New Lisbon, NJ 08064
(609) 894–9342

Pinelands National Reserve was authorized as an affiliated area of the National Park Service in 1978 to assist in shaping the future of the last vast forested area on the Atlantic coast between Boston and Richmond. The Pinelands National Reserve comprises 1.1 million acres (1,700 square miles) of forests, farms, and scenic towns. The reserve includes portions of seven southeastern New Jersey counties.

Congress created the Pinelands National Reserve so that governments at all levels could shape the future and balance protection of the area's natural resources with development in this mostly rural region of a heavily populated state. The Pinelands comprise more than a quarter of New Jersey. Nearly 40 percent of the area is publicly owned. The reserve includes fifty-six municipalities and is home to 500,000 residents.

Fifteen appointed members of the Pinelands Commission have produced a management plan in which an inner region of the reserve has been designated a preservation area. Long-time Pinelands villages and remains of historic towns dot this largely forested landscape where compatible agriculture, horticulture, and recreation uses are permitted. The preservation area is surrounded by a designated protection area in which orderly development is permitted as long as it maintains the character of the existing environment.

The Pinelands is home to 150 species of birds, about sixteen species of fish, and more than thirty species of mammals. The reserve contains approximately 580 native species and 270 introduced species of plants, including over 12,000 acres of dwarf pine and oak. An immense acquifer underlying the Pinelands is estimated to contain more than 17 trillion gallons of water.

FACILITIES: Food and lodging are available in small towns throughout Pinelands National Reserve. *Pinelands Guide,* a booklet describing recreational resources, historic sites, and nature centers, is available free from the Pinelands Commission at the New Lisbon address above.

CAMPING: Public and private campgrounds are scattered throughout the area. Allaire State Park, Bass River State Forest, Belleplain State Forest, Wharton State Forest, and Lebanon State Forest have campgrounds with hot showers.

Sagamore Hill National Historic Site

NEW YORK

STATE TOURIST INFORMATION
(800) 225–5697

ELEANOR ROOSEVELT NATIONAL HISTORIC SITE
519 Albany Post Road
Hyde Park, NY 12538
(914) 229–9422

Eleanor Roosevelt National Historic Site was authorized in 1977 and comprises 180 acres including Val-Kill, Mrs. Roosevelt's home. The site contains fields, wetlands, a pond, and the cottage where Eleanor Roosevelt entertained friends and dignitaries during her long years of public service. The historic site is located in southeastern New York, approximately 6 miles north of Poughkeepsie on U.S. 9G, ½-mile north of the intersection of St. Andrews Road and Route 9G.

Eleanor Roosevelt was born in 1884 in New York City. In 1905, she was given in marriage to her distant cousin, Franklin D. Roosevelt, by her uncle, President Theodore Roosevelt. Following Franklin's polio attack in 1921, she became increasingly active in politics. By the time Franklin was first elected president in 1932, Eleanor was active in a number of causes and soon began touring the country on a variety of political missions.

Mrs. Roosevelt resided at Val-Kill after her husband's death in 1945. She was called to public service by President Harry S Truman. As chairman of the Human Rights Commission of the United Nations, she was largely responsible for the Universal Declaration of Human Rights, which was passed in 1948. This was followed by writing, lecturing, hosting a television talk show, participating in human rights organizations, and actively working in the

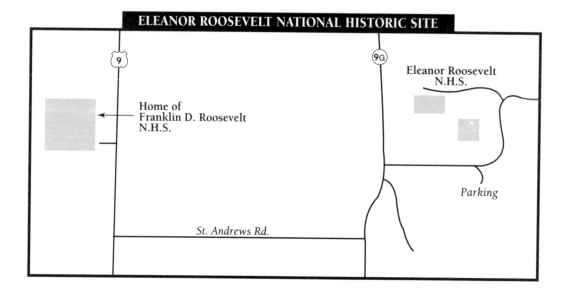

Democratic party. Eleanor Roosevelt died on November 7, 1962, and was buried in Hyde Park next to her husband.

Val-Kill grew out of an idea of Franklin D. Roosevelt's when he suggested in 1924 that Mrs. Roosevelt and two of her friends might like to build a cottage on the Val-Kill stream, a favorite picnic spot. A fieldstone cottage was built in 1925, and the following year a building was constructed to house a furniture factory. In 1929, a second factory building was added. When the business ceased to operate in 1936, the building was converted by Mrs. Roosevelt into a home of her own. For the next twenty-six years, Mrs. Roosevelt spent much of her time at Val-Kill, where she entertained people from all walks of life.

The site is closed in January and February. Hours of operation during the remainder of the year are subject to change. Call (914) 229–9115 for information. Tours are conducted every half-hour and include a film of Mrs. Roosevelt's career and a tour of the furnished rooms of her home. All group reservations must be made at least ten days in advance.

FACILITIES: No food or lodging is available at the site, but both can be found in the town of Hyde Park.

CAMPING: (See the camping section under Vanderbilt Mansion National Historic Site.)

FIRE ISLAND NATIONAL SEASHORE

120 Laurel Street
Patchogue, NY 11772
(516) 289–4810

Fire Island National Seashore contains nearly 20,000 acres and was authorized in 1964 to preserve the natural features and recreational opportunities of a barrier island off the south shore of Long Island. The island can be reached by automobile via bridges from Bayshore and Shirley on each end of the park. Visitors must park at the Robert Moses State Park or Smith Point County Park lots and walk to Fire Island National Seashore; driving is not permitted. Visitors may also take ferries from Bayshore (516–665–5045), Sayville (516–589–8980), and Patchogue (516–475–1636) from May to November.

The barrier beach of Fire Island stretches 32 miles, with a width of from 200 yards to ½ mile. In addition to a wide beach on the Atlantic side, the island contains pines, patches of seaside plants, and hidden hardwood groves. The Sunken Forest at Sailors Haven is a 200-year-old forest full of holly, sassafras, tupelo, and shadblow providing a canopy with vines of catbrier and wild grape climbing from the forest floor. Fire Island is also a habitat for a wide variety of wildlife, including songbirds, deer, waterfowl, and foxes.

Visitor centers with information, exhibits, interpretive activities, and nature trails are at Sailors Haven, Watch Hill, and Smith Point. Lifeguards and interpretive rangers work at Watch Hill and Sailors Haven during July and August. The first two locations also provide marinas, guarded swimming beaches, change rooms, and showers. A restaurant and a snack bar are available at Watch Hill, and a snack bar is available at Sailors Haven. Smith Point is the gateway to New York State's only federal wilderness area, which stretches from Smith Point to Watch Hill. Watch Hill is noted for its rich and beautiful salt marsh, with an elevated boardwalk nature trail. The historic Fire Island Lighthouse at the western end of the National Seashore is open to the public. Call for dates and hours of operation. The former Keepers Quarters has been renovated as a visitor center with exhibits on the island's history. Park at Field 5 of the adjacent Robert Moses State Park and walk in 0.6 mile. There are no roads on the island except for the two entrance roads noted above.

The William Floyd Estate (516–399–2030) is a detached unit of the National Seashore located on Washington Avenue in Mastic Beach. This 275-year-old home of a signer of the Declaration of Independence is open seasonally for house tours. Call for dates and times.

FACILITIES: No lodging is available on the island. Food service and groceries are provided by concessioners at Sailors Haven and Watch Hill. Restrooms are also at these two locations. Complete facilities—including hotels and restaurants—are available in neighboring communities. Lodging information can be obtained from the Fire Island Tourism Bureau (516–563–8448).

CAMPING: At Watch Hill (twenty-eight sites, two group camps) camping is available by reservation only from May 15 to October 15 (516–597–6633). No toilets or water are available during the remainder of the year. Access is by private boat or scheduled ferry only.

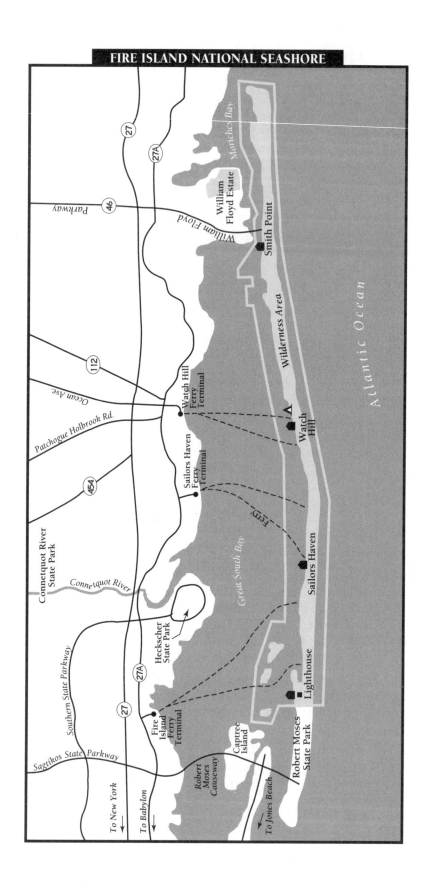

FIRE ISLAND NATIONAL SEASHORE

FISHING: Fishermen can fish in the surf for striped bass, bluefish, and weakfish. Great South Bay and Moriches Bay offer bluefish, blackfish, fluke, weakfish, kingfish, and winter flounder. Clamming and crabbing are also popular activities on the island.

FORT STANWIX NATIONAL MONUMENT

112 East Park Street
Rome, NY 13440
(315) 336–2090

Fort Stanwix National Monument contains approximately sixteen acres and was authorized in 1935 (acquisition was not completed until 1973) to preserve the site of an important stand by American forces during the Revolutionary War. The fort is located in central New York in the city of Rome. State highways 26, 46, 49, 69, and 365 pass within sight of the monument.

Fort Stanwix was constructed by British forces in 1758 to protect an important portage between the Mohawk River and a water passage to Lake Ontario. After England conquered Canada in 1760, the post lost much of its importance until it was occupied by Americans in the summer of 1776 to protect against British invasion from the north. In 1777, a major siege against the fort was successfully repulsed. This marked the end of military actions against Stanwix, although the fort was garrisoned until 1781.

The reconstructed fort is open from 9:00 A.M. to 5:00 P.M. daily except Thanksgiving Day and Christmas Day. A city garage on James Street is available for visitor parking. Park personnel are stationed inside the entrance to provide directions to the visitor center, which contains exhibits and a movie. The fort also contains a small museum, and living-history programs take place throughout the day during summer months.

FACILITIES: No food or lodging is available in the park, but both are nearby in Rome. A Quality Inn is across the street from the fort. Drinking water and restrooms are located inside the entrance.

CAMPING: No camping is permitted on the monument grounds. Delta Lake State Park (110 sites), 6½ miles northeast on State Highway 46, offers campsites with tables, grills, flush toilets, showers, and a swimming beach. A private campground with hookups is located off Route 365, 7 miles west of Rome.

GATEWAY NATIONAL RECREATION AREA

Floyd Bennett Field, Building 69
Brooklyn, NY 11234
(718) 338–3338

Gateway National Recreation Area contains over 26,000 acres and was established in 1972 to provide recreational activities for the millions of people living in the New York City area. The park comprises four separate sections located in the New York City harbor area in both New York and New Jersey. All units are accessible by auto and by mass transit.

Gateway National Recreation Area is truly a gateway. Over the years, this land area surrounding New York harbor has formed a natural gateway for trade goods and millions of immigrants. The recreation area comprises four units. The Sandy Hook Unit in New Jersey and the Breezy Point Unit in New York are two arms of land that stretch across the water toward one another. The other two units, Staten Island and Jamaica Bay, lie within the arms. The units contain a variety of natural and historical items of interest to visitors, including beaches, dunes, bays, wooded uplands, a holly forest, a wildlife refuge, airfields, forts, and the nation's oldest operating lighthouse. Facilities are available for numerous recreational activities.

Breezy Point Unit (718–474–4600): a fine ocean beach, Jacob Riis Park, with opportunities for swimming, surf fishing, softball, baseball, football, paddleball, rugby, and handball. The unit also includes Fort Tilden, a naval air station and one of the first stations of the U.S. Lifesaving Service. Rangers lead groups on guided walks, while craft shows and theatrical performances take place at Riis Park in spring and fall.

Jamaica Bay Unit (718–338–3829): the Jamaica Bay Wildlife Refuge (718–474–0613) provides a habitat for more than 300 species of birds and is open year-round. A bay provides fishing, while special programs take place at Canarsie Pier, Plumb Beach, Dead Horse Bay, Frank Charles Park, and Floyd Bennett Field. The latter was New York's first municipal airport and currently serves as park headquarters.

Sandy Hook Unit (908–872–0115): the site of the oldest continually operating lighthouse in North America and a series of forts from colonial times, with the last fort still largely intact. Tours of the fort and a holly forest are offered daily. There are lectures and special events including puppet shows and lifesaving demonstrations during summer months and weekly tours and presentations in other seasons.

Staten Island Unit (718–351–8700): a hangar complex at Miller Field served seaplanes of the U.S. Air Service following World War I. Sports facilities and calm waters for fishing and swimming are at Great Kills Park. Guided walks and star watches are offered for the general public.

FACILITIES: Snack bars, food service, and vending machines are available throughout the four units on a seasonal basis. Marinas are located in the Staten Island and Jamaica Bay units.

CAMPING: Four primitive campsites in the Sandy Hook Unit are available by reservation only for organized youth groups. No other camping facilities are available in the park areas.

FISHING: Fishing for flounder, fluke, striped bass, and bluefish is available at various locations around the park.

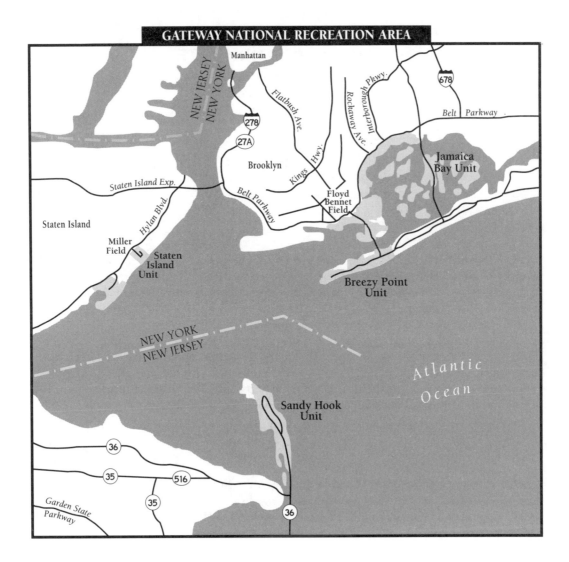

HOME OF FRANKLIN D. ROOSEVELT
NATIONAL HISTORIC SITE

519 Albany Post Road
Hyde Park, NY 12538
(914) 229–9115

Franklin D. Roosevelt's 264-acre homesite was designated a national historic site in 1944 to preserve the birthplace and lifetime residence of our thirty-second president. The home is located in southeastern New York, approximately 6 miles north of Poughkeepsie via U.S. 9.

Franklin D. Roosevelt was born (January 30, 1882) and raised in this home. As governor of New York (1928–1932), Roosevelt came back to Hyde Park often, and three days after his death on April 12, 1945, he was buried here. Seventeen years later, Eleanor Roosevelt was buried beside her husband.

The hours of operation are subject to change. Call (914) 229–9115 for information. The site is closed Thanksgiving Day, Christmas Day, and New Year's Day. A leaflet providing additional information is available. Next to the site, the Roosevelt Library and Museum includes the president's study, his ship models, gifts, and exhibits about his life. The graves of Franklin and Eleanor are in a rose garden area between the house and library. Plan a full day to see the home, library, Vanderbilt Mansion, and Eleanor Roosevelt's Val-Kill retreat.

FACILITIES: No food or lodging is available at the site, but both may be found just outside the park. Restrooms and drinking water are provided in a visitor facility in the stable/garage and in the library. The facility also contains a bookstore and Hudson Valley tourism information.

CAMPING: No camping is permitted at the site. Mills-Norrie State Park, 5 miles north on Highway 9, offers sites with flush toilets, showers, fishing, boating, and nature trails. The park's camping section is seldom filled, even on weekends (914–889–4646).

MARTIN VAN BUREN NATIONAL HISTORIC SITE

P.O. Box 545
Kinderhook, NY 12106
(518) 758–9689

Martin Van Buren National Historic Site in rural Columbia County was authorized in 1974 to preserve the home of the eighth president of the United States. The site is located in eastern New York, approximately 20 miles south of Albany via Highway 9. It is just southeast of the village of Kinderhook on Route 9H.

Martin Van Buren was born in Kinderhook in 1782. At age fourteen, he was apprenticed in a local law office. Six years later, he decided to complete his apprenticeship in New York City under the supervision of an old friend, William Van Ness. Here he made important personal connections before returning to Kinderhook to practice law.

Following his marriage to Hannah Hoes in 1807, Van Buren and his wife moved to Hudson, New York, where he commenced an ambitious political career. Over the years he held positions as county surrogate, state senator, state attorney general, U.S. senator, governor of New York, vice-president, and, from 1837 to 1841, president of the United States. Van Buren was defeated for reelection in 1840, partially because of his opposition to the annexation of Texas.

Martin Van Buren purchased the Lindenwald estate in 1839 while serving as U.S. president. The home originally belonged to a local judge who had built it in 1797, and it is named after the linden trees growing on the estate. Numerous changes were made to the house by Van Buren during his twenty-one-year residence; he died at Lindenwald in 1862. The mansion has been restored by the National Park Service to its 1840–1862 appearance.

The site is open daily from 9:00 A.M. to 4:30 P.M., mid-May through October. From November 1 through December 5 the site is open Saturday and Sunday, 9:00 A.M. to 4:30 P.M. The site is closed from December 6 to mid-May. Guided tours of the house and grounds and other interpretive programs are provided by rangers. Reservations are required for groups of ten or more. A fifteen-minute audio-slide presentation is given inside the home. Van Buren's grave is in the Kinderhook Village Cemetery.

FACILITIES: Information about tours, fees, special events, food and lodging can be obtained at the Gatehouse along Old Post Road, which is staffed by rangers. A bookstore and restrooms are located in the gatehouse.

CAMPING: No camping is permitted at the site. Lake Taghkanic State Park, approximately 15 miles southeast of Kinderhook via the Taconic State Parkway, offers campsites with tables, grills, flush toilets, swimming, and fishing. Many privately owned campgrounds are also in the vicinity.

NEW YORK CITY PARKS

c/o National Park Service Manhattan Sites
26 Wall Street
New York, NY 10005

1. **Castle Clinton National Monument** (southern tip of Manhattan Island in Battery Park; 212–344–7220): This structure, built from 1808 to 1811, was used for the military defense of New York harbor and New York City until 1821. Subsequently, it opened as Castle Garden, a promenade and entertainment center, and in 1855 became an immigrant landing depot through which more than 8 million people entered the United States from 1855 to 1890.

2. **Ellis Island** (212–363–3200/3201): The immigration processing station for 12 million Americans from 1892 to 1924 is operated as part of the Statue of Liberty National Monument. The museum contains three stories of exhibits, displays, artifacts, and photos that explain the immigrants' trip across the ocean, processing at Ellis Island, and assimilation into the United States. A twenty-eight-minute film, "Island of Hope, Island of Tears," is shown continuously in two theaters. Ellis Island is open seven days a week except Christmas from 9:30 A.M. to 5:00 P.M. and is accessible by Statue of Liberty Circle Line Ferry from Battery Park in Manhattan and Liberty State Park in Jersey City, New Jersey.

3. **Federal Hall National Memorial** (15 Pine Street; 212–264–8711): This building, originally constructed as the Customs House of New York Port, is on the site of Federal Hall, the first capitol of the United States. It is also where the Second Continental Congress convened in 1785, where George Washington took the oath as first U.S. president on April 30, 1789, and where the Bill of Rights was adopted in 1789. The memorial contains a museum and provides a film, displays, and audiovisual exhibits.

4. **General Grant National Memorial** (Riverside Drive and 122nd Street; 212–666–1640): This granite structure, commonly known as Grant's Tomb, contains the tombs of Union Commander and U.S. President Ulysses S. Grant and his wife. The memorial is open daily from 9:00 A.M. to 5:00 P.M. Wednesday through Sunday.

5. **Hamilton Grange National Memorial** (287 Convent Avenue between West 141st Street and West 142nd Street; 212–283–5154): This was the home of Alexander Hamilton, first secretary of the treasury. It was named "The Grange" after Hamilton's grandfather's estate in Scotland. Visitors will find an interpretive program planned around drama, music, and colonial crafts. The memorial is open daily from 9:00 A.M. to 5:00 P.M.

6. **Statue of Liberty National Monument** (Liberty Island in New York Harbor; 212–363–3200/3201): The famous 152-foot copper sculpture was given to the United States by France in 1886 in commemoration of the alliance between the two nations during the American Revolution. A museum in honor of the immigrants who came to America is located in an addition to the statue's pedestal. An elevator and stairway lead to the top of the pedestal. From here, a spiral stairway equivalent to twelve stories leads to the statue's crown. Both the statue and museum are open daily except Christmas from 9:30 A.M. to 5:00 P.M. with extended hours in summer. Boats from Battery Park run from 9:00 A.M. to 4:00 P.M. daily.

7. **Theodore Roosevelt Birthplace National Historic Site** (28 East Twentieth Street; 212–260–1616): This four-story reconstructed Victorian brownstone home was the birthplace and boyhood home of our twenty-sixth president. The home has five rooms restored

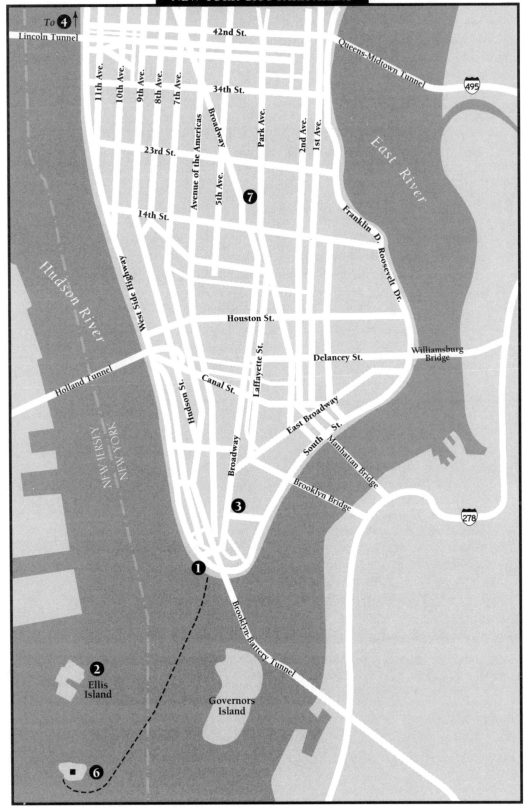

To **4**

Lincoln Tunnel

42nd St.

Queens-Midtown Tunnel

11th Ave.

10th Ave.

9th Ave.

8th Ave.

7th Ave.

34th St.

Broadway

Park Ave.

2nd Ave.

1st Ave.

East River

Avenue of the Americas

5th Ave.

23rd St.

7

14th St.

Franklin D. Roosevelt Dr.

West Side Highway

Hudson River

Houston St.

Hudson St.

Laffayette St.

Delancey St.

Williamsburg Bridge

Holland Tunnel

Canal St.

NEW JERSEY

NEW YORK

Broadway

East Broadway

South St.

Manhattan Bridge

3

Brooklyn Bridge

278

1

Brooklyn-Battery Tunnel

2

Ellis Island

Governors Island

6

to their 1865 appearance and contains numerous items relating to Roosevelt's career. The historic site is open for guided tours from 9:00 A.M. to 4:00 P.M. daily except Thanksgiving Day, Christmas Day, and New Year's Day.

SAGAMORE HILL NATIONAL HISTORIC SITE

20 Sagamore Hill Road
Oyster Bay, NY 11771
(516) 922–4447

Sagamore Hill National Historic Site was authorized in 1962 to preserve the estate of President Theodore Roosevelt. President Roosevelt used this estate as his permanent residence from 1885 until his death in 1919. The site is on the north shore of Long Island, at the end of Cove Neck Road, near the village of Oyster Bay. To reach the site by car, take the Long Island Expressway (Interstate 495) eastbound, to exit 41 North (State Highway 106). Follow State Highway 106 north toward Oyster Bay. Follow the brown historic site signs to Sagamore Hill. The site is 30 miles from the Queens Midtown Tunnel. It can also be reached by the Long Island Railroad from New York City's Pennsylvania Station at Seventh Avenue and West Thirty-third Street. A taxi is required to reach the site from the Oyster Bay railroad station.

Sagamore Hill was purchased by Theodore Roosevelt shortly after his graduation from Harvard University. The twenty-three-room Queen Anne–style mansion was completed in 1885 and served as his summer White House from 1902 to 1908.

The mansion is furnished with artifacts from the Roosevelt family. Skirting the west and south sides of the house is the piazza, a large field once used for political rallies. Nearby is the Old Orchard Museum, the former home of the President's oldest son, Brigadier General Theodore Roosevelt, Jr. The Old Orchard Museum contains exhibits relating to the lives of Theodore Roosevelt and his family. There is also a nature trail leading from Old Orchard Museum to the salt marsh and beach on the shore of Cold Spring Harbor.

FACILITIES: Neither lodging nor food is available at the site. Restrooms are located in the museum and near the parking lot. No picnicking is permitted on the grounds.

CAMPING: No camping is permitted at the site. Wildwood State Park, located 60 miles farther east on Long Island, offers camping facilities.

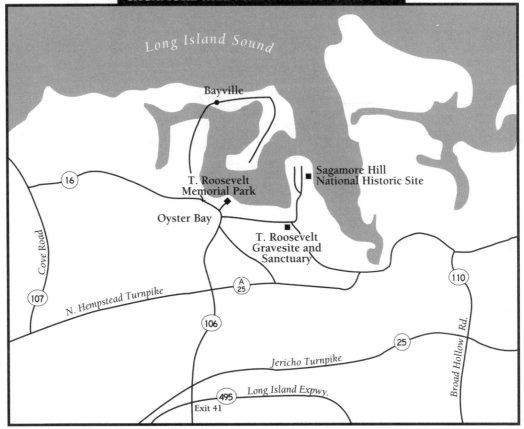

Long Island Sound

Bayville

16

T. Roosevelt
Memorial Park

Sagamore Hill
National Historic Site

Oyster Bay

Cove Road

T. Roosevelt
Gravesite and
Sanctuary

107

N. Hempstead Turnpike

A 25

110

106

25

Jericho Turnpike

Broad Hollow Rd.

495 Long Island Expwy.

Exit 41

ST. PAUL'S CHURCH NATIONAL HISTORIC SITE

897 South Columbus Avenue
Mount Vernon, NY 10550
(914) 667–4116

This affiliated area of the National Park Service was designated a national historic site in 1943 to memorialize and help preserve the eighteenth-century St. Paul's Church and its rich American history. The site is located just north of New York City in the town of Mount Vernon at 897 South Columbus Avenue.

The original St. Paul's parish was established in 1665, with the first recorded church built in 1692. The present building was constructed during the period 1763–82. The church is best known as the site of the 1733 election whereby Quakers were denied the right to vote because of their religious convictions. Following the election, John Peter Zenger printed a newspaper article on the injustice of the event. After printing subsequent articles criticizing the governor, he was arrested and tried for libel. Zenger was found innocent in a decision that established

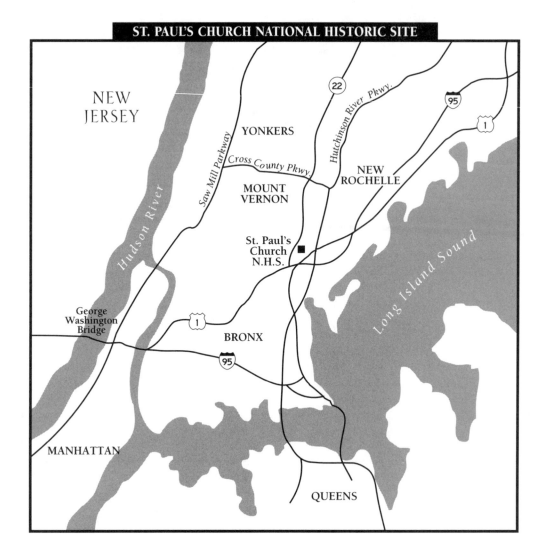

truth as a defense against libel, which led to the foundation for the principle of freedom of the press in the Bill of Rights. Later, during the Revolutionary War, St. Paul's was used as a barracks and hospital by Hessian troops. After the American Revolution, in 1787, it was used as Westchester County's courthouse. Aaron Burr practiced law here.

The site is open Monday through Friday year-round with the exception of holidays. Hours are 9:00 A.M. to 5:00 P.M. Free tours of the church, museum, grounds, and cemetery are available by appointment. Special tours of the cemetery are given on the last Sunday of each month at 2:00 P.M. April through October. Adjacent to the church, the Bill of Rights Museum is located in the former carriage shed–parish hall. Exhibits include artifacts, pictures, and maps relating to the history of St. Paul's and the American Revolution in this area. Included are a working replica of an eighteenth-century printing press, handcrafted dioramas, and a legislative journal from the first session of congress.

FACILITIES: Most visitor services are available nearby. A museum shop is at the site.

SARATOGA NATIONAL HISTORICAL PARK

648 Route 32
Stillwater, NY 12170
(518) 664–9821

Saratoga National Historical Park comprises 2,824 acres and was authorized in 1938 to commemorate the site of an important American victory over the British in 1777. The Battle of Saratoga (Freeman's Farm) is considered the turning point of the American Revolution. The park is located in eastern New York, 30 miles north of Albany via U.S. 4 and State Highway 32.

In the summer of 1777, British forces under General John Burgoyne left Canada to invade the united colonies (states), which were seeking independence. The expedition started with approximately 9,000 men with an aim to advance down the Champlain Valley to the Hudson River, and from there to Albany. Once in possession of Albany, Burgoyne would open up communications with New York City and wait for further instructions.

At first Burgoyne succeeded, with Fort Ticonderoga falling and the Americans retreating, but the American forces under General Philip Schuyler delayed him by destroying roads and bridges. By the time Burgoyne reached the Freeman Farm, Schuyler had been replaced by General Horatio Gates, who fortified a strong position on Bemis Heights, 2 miles north of Stillwater.

The British forces, by then reduced to 6,000 men by deaths, desertions, and garrisoning the supply line, met the larger American force on September 19. The fighting ended indecisively at nightfall. The armies waited for two and one half weeks before Burgoyne again attempted to pass the American lines on October 7. The second battle resulted in the loss of key positions on the British lines and forced Burgoyne to retreat to Saratoga (modern-day Schuylerville), where he surrendered on October 17, 1777. The victory at Saratoga is considered the turning point of the American Revolution and one of the world's most decisive battles.

The park's visitor center is open 9:00 A.M. to 5:00 P.M. daily except Thanksgiving Day, Christmas Day, and New Year's Day. It contains exhibits and a twenty-one-minute film. A 9-mile, self-guided auto-tour route begins near here; guide booklets are available in the visitor center. The tour road is open, weather permitting, from April 1 to November 30. Extended hours are posted from June through August. The tour includes ten stops with historic markers, interpretive signs, trails, and the restored Neilson House, which is open in summer from 10:00 A.M. to 4:00 P.M.

Two related sites are under park jurisdiction. Guided tours are available through the restored country home of General Schuyler. The Saratoga Monument, a 155-foot-tall stone spire erected for the centennial of the surrender, is also open to the public. The sites are located approximately 8 miles north of the battlefield in Schuylerville and can be reached by taking Route 4 or Route 32. Directions and maps are available at the visitor center. The sites are open in summer from 9:00 A.M. to 5:00 P.M., Wednesday through Sunday.

FACILITIES: No food or lodging is available in the park. Modern restrooms and drinking water are in the visitor center.

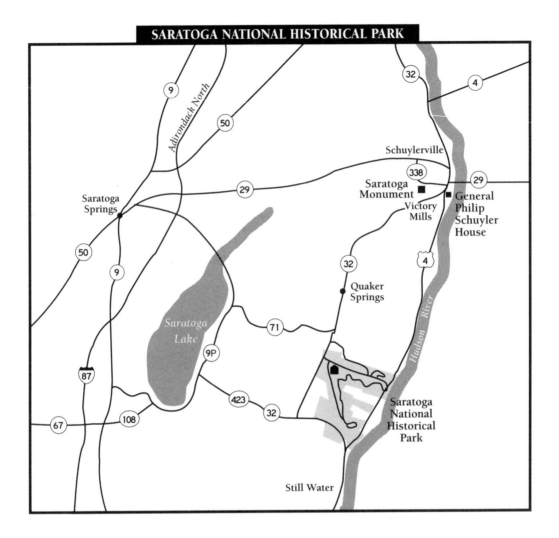

SARATOGA NATIONAL HISTORICAL PARK

CAMPING: No camping is permitted in the park. Moreau Lake State Park is a short distance north off Interstate 87 (exit 17). Moreau Lake offers tables, grills, water, flush toilets, swimming, and fishing (518–793–0511).

FISHING: Fishing is permitted in the park. Information is available at the visitor center.

THEODORE ROOSEVELT INAUGURAL NATIONAL HISTORIC SITE

641 Delaware Avenue
Buffalo, NY 14202
(716) 884–0095

Theodore Roosevelt Inaugural National Historic Site contains one acre and was authorized in 1966 to preserve the house where Theodore Roosevelt took the oath of office as president of the United States on September 14, 1901, following the assassination of President William McKinley. The home is located in western New York state in the city of Buffalo. In Buffalo, the site is at 641 Delaware Avenue, near North Street.

On September 6, 1901, while attending a reception at the Pan-American Exposition in Buffalo, New York, President William McKinley was shot by an anarchist. Vice-President Theodore Roosevelt, on a speaking engagement in Vermont, was summoned to Buffalo following the shooting. He stayed at the Ansley Wilcox home until September 10 when it appeared that McKinley was out of danger. Roosevelt then joined his family for a vacation in New York's Adirondack Mountains. On September 13, McKinley's condition suddenly worsened and Roosevelt was notified to return to Buffalo as soon as possible. The vice-president arrived in Buffalo on September 14 at 1:30 P.M., eleven hours after McKinley's death. Roosevelt took the oath of office in the Wilcox Library at 3:30 P.M. He wore borrowed clothing and no photographs were taken.

The restored house is open (fee charged) Monday through Friday from 9:00 A.M. to 5:00 P.M. and on Saturday and Sunday from noon until 5:00 P.M. The site offers an informational slide presentation, two recently updated exhibit areas, and four restored period rooms that may be seen on a guided tour. The site is closed on major holidays. A parking lot is in the rear of the house and can be reached from Franklin Street (one-way north).

FACILITIES: No dining facilities are available at the site. Several restaurants and hotels are within walking distance of the site along Delaware avenue.

CAMPING: No camping is permitted at the site. Darien Lakes, Letchworth, Four Mile Creek, and Joseph Davis state parks all offer camping within a 30-mile radius of Buffalo. Campgrounds are also across the border in Canada.

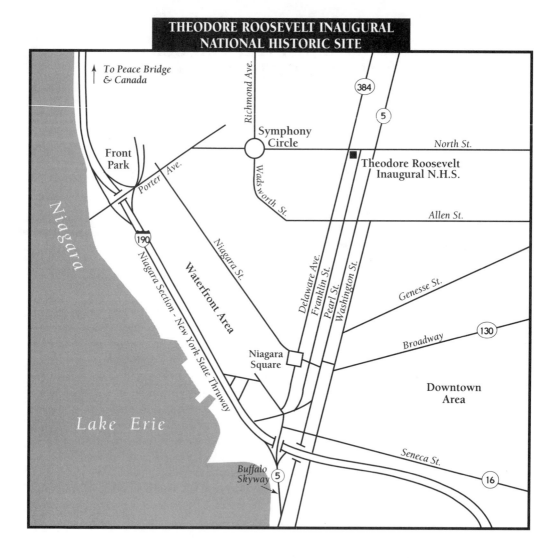

VANDERBILT MANSION NATIONAL HISTORIC SITE

249 Albany Post Road
Hyde Park, NY 12538
(914) 229–9115

Vanderbilt Mansion National Historic Site comprises 212 acres and was designated a part of the National Park Service in 1940 to preserve a lifestyle and era through one of the elegant mansions built around the turn of the century. The park is located in southeast New York, 6 miles north of Poughkeepsie via U.S. 9. It is just north of the village of Hyde Park on a bluff overlooking the Hudson River.

In 1895, this estate was purchased by Frederick Vanderbilt (one of four grandsons of Cornelius Vanderbilt) as a spring-fall cottage where he could pursue his interests in purebred livestock and horticulture. In 1896, a then-existing mansion was torn down, and construction commenced on the present fifty-four-room, $660,000 (excluding furnishings) structure. After the home's completion in 1899, the Vanderbilts lived here in the spring and fall and made the estate the scene of lavish parties that included the rich and famous.

Hours of operation are subject to change (914–229–9115). The site is closed Thanksgiving Day, Christmas Day, and New Year's Day.

The visitor center is located in the Pavilion, which served as housing when there was an overflow of guests and also as an occasional winter home. The mansion's interior and its furnishings are especially stunning. Signs explaining each room's use and furnishings are located at doorways in the mansion. Visitors should also walk a short distance to the large garden area. Volunteers, using donated funds, have completed several beds of flowers matching their 1938 grandeur.

FACILITIES: No food or lodging is available at the site, although both may be found a mile south in Hyde Park. Restrooms and a drinking fountain are located in the visitor center. Cabins are available in Mills-Norrie State Park (see camping section).

CAMPING: No camping is permitted at the site. Mills-Norrie State Park, 3½ miles north on Highway 9, offers nice shaded sites with tables, flush toilets, hot showers, fishing, boating, a marina, and nature trails. The park's camping section is seldom filled, even on weekends (914–889–4646).

FISHING: Fishing is available at the site; a valid New York fishing license is required. The small creek, however, is not stocked, and most fish are smaller than the size allowed for removal.

Vanderbilt Mansion National Historic Site

WOMEN'S RIGHTS NATIONAL HISTORICAL PARK
P.O. Box 70
Seneca Falls, NY 13148
(315) 568–2991

Women's Rights National Historical Park comprises five acres and was authorized in 1980 to commemorate the beginning of the women's struggle for equal rights. The park includes the site of the 1848 Women's Rights Convention and the homes and offices of a number of early women's rights activists. The historical park is in western New York, in the town of Seneca Falls, approximately midway between Rochester and Syracuse. The park is a fifteen-minute-drive south of the New York thruway, exit 41 via Route 414 and Route 5/20.

The industrial revolution of the early 1800s had a significant impact on the women of America. Although asked to work and earn outside income, women were required to turn over incomes to their husbands in addition to receiving lower wages for comparable work. Women also were not permitted to own property, enter a profession other than teaching, attend college, inherit their husbands' estates, or vote.

Nowhere did the change in women's lives become more apparent than in Seneca Falls, New York. Situated near the Great Western Turnpike, the Erie Canal, and a major railroad, the town was a major crossing point for a wide variety of individuals and ideas. In early July 1848, five courageous women met to discuss their difficulties in reconciling family and public responsibilities. This meeting led to the first Women's Rights Convention on July 19 and 20. This convention marked the formal beginning of the women's rights movement in the United States.

The park incorporates four historic buildings: the site of the convention and the homes of three individuals instrumental in the movement. The visitor center in downtown Seneca Falls (116 Fall Street) is open daily, 9:00 A.M. to 5:00 P.M., except Thanksgiving, Christmas, and New Year's Day. Interpretive talks and walking tours are scheduled from June through September. Guided tours of the restored Elizabeth Cady Stanton house are offered year-round.

Other places of interest in Seneca Falls include the National Women's Hall of Fame at 76 Fall Street, the Seneca Falls Urban Cultural Park Visitor Center at 115 Fall Street, lower level, and the Seneca Falls Historical Society Museum at 55 Cayuga Street. A number of interesting buildings remain standing near the downtown area.

FACILITIES: Food and lodging are available in Seneca Falls. Restrooms and drinking water are in the visitor center.

CAMPING: Cayuga Lake State Park, located 3 miles east of Seneca Falls, offers 286 camping sites with tables, grills, flush toilets, a dump station, showers, fishing, boating, and swimming from mid-May to mid-October. Electric hookups are provided at thirty-six sites: From downtown Seneca Falls, drive 2 miles east on Bayard Street and 1 mile south on State Highway 89 (315–568–5163). The park is quite nice.

NORTH CAROLINA

BLUE RIDGE PARKWAY

400 BB&T Building
Asheville, NC 28801
(704) 271–4779

This first national parkway comprises more than 81,000 acres along 470 miles of road that follow the crest of the Blue Ridge Mountains. The parkway, located in western North Carolina and Virginia, connects Great Smoky Mountains National Park and Shenandoah National Park.

The Blue Ridge Parkway is almost too good to be true. It provides quiet, leisurely (45 miles per hour maximum) travel on a road that is free of trucks, billboards, and beer cans through a largely undeveloped stretch of the southern Appalachians. The complete drive without stops takes approximately 16 hours. The scenery is beautiful, and the parkway is generally uncrowded. Along the way, motorists will find trails, wayside exhibits, museums, picnic areas, craft centers, and campgrounds. A detailed map of the entire route may be obtained at any of eleven visitor centers that are open May through October. Visitors also will find a schedule of guided walks, living-history programs, craft demonstrations, and evening talks that take place along the parkway.

Of particular interest is Mabry Mill, which contains a water-powered gristmill and blacksmith shop along with other pioneer exhibits. For craft lovers, the Parkway Craft Center at the Moses H. Cone Memorial Park, the Northwest Trading Post, and the Folk Art Center near Asheville offer outstanding examples of local handicrafts.

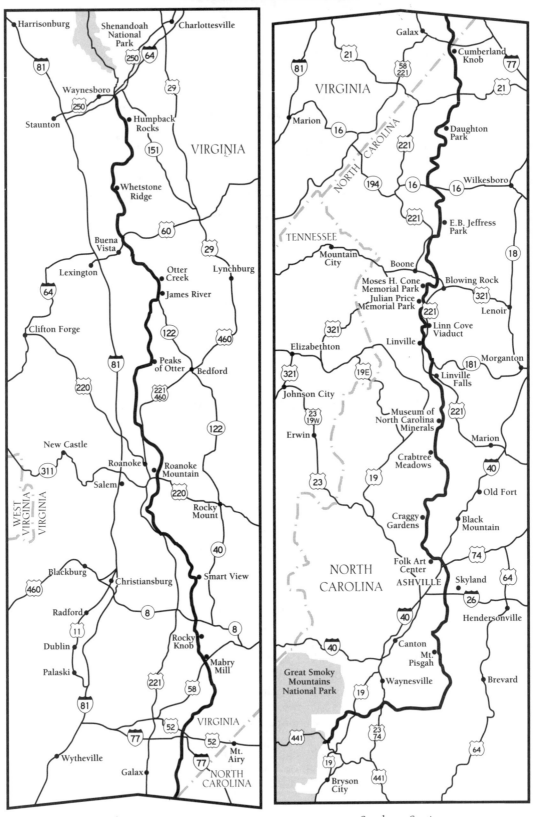

Northern Section

Southern Section

FACILITIES: Restaurants, gas stations, and picnic areas are located along the parkway and in nearby towns. Food, lodging, and gasoline are available at Peaks of Otter (703–586–1081), Doughton Park (919–372–4499), and Mount Pisgah (704–235–8228). Lodging only is at Rocky Knob (703–593–3503), and food only is at Whetstone Ridge Otter Creek, Mabry Mill, and Crabtree Meadows.

CAMPING: Campgrounds with tables, grills, water, flush toilets, and dump stations are at Otter Creek (sixty-seven spaces), Roanoke Mountain (105 spaces), Julian Price Park (197 spaces), Linville Falls (seventy-five spaces), Crabtree Meadows (ninety-three spaces), Mt. Pisgah (140 spaces), Peaks of Otter (148 spaces), Rocky Knob (109 spaces), and Doughton Park (136 spaces). Campgrounds are open from May 1 to November 1. Winter camping (limited facilities) is occasionally available, depending on weather.

FISHING: Streams contain brook, rainbow, and brown trout; some waters managed as native trout streams require reduced limits. Price Lake contains rainbow trout, and bass and bluegills are found in Bass Lake.

CAPE HATTERAS NATIONAL SEASHORE
Route 1, Box 675
Manteo, NC 27954
(919) 473–2111

Cape Hatteras National Seashore was authorized as part of the National Park Service in 1937 to protect 45 square miles of beach land along Atlantic barrier islands. The seashore is located in eastern North Carolina and is reached from the north via U.S. Highway 158, from the west by highways 64 or 264, and from the south via ferries from Cedar Island or Swan Quarter.

From the time of the first English settlement in the New World on Roanoke Island in 1585 to the first successful flight of a powered airplane at Kill Devil Hill in 1903, this area along North Carolina's coast has a rich human history. Pirates roamed the ocean and inlets here along a cape made famous by its shipwrecks. At Coquina Beach, the remains of a four-masted schooner stranded in 1921 are accessible to visitors.

A wide variety of recreational activities are available, including beachcombing, surfing, sailing, fishing, and nature study. The park's main visitor center at Cape Hatteras Light Station contains exhibits, and personnel are on duty to answer questions. Additional visitor centers are at Bodie Island and Ocracoke Island.

FACILITIES: A number of concessioners operate fishing piers and sell tackle, bait, and beverages. A marina is located near Oregon Inlet.

CAMPING: Campgrounds with tables, grills, flush toilets, cold-water showers, and dump stations are at Cape Point (202 spaces), Frisco (128 spaces, no dump station), Ocracoke (136 spaces), and Oregon Inlet (120 spaces). Cape Point, Ocracoke, and Oregon Inlet are open from Memorial Day to Labor Day. The other two are open from late May to Labor Day. Reservations may be made for Ocracoke Campground for camping from Memorial Day through Labor Day.

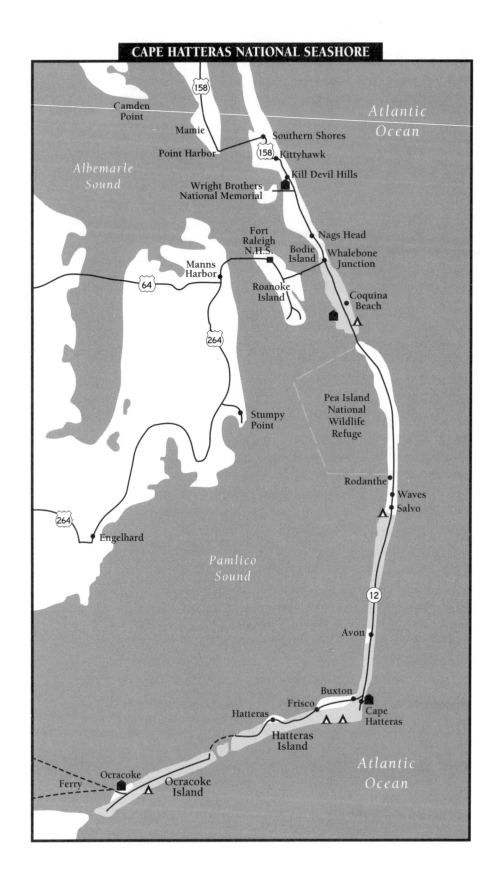

Camden
Point

Atlantic
Ocean

Mamie

Southern Shores

Point Harbor

158

Kittyhawk

158

Albemarle
Sound

Kill Devil Hills

Wright Brothers
National Memorial

Nags Head

Fort
Raleigh
N.H.S.

Bodie
Island

Whalebone
Junction

Manns
Harbor

64

Roanoke
Island

Coquina
Beach

264

Pea Island
National
Wildlife
Refuge

Stumpy
Point

Rodanthe

Waves

Salvo

264

Engelhard

Pamlico
Sound

12

Avon

Buxton

Frisco

Hatteras

Cape
Hatteras

Hatteras
Island

Atlantic
Ocean

Ocracoke

Ferry

Ocracoke
Island

FISHING: A variety of saltwater fish are taken from the surf, the piers, and deep-sea chartered boats. These include channel bass, mullet, striped bass, bluefish, spot, marlin, sailfish, dolphin, and amberjack. A few freshwater ponds contain bass and bluegill.

CAPE LOOKOUT NATIONAL SEASHORE

131 Charles Street
Harkers Island, NC 28531
(919) 728–2250

Cape Lookout National Seashore was authorized in 1966 to protect 55 miles of primitive barrier islands on the lower Outer Banks, including beaches, dunes, salt marshes, and the Cape Lookout Lighthouse. The seashore is located in eastern North Carolina, southwest of Cape Hatteras. There are no bridges to the islands. Passenger-only ferry service is available from Harkers Island to the Cape Lookout Lighthouse area, and between Ocracoke and Portsmouth Village. Vehicle ferry service for four-wheel-drive vehicles or ATVs is available from Davis to Great Island Bay and from Atlantic to Long Point. There are no roads on the seashore.

The narrow ribbons of sand running from Ocracoke Inlet on the northeast to Beaufort Inlet on the southwest are continuously being changed by wind, waves, and currents. The islands are composed mostly of bare beaches and low dunes covered by scattered grasses, flat grasslands with dense vegetation, and large expanses of salt marshes on the west side. Mammals are relatively rare, but on Shackleford there is a population of horses formerly pastured in the area that became wild. Also on this island, visitors will find an extensive maritime forest.

The lighthouse built on Cape Lookout in 1859 is still in operation but closed to the public. The nearby Keeper's Quarters, which was built in 1873, is open seasonally as a visitor center. Portsmouth Village was established at the north end of the seashore in 1753. Originally a busy transshipment point for ship cargoes to the mainland, today it is a ghost village. Information on reaching Portsmouth Village or the Cape Lookout lighthouse may be obtained by writing or calling headquarters on Harkers Island or through its web site: www.nps.gov/calo/.

FACILITIES: There are no facilities of any kind on the islands. There is also little shade, so proper clothing is a must. Water must be taken in, and any trash should be carried out.

CAMPING: Primitive camping is permitted, although there is no water, and toilet facilities are limited. No camping is permitted at Portsmouth Village or near the lighthouse.

FISHING: A variety of saltwater fish are taken from the surf, including channel bass, flounder, bluefish, spot, croaker, and sea trout.

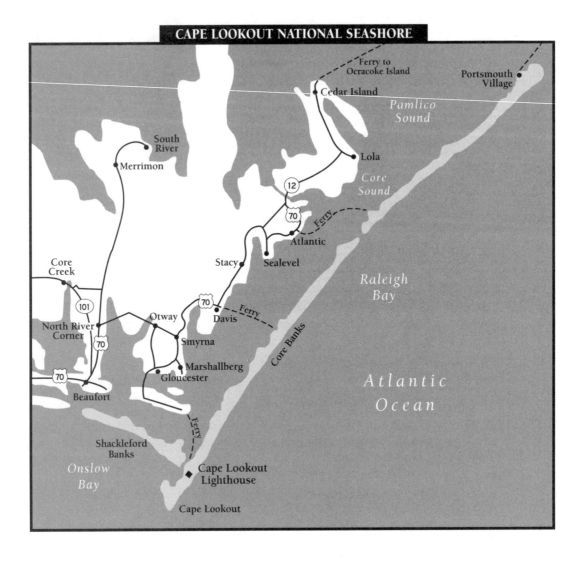

Ferry to Ocracoke Island

Portsmouth Village

Cedar Island

Pamlico Sound

South River

Merrimon

Lola

Core Sound

12

70

Ferry

Atlantic

Stacy

Sealevel

Core Creek

Raleigh Bay

101

70

Otway

Davis

Ferry

North River Corner

70

Smyrna

Core Banks

Marshallberg

Gloucester

70

Atlantic Ocean

Beaufort

Ferry

Shackleford Banks

Onslow Bay

Cape Lookout Lighthouse

Cape Lookout

CARL SANDBURG HOME NATIONAL HISTORIC SITE

1928 Little River Road
Flat Rock, NC 28731
(704) 693–4178 and 698–5627

Carl Sandburg Home National Historic Site comprises 250 acres and was authorized in 1968 to preserve the farm home where this famous American author spent the last twenty-two years of his life. The park is located in western North Carolina, 26 miles south of Asheville via Interstate 26.

When Carl Sandburg and his family moved from Michigan to this farm (named "Connemara") in 1945, he had already produced much of his outstanding literary work, such as the two-volume *Abraham Lincoln: The Prairie Years* (1926) and the four-volume *Abraham Lincoln: The War*

Years (1940). He had also spent many years pursuing a career in journalism. While living here, he continued his writing, including the only novel, *Remembrance Rock* (1948), and an autobiography, *Always the Young Strangers* (1953). In 1967, Carl Sandburg died at age eighty-nine.

The site is open 9:00 A.M. to 5:00 P.M. daily except Christmas Day. An information station with films and literature is in the basement of the main house. Guided tours of the home begin here. Following the tour, visitors are invited to walk around the farm and visit the numerous buildings. Mrs. Sandburg raised prize-winning goats at the barn. Trails to Little Glassy Mountain (0.2 mile) and Big Glassy Mountain (1.3 miles) begin near the house. Readings are presented periodically throughout the day during summer months. Allow two to three hours for a visit.

FACILITIES: No food service or lodging is available. Restaurants and motels are in Hendersonville, 3 miles north.

CAMPING: No camping is permitted at the site. Camping is available on U.S. 64E. Pleasant Ridge State Park offers camping facilities across the South Carolina border on U.S. 25.

FORT RALEIGH NATIONAL HISTORIC SITE
Route 1, Box 675
Manteo, NC 27954
(919) 473–5772

Fort Raleigh National Historic Site comprises 513 acres and was established in 1941 to commemorate the first attempted English settlement in North America. It was expanded in 1990 to include associated historical events. The park is located in eastern North Carolina, 3 miles north of Manteo via U.S. 64. (For a map of the vicinity, see Cape Hatteras National Seashore.)

In 1585, under the sponsorship and aid of Sir Walter Raleigh, a military venture was sent to establish an initial English settlement in a new colony called Virginia. After selecting the north end of Roanoke Island, the group built a fort and set out to explore the surrounding territory. Later, becoming short on food, the expedition set sail to England with Sir Francis Drake. By 1587, two additional groups totaling 115 men, women, and children had been dropped off at the earlier settlement. When English ships next returned in 1590, however, the colony had mysteriously disappeared.

The visitor center contains exhibits, excavated artifacts, and a film to help interpret the site. Visitors will also find the restored fort, which was part of the settlement site of 1585 and 1587. The Thomas Hariot Nature Trail begins near the fort. During summer months, a symphonic drama (fee charged) is produced in the Waterside Theatre. Adjacent to the site, the Elizabethan Garden (fee charged) is maintained by a private organization.

FACILITIES: Restrooms and drinking water are available in the visitor center. Lodging and food service can be found in nearby communities.

CAMPING: No camping is permitted at the site. A private campground is located nearby, and a number of National Park Service campgrounds are available at Cape Hatteras National Seashore.

GUILFORD COURTHOUSE NATIONAL MILITARY PARK

2332 New Garden Road
Greensboro, NC 27410
(910) 288–1776

Guilford Courthouse National Military Park comprises 220 acres and was established in 1917 to memorialize an important 1781 battle that opened the campaign that was to end the American Revolution. Guilford Courthouse is located in north-central North Carolina, 6 miles northwest of downtown Greensboro. Follow U.S. 220 northwest and turn east on New Garden Road.

After England had resigned itself to losing its northern colonies and began concentrating forces in the South, British General Charles Cornwallis commenced a campaign that was designed to subdue North and South Carolina. After weeks of pursuing a force led by General Nathanael Greene, the latter's Continental troops took position at Guilford Courthouse and invited Cornwallis to attack. Although the bloody battle on March 15, 1781, resulted in Greene's withdrawing his troops, the British losses were severe; seven months later, the surrender of Cornwallis at Yorktown sealed the fate of England's ambitions in America.

The park is open daily except Christmas Day and New Year's Day, from 8:30 A.M. to 5:00 P.M. The visitor center contains exhibits and a twenty-minute film program to help interpret the campaign and battle. Park personnel are on duty in the center to help visitors. A one-way auto road and bicycle trail begins at the visitor center. Exhibits and audio messages are located at stops along the road.

FACILITIES: Food service and lodging are not available in the park but may be found nearby in Greensboro. Modern restrooms and drinking water are in the visitor center.

CAMPING: No camping is permitted in the park. The city of Greensboro operates a nice campground south of town with tables, grills, flush toilets, and showers.

MOORES CREEK NATIONAL BATTLEFIELD

P.O. Box 69
Currie, NC 28435
(919) 283–5591

Moores Creek National Battlefield comprises eighty-six acres and was established in 1926 to commemorate a 1776 battle between North Carolina patriots and loyalists. The battlefield is located in southeastern North Carolina, 20 miles northwest of Wilmington via U.S. 421 and State Highway 210. The battlefield can also be reached by taking State Highway 210 west from the Rocky Point exit off Interstate 40.

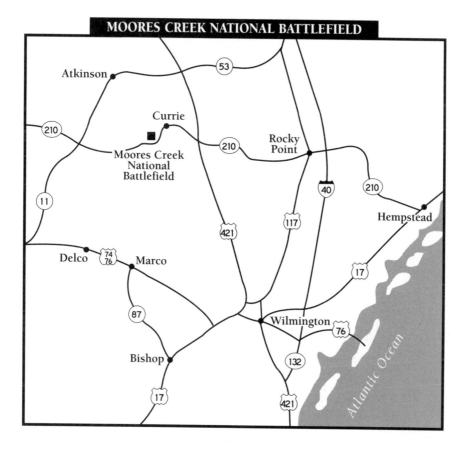

MOORES CREEK NATIONAL BATTLEFIELD

To reestablish strong British authority in the Carolinas, an army of 1,600 loyalists was recruited to march to the coast and join British troops. At Moores Creek on February 27, 1776, they were met by 1,000 patriots who not only halted the advance but also turned the loyalist retreat into a rout. The victory ended British authority in the colony and helped delay a full-scale invasion of the South. On April 12, 1776, North Carolina was the first colony to instruct its delegation to the Continental Congress to vote for independence.

The battlefield is open daily except Christmas Day and New Year's Day, from 9:00 A.M. to 5:00 P.M. (extended to 6:00 P.M. on summer weekends). A visitor center contains an audiovisual program and exhibits interpreting the conflict. Included in the center are original weapons and a diorama. Conducted tours and self-guiding walks begin here and lead past monuments and the patriot defense lines. A living-history program is presented on Saturday and Sunday afternoons during summer.

FACILITIES: No lodging is available in the park. A soft-drink machine is at the visitor center. Restrooms and drinking water are provided at the visitor center and at Patriots Hall.

CAMPING: No camping is permitted on the battlefield grounds. Carolina Beach State Park has camping facilities south of Wilmington on U.S. 421.

WRIGHT BROTHERS NATIONAL MEMORIAL

c/o Cape Hatteras National Seashore
Route 1, Box 675
Manteo, NC 27954
(919) 473–2111

Wright Brothers National Memorial comprises 431 acres and was authorized in 1927 to commemorate the site of the first sustained flight in a heavier-than-air machine. The flight was made here by Wilbur and Orville Wright on December 17, 1903. The park is located in eastern North Carolina, 50 miles southeast of Elizabeth City. It is approximately midway between Kitty Hawk and Nags Head on U.S. 158. (For an area map, see Cape Hatteras National Seashore.) The First Flight Airstrip, a 3,000-foot runway (VFR) with aircraft parking (limited to 24 hours per visit), is available for those wishing to arrive at the memorial by private aircraft.

Although the Wright brothers experimented at their home in Dayton, Ohio, they needed a location with relatively constant winds to test their aircraft designs. After checking weather bureau records, they decided upon the Kitty Hawk area. The brothers made more than 1,000 glider flights from the top of Kill Devil Hill in 1900, 1901, and 1902. Finally, on December 17, 1903, their motor-driven machine lifted off level sand and traveled 120 feet in 12 seconds. This was the first successful powered, man-carrying airplane flight in history. They made three more successful flights that day.

The visitor center contains exhibits and full-scale reproductions of the 1902 glider and the 1903 flying machine. The original motor-driven plane is in the Smithsonian Institution in Washington, D.C. A 60-foot granite memorial stands atop Kill Devil Hill, where many of the glider flights originated. Nearby are two reconstructed wooden buildings duplicating the Wrights' 1903 camp.

FACILITIES: Restrooms and water are available in the visitor center. Lodging and food service can be found in nearby communities.

CAMPING: No camping is permitted on the memorial grounds. A number of National Park Service campgrounds are located to the south in Cape Hatteras National Seashore.

OHIO

STATE TOURIST INFORMATION
(800) 282–5393

CUYAHOGA VALLEY NATIONAL RECREATION AREA
15610 Vaughn Road
Brecksville, OH 44141
(216) 524–1497

This 33,000-acre recreation area was established in 1975 to preserve the rural Cuyahoga River Valley, which links the two urban centers of Cleveland and Akron. The park is located in northeastern Ohio along a north–south strip paralleled on the west by Interstate 77 and on the east by State Highway 8.

Within a heavily populated urban area that was once the western boundary of the United States, Cuyahoga Valley offers a place to enjoy a wildflower walk, hike or bike along miles of trails, or hear a traditional music concert. The park's main visitor attraction is the Ohio & Erie Canal Towpath Trail, a 19-mile, multi-use trail extending the length of the park alongside remnants of the canal.

The Canal Visitor Center is at the north end of the park in a restored house next to the canal. Inside, visitors find information, exhibits, publications, and a museum of canal history. Park rangers and volunteers conduct canal lock demonstrations at the adjacent Lock 38 seasonally on weekends and holidays. The visitor center is located on Canal Road, south of Rockside Road in the village of Valley View, and is open daily from 8:00 A.M. to 5:00 P.M., except Thanksgiving, Christmas, and New Year's days (216–524–1497).

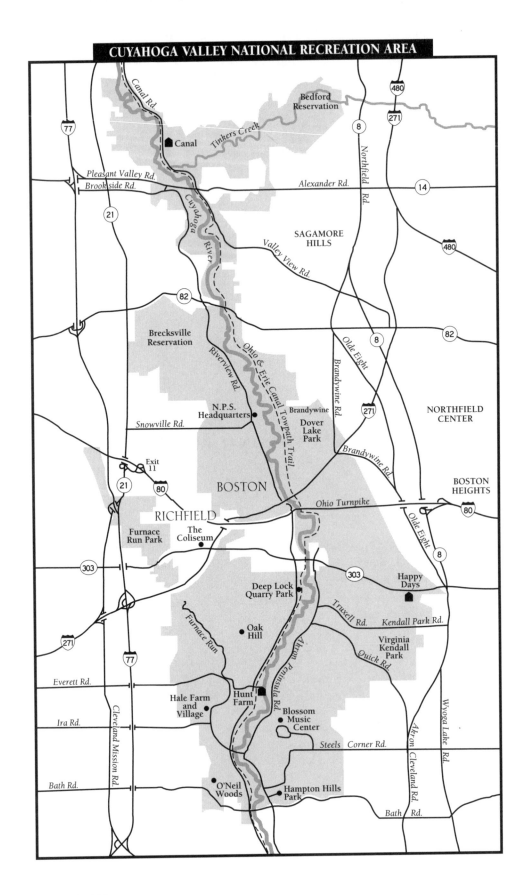

CUYAHOGA VALLEY NATIONAL RECREATION AREA

Canal Rd.

Tinkers Creek

Bedford Reservation

Canal

Pleasant Valley Rd.

Brookside Rd.

Alexander Rd.

Northfield Rd.

Cuyahoga River

SAGAMORE HILLS

Valley View Rd.

Brecksville Reservation

Riverview Rd.

Ohio & Erie Canal Towpath Trail

Olde Eight

Brandywine Rd.

NORTHFIELD CENTER

N.P.S. Headquarters

Snowville Rd.

Brandywine Dover Lake Park

Brandywine Rd.

Exit 11

BOSTON

Ohio Turnpike

Olde Eight

BOSTON HEIGHTS

RICHFIELD

Furnace Run Park

The Coliseum

Deep Lock Quarry Park

Happy Days

Furnace Run

Oak Hill

Truxell Rd.

Kendall Park Rd.

Virginia Kendall Park

Quick Rd.

Akron Peninsula Rd.

Everett Rd.

Hale Farm and Village

Hunt Farm

Blossom Music Center

Cleveland Mission Rd.

Ira Rd.

Steels Corner Rd.

Wyoga Lake Rd.

Akron Cleveland Rd.

Bath Rd.

O'Neil Woods

Hampton Hills Park

Bath Rd.

Happy Days Visitor Center, located on State Route 303, offers information and a variety of activities. The rustic building was built by the Civilian Conservation Corps in the 1930s as a day camp for inner-city children. A network of trails leads from here through the Virginia Kendall unit of the park. The popular Cuyahoga Valley Lyceum Series of lectures, concerts, and dramatic presentations is presented at the visitor center each January through March. Visitor center hours are limited in off-season (216–650–4636).

A third facility, Hunt Farm Visitor Information Center, is in the south end of the park near the intersection of Bolanz and Riverview roads. The Hunt Farm property is typical of the small family farms that dotted the Cuyahoga Valley in the late nineteenth century. The building is open seasonally and houses exhibits about the area's agricultural history (212–650–4636).

There are a variety of other things to see and do in the park. The Stephen Frazee house is open seasonally, providing visitors a glimpse of life in Ohio's Western Reserve during the early period of settlement. Hale Farm and Village, a restored 1800s farm and village, is operated by the Western Reserve Historical Society. The Cuyahoga Valley Scenic Railroad runs from Cleveland to Akron and offers excursions year-round. The Cleveland Orchestra spends its summers at Blossom Music Center. Summer stock is performed at Porthouse Theatre, which is owned and operated by Kent State University. Cleveland Metroparks and Metro Parks, serving Summit County, manage the Bike and Hike Trail, which extends from Bedford to Kent. A connector trail along Holzhauer Road provides access to the Towpath Trail. There are also golf courses, a water park, two ski resorts, and businesses that offer bicycle rentals and carriage rides.

FACILITIES: Food service is available nearby. Restrooms, drinking water, and picnic facilities are located throughout the park area.

CAMPING: No camping facilities are provided within the park, but lodging is available nearby.

FISHING: Several ponds and fishing piers are located within the park; an Ohio license is required.

DAVID BERGER NATIONAL MEMORIAL

c/o Jewish Community Center
3505 Mayfield Road
Cleveland Heights, OH 44118
(216) 382–4000

David Berger National Memorial was authorized in 1980 to honor the memory of the eleven Israeli athletes who were assassinated at the 1972 Olympic Games in Munich, Germany. David Berger, an American citizen, was one of the eleven. The memorial is located at the Jewish Community Center on U.S. Highway 322 in Cleveland Heights, a suburb on the east side of Cleveland, Ohio.

David Berger was raised in Shaker Heights, Ohio, where he was a merit scholar. Subsequently, he graduated from Tulane University and received both an M.B.A. and a law degree from Columbia University. In 1970, David moved to Israel, where he worked with the physically handicapped and continued to lift weights in training to make the 1972 Olympic Games as a member of Israel's team. It was at the twentieth Olympiad where David Berger and ten of his teammates were killed.

The memorial is a steel sculpture designed by David E. Davis. It consists of the five inter-locking rings of the Olympic symbol broken into ten semicircles and placed on eleven steel segments to symbolize the eleven individuals who died in Munich.

FACILITIES: Food and lodging are available nearby in Cleveland Heights.

CAMPING: No camping is permitted at the memorial.

DAYTON AVIATION HERITAGE NATIONAL HISTORICAL PARK

P.O. Box 9280
Wright Brothers Station
Dayton, OH 45409
(513) 225–7705

Dayton Aviation Heritage National Historical Park comprises eighty-six acres and was established in 1992 to preserve the area's aviation heritage and commemorate the legacies of Wilbur Wright, Orville Wright, and their friend, poet Paul Laurence Dunbar. The historical park is comprised of four units in and near the city of Dayton, in southwestern Ohio.

Orville and Wilbur Wright, two self-educated residents (both were a few credits short of high school graduation) of Dayton, Ohio, built and flew the world's first human-controlled heavier-than-air powered flying machine in 1903. They later built and flew the world's first practical and controllable airplane. The Wrights were able to apply scientific methodology to the mechanical knowledge they honed, first in the printing business, and later in their now-famous bicycle shop. The brothers designed and constructed both the planes and the internal combustion engines that powered them. The Wrights later operated a local flying school that trained over a hundred aviators.

The historical park is comprised of four units:

1. **Wright Cycle Shop** and **Hoover Block** (22 South Williams Street): The last remaining building in Dayton occupied by the brothers' bicycle business. The Hoover Block served as one site of the Wright's printing business. This is the location for the National Park Service office.

2. **Paul Laurence Dunbar House** (219 North P. L. Dunbar Street): Home purchased by Wright friend Paul Dunbar for his mother. Dunbar, an African-American who achieved distinction as a writer of novels, plays, short stories, and poems, purchased this home in 1903. He died here in 1906.

3. **Wright Hall** (2001 South Patterson Boulevard): The restored 1905 Wright Flyer III, the first practical aircraft capable of controlled flight, is on display at Wright Hall in Carillon Historical Park.

4. **Huffman Prairie Flying Field** (Wright-Patterson Air Force Base): This was the location for two years of Wright flights following their successful powered flights in 1903 at Kitty Hawk,

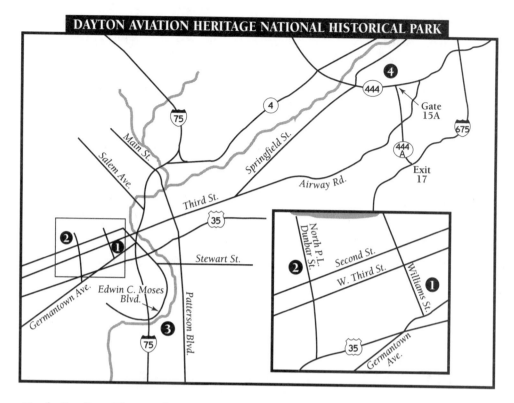

North Carolina. The Wrights eventually established what became the world's first permanent flying school. The U.S. Air Force Museum at the base is also a worthwhile stop.

FACILITIES: Restrooms and drinking water are in the National Park Service Office at 22 South Williams Street.

CAMPING: No camping is available in the historical park.

JAMES A. GARFIELD NATIONAL HISTORIC SITE

8095 Mentor Avenue
Mentor, OH 44060
(216) 255–8722

James A. Garfield National Historic Site comprises approximately eight acres and was authorized in 1980 to preserve Lawnfield, the site from which James Garfield conducted his successful campaign to become the twentieth president of the United States. The site is in northeastern Ohio, east of Cleveland, in the town of Mentor.

James A. Garfield was born in 1831 in a log cabin in Moreland Hills, Ohio. From work as a horse driver on the Ohio Canal, Garfield went on to become a teacher, minister, headmaster, college president, U.S. senator, U.S. representative, and president of the United States. Four months after assuming the office of president, James Garfield was shot on July 2, 1881, at forty-nine years of age. The president died on September 19, 1881, from the infection that developed from the wound.

Garfield originally purchased Lawnfield in 1876 as a rundown one-and-one-half-story farmhouse on 118 acres of land. He later added an additional story and purchased another forty acres of land. Following President Garfield's death, his widow added another wing to house a service area (kitchen, laundry, and maid's quarters) and a memorial library.

The house and grounds are owned by the National Park Service, and the original furnishings are owned by the Western Reserve Historical Society. The society administers the site for the National Park Service. The site is open for self-guided tours Tuesday through Saturday from 10:00 A.M. to 5:00 P.M. and Sunday from noon to 5:00 P.M. The site is closed on Monday. A fee is charged for entrance. In 1996, the site closed for two to three years of restoration.

FACILITIES: Food and lodging are available nearby in the town of Mentor.

CAMPING: No camping is permitted at the site. Punderson State Park, approximately 20 miles south of Mentor via Ohio Highway 44, offers 201 sites with tables, grills, flush toilets, showers, and fishing (216–564–1195).

HOPEWELL CULTURE NATIONAL HISTORICAL PARK

16062 State Route 104
Chillicothe, OH 45601
(614) 774–1126

Established in 1923 as Mound City Group National Monument, the name was changed in 1992 to Hopewell Culture National Historical Park as the park expanded to include three other sites. Only the Mound City Group is open to visitors. The park is located in south-central Ohio, 4 miles northwest of Chillicothe via State Highway 104.

Two thousand years ago, peoples of the Hopewell culture constructed Mound City, a square earthen wall enclosure containing at least twenty-three mounds in a thirteen-acre area. Later named after an 1891 excavation at a farm owned by Mordecai Hopewell, the culture flourished across much of eastern North America during a period from 2,000 to 1,500 years ago. The classic Hopewell sites are located in central and southern Ohio.

The Hopewell peoples were among the first to cultivate plants in North America, although they also relied on hunting and gathering. They were skilled artisans who were part of an extensive network through which artifacts and raw materials flowed. Copper ornaments and breastplates, stone effigy pipes, delicately chopped flint blades and other objects have been found buried under their mounds. Many of these items were obtained from distant areas such as the present-day Yellowstone National Park area in Montana and Wyoming.

The park visitor center is open daily from 8:30 A.M. to 5:00 P.M., except Thanksgiving,

Christmas, and New Year's Days. The visitor center contains a small museum, an auditorium where the fifteen-minute-long video *Legacy of the Mound Builders* is shown, and a book sales area. It is also the beginning point for a self-guided walk through Mound City. Ranger-conducted walks and special programs are scheduled during the summer.

FACILITIES: Park facilities are wheelchair-accessible. Restrooms and water are available in the visitor center; food and lodging are available in Chillicothe.

CAMPING: No camping is permitted on the park grounds. Private campgrounds are available in Chillicothe and a number of state parks with camping facilities are within 30 miles of the park.

PERRY'S VICTORY AND
INTERNATIONAL PEACE MEMORIAL
P.O. Box 549
Put-in-Bay, OH 43456
(419) 285–2184

Perry's Victory and International Peace Memorial comprises nearly twenty-six acres and was incorporated into the National Park Service in 1936. The Monument commemorates Commodore Oliver Hazard Perry's victory on Lake Erie in one of the most decisive naval battles of the War of 1812 and the resulting international peace between Canada and the United States. The park is located in northern Ohio on the Lake Erie island of South Bass. In season, automobile and passenger ferries operate from Catawba Point and passenger-only ferries operate from Port Clinton. There is year-round air service to the island from the Port Clinton and Sandusky airports.

Early in the War of 1812, British ships controlled Lake Erie, an important lifeline for American troops and supplies in the Old Northwest. On September 10, 1813, this stranglehold was broken when nine vessels under the command of Commodore Oliver Hazard Perry won a decisive victory over six British warships under the command of Robert Heriott Barclay, about 10 miles northwest of South Bass Island. Since the end of the War of 1812, peaceful relations have existed between the United States and Canada, and with Great Britain before her. Canada and the U.S. share the world's longest undefended border of more than 4,000 miles, and the lessons of peace through negotiation and arbitration are still honored through the 1817 Rush-Bagot Agreement, one of the first disarmament treaties. It is still in effect today.

The park is best known for the granite memorial shaft built between 1912 and 1915 that rises 352 feet above its 45-foot-wide base. Visitors may ride an elevator from the second floor of the Memorial to an observation platform 317 feet above Lake Erie (fee charged). The memorial is open from mid-May to early October and is open by appointment during the rest of the year.

FACILITIES: A full range of tourist facilities is available on the island in season. Full services are also available in mainland communities.

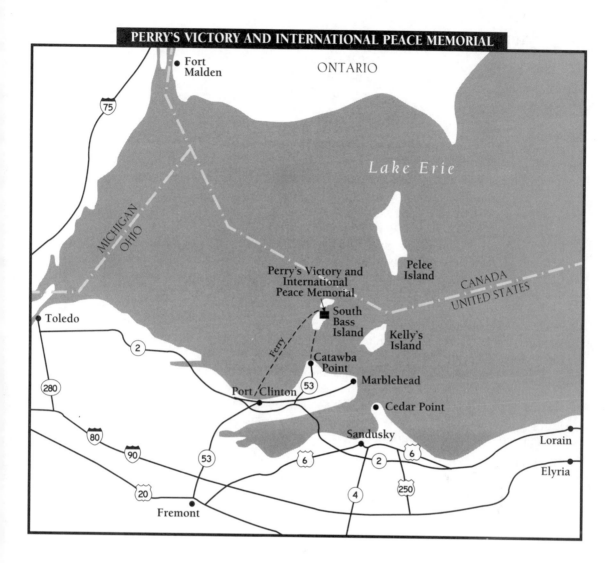

CAMPING: Camping is not available at the memorial. South Bass Island State park offers 130 sites with primitive camping on the island (no reservations; 419–285–2112). On the mainland, East Harbor State Park, northeast of Port Clinton, provides 570 sites with modern bathhouse facilities (no reservations; 419–734–5857).

FISHING: Fishing is available in Lake Erie from the memorial grounds; an Ohio license is required. Catches include bass, catfish, crappie, pike and walleye.

Perry's Victory and International Peace Memorial (opposite page)

WILLIAM HOWARD TAFT NATIONAL HISTORIC SITE

2038 Auburn Avenue
Cincinnati, OH 45219
(513) 684–3262

William Howard Taft National Historic Site comprises three acres and was authorized in 1969 to preserve the birthplace and boyhood home of the only person to
serve as both chief justice and president of the United States. The park is located
at 2038 Auburn Avenue in the city of Cincinnati (see accompanying map).

This two-story brick home was purchased by William Howard Taft's father in 1851, and it was
here that William Howard was born on September 15, 1857. After attending public schools in
Cincinnati, he graduated second in his class at Yale and then returned to Ohio to earn a law
degree from Cincinnati Law School. Among Taft's many important positions were those of solic-
itor general of the United States, twenty-seventh president of the United States (1909–1913),
professor of constitutional law at Yale, and chief justice of the United States (1921–1930).
William Howard Taft died in Washington, D.C., on March 8, 1930, and was buried in Arlington National Cemetery.

Four restored rooms reflect the family life of the Tafts during the years 1857 to 1877.
Museum exhibits emphasize the long and dedicated public career of William Howard Taft and
the Taft family. The site is open from 10:00 A.M. to 4:00 P.M. seven days a week, except Thanksgiving, Christmas, and New Year's Day. An elevator is available. Admission is free. Reservations
are required for groups of ten or more.

FACILITIES: Drinking water and restrooms are available in the restored home. They are handicapped accessible.

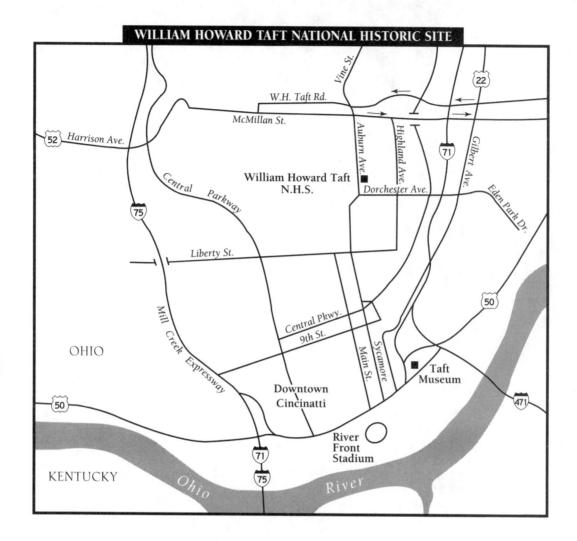

WILLIAM HOWARD TAFT NATIONAL HISTORIC SITE

Vine St.

W.H. Taft Rd.

McMillan St.

22

52 Harrison Ave.

Auburn Ave.

Highland Ave.

71

Gilbert Ave.

75

Central Parkway

William Howard Taft N.H.S.

Dorchester Ave.

Eden Park Dr.

Liberty St.

50

Mill Creek Expressway

OHIO

Central Pkwy.
9th St.

Main St.

Sycamore

Taft Museum

Downtown Cincinatti

50

River Front Stadium

471

71

KENTUCKY

75

Ohio River

PENNSYLVANIA

STATE TOURIST INFORMATION
(800) 847–4862

ALLEGHENY PORTAGE RAILROAD
NATIONAL HISTORIC SITE
P.O. Box 189
Cresson, PA 16630
(814) 886–6100

Allegheny Portage Railroad National Historic Site comprises 1,476 acres and was authorized in 1964 to commemorate the first railroad crossing the Allegheny Mountains, which operated from 1834 to 1855. The park is located in central Pennsylvania, 12 miles west of Altoona via U.S. highways 220 and 22. The visitor center can be reached from the Gallitzin Road exit off U.S. 22. (See the area map under Johnstown Flood National Memorial.)

Alarmed by the growth of New York City and Baltimore, the Pennsylvania legislature authorized funding for construction of a canal to the West in 1826. Crossing the Alleghenies presented the greatest problem, and a number of possibilities were considered. It was finally decided to build a portage railroad that would lift and lower cars from one level to another along a series of inclined planes. The 36-mile railroad consisted of five planes on each side of the mountain with a stationary steam engine providing power at the top of each plane. By 1854, the Pennsylvania Railroad was able to provide continuous rail service between the eastern seaboard and the Ohio Valley, thereby making the portage obsolete.

Independence National Historical Park (opposite page)

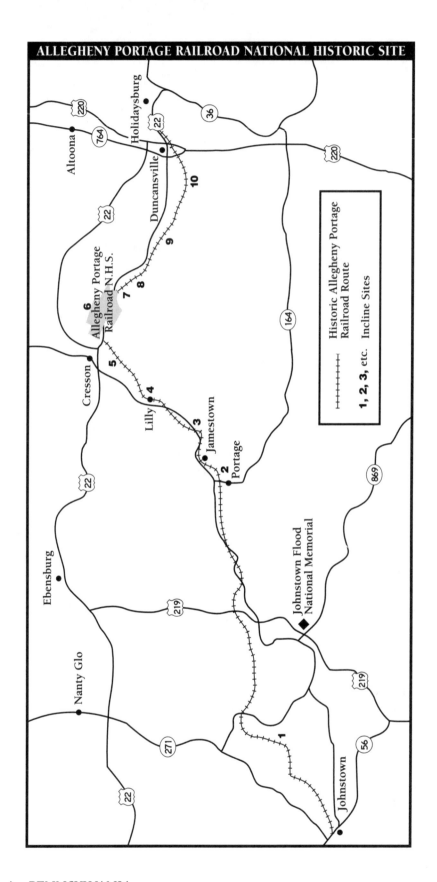

ALLEGHENY PORTAGE RAILROAD NATIONAL HISTORIC SITE

The Summit Level Visitor Center tells the story of the portage railroad through exhibits and a twenty-minute film. The visitor center is open daily from 9:00 A.M. to 5:00 P.M. (to 6:00 P.M. during summer). Other park features include inclined planes 6, 8, 9, and 10, the historic Lemon House, Engine House #6 exhibit building, Skew Arch Bridge, the Staple Bend Tunnel, stone culverts, and stone railroad ties. A variety of interpretive programs are offered during the summer including guided walks, costumed demonstrations and Evenings on the Summit Programs, which are offered on Saturdays.

FACILITIES: No food or lodging is available in the park, but there are restrooms, grills, and picnic tables. Restaurants and lodging are in Cresson.

CAMPING: No camping is permitted at the site. Prince Gallitzin State Park, approximately 20 miles northwest of Altoona, provides camping facilities with tables, grills, flush toilets, showers, swimming, and fishing.

DELAWARE AND LEHIGH NAVIGATION CANAL NATIONAL HERITAGE CORRIDOR

c/o DLNCNHC Commission
10 East Church Street
Room P-208
Bethlehem, PA 18018
(215) 861–9345

Delaware and Lehigh Navigation Canal National Heritage Corridor was authorized in 1988 to conserve and interpret the valleys' heritage and to enhance the region's quality of life. The National Heritage Corridor stretches for 150 miles in eastern Pennsylvania along the historic routes of the Delaware Canal and the Lehigh Navigation System.

The eastern Pennsylvania region encompassed by the Delaware and Lehigh Navigation Canal National Heritage Corridor has witnessed a progression of peoples, including the Lenape Indians, who built their villages where trails and waterways met. Later, European settlers, including William Penn's Quakers and the Moravians, who settled Bethlehem, used these trails to journey to the region.

Poor roads hindered the region's development and resulted in a concentration of industry and settlements (many of which are still visible today) in areas with easy access to water. The need to transport goods and raw materials and to move large amounts of anthracite coal from the coal fields of Carbon County and the Wyoming Valley led to construction of the Lehigh Navigation System and the Delaware Canal. These waterways were built in stages between 1817 and 1845 and saw their most active period from the 1830s to the 1860s. The canals eventually succumbed to competition from railroads and highways, although the Delaware Canal and portions of the Lehigh Navigation System continued to operate until 1942. Today, the well-preserved Delaware Canal is the most completely intact towpath canal in the nation.

The land encompassed by the National Heritage Corridor provides a wide variety of places, activities, and experiences for visitors. These include parks, trails, scenic landscapes, historic

DELAWARE AND LEHIGH NAVIGATION CANAL
NATIONAL HERITAGE CORRIDOR

villages, historic structures, museums, and, of course, the waterways. Visitors may tour a restored Quaker village at Historic Fallsington, ride a mule-drawn canal boat at New Hope or Hugh Moore Park, and travel up the Lehigh Gorge on a steam train from Jim Thorpe's historic railroad station.

For information on sights and activities, write: Carbon County Tourist Promotion Agency, 1004 Main Street, Stroudsburg, PA 18360 (717–424–6050); Lehigh Valley Convention and Visitors' Bureau, P.O. Box 2605, Lehigh Valley, PA 18001 (800–747–0561); and Bucks County Tourist Commission, P.O. Box 912, Doylestown, PA 18901 (215–345–4552).

FACILITIES: Food and lodging, including historic bed-and-breakfast facilities, are available throughout the corridor. The Weisel Youth Hostel is adjacent to Nockamixon State Park, and the Solly House Hostel is within Tyler State Park. Family cabins are available by reservation at Nockamixon and Ralph Stover state parks.

CAMPING: Camping is available at Hickory Run State Park, at Tinicum County Park, and at numerous private campgrounds. Wy-Hit-Tuk County Park on the Delaware Canal offers canoe camping.

FISHING: Rainbow, brook, and brown trout are in smaller streams. The Delaware and lower Lehigh offer shad, smallmouth bass, walleye, and muskellunge. Allentown's Little Lehigh and Bethlehem's Monacacy Creek offer good fishing. Lakes at Francis Walter Dam and at Beltzville and Nockamixon state parks are stocked. A state fishing license is required.

DELAWARE NATIONAL SCENIC RIVER; DELAWARE WATER GAP NATIONAL RECREATION AREA
Bushkill, PA 18324
(717) 588–2451

Delaware Water Gap National Recreation Area was authorized in 1965 to preserve 70,000 acres of relatively unspoiled land containing historical features and providing numerous recreational opportunities. The park is located on both the Pennsylvania and New Jersey sides of the 40-mile-long Delaware National Scenic River. The southern section of the park is intersected by Interstate 80.

Delaware Water Gap and Delaware National Scenic River lie between the Kittatinny Ridge of New Jersey and the Pocono Plateau of Pennsylvania in a region that was a resort haven for wealthy vacationers during the late nineteenth and early twentieth centuries. Except for this brief period, civilization generally bypassed this area.

Just off the Interstate 80 bridge on the New Jersey side of the river, Kittatinny Point Visitor Center contains exhibits explaining how Kittatinny Ridge and the Delaware Water Gap were created. Nearby in Pennsylvania, at Resort Point, the stone foundation of a large hotel that burned in 1931 is still visible; at Slateford, a restored farm site may be toured.

While driving toward the park's northern end, additional points of interest are a nature trail for disabled persons at the Pocono Environmental Education Center (717–828–2319) and a visitor center and scenic trail at Dingmans Falls.

Delaware Water Gap National Recreation Area (next two pages)

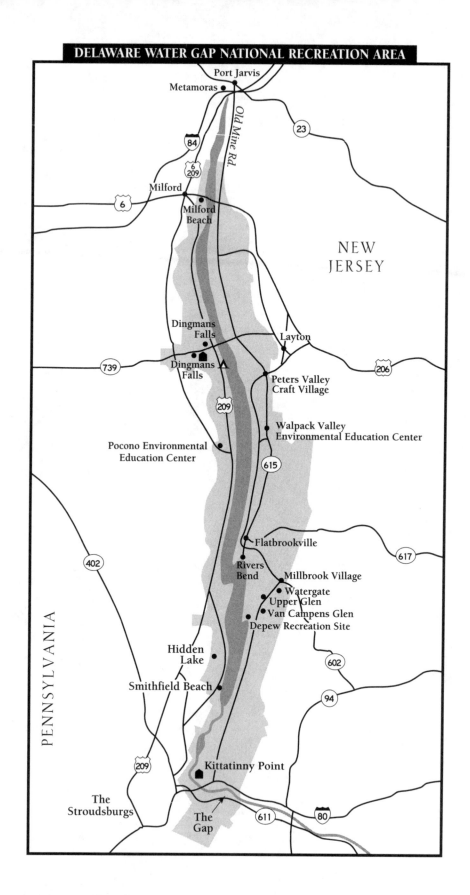

DELAWARE WATER GAP NATIONAL RECREATION AREA

Port Jarvis

Metamoras

84

6
209

23

Milford

6

Milford
Beach

NEW
JERSEY

Dingmans
Falls

Layton

739

Dingmans
Falls

Peters Valley
Craft Village

206

209

Walpack Valley
Environmental Education Center

Pocono Environmental
Education Center

615

402

Flatbrookville

617

Rivers
Bend

Millbrook Village

Watergate
Upper Glen

Van Campens Glen

Depew Recreation Site

602

Hidden
Lake

Smithfield Beach

94

PENNSYLVANIA

209

Kittatinny Point

The
Stroudsburgs

The
Gap

611

80

Old Mine Rd.

At Millbrook Village, visitors can take an enjoyable walking tour of a re-created town of the late 1800s. Buildings include period homes, a blacksmith shop, general store, church, school, wagon shop, woodworker's shop, weaving and spinning house, cabin, and barn. Village grounds are open daily from 9:00 A.M. to 5:00 P.M. year-round. From April through October selected buildings are open to the public and crafts are demonstrated on weekends. From November through March only the grounds are open. A nineteenth-century folk-life festival is held on the first full weekend of October each year.

Peters Valley Craft Center is a community of artisans skilled in woodworking, fibers, black-smithing, ceramics, fine metals, and photography. Selected studios are open to visitors daily from 2:00 P.M. to 4:00 P.M. June 1 through August 31 (201–948–5200).

A variety of natural and cultural interpretive programs are offered during the year. Contact the park for additional information.

FACILITIES: No commercial food or lodging establishments are available in the park, but both can be found in towns along the roads. An American Youth Hostel provides overnight accom-modations near the northern end of the park on the New Jersey side. Picnic areas and restrooms are located throughout the recreation area, while boat launching ramps are at the Gap, Ding-mans Ferry, Poxono, Smithfield Beach, and Milford Beach.

CAMPING: Dingmans Campground, operated by a concessioner just south of Dingmans Ferry, offers more than one hundred sites with water, tables, fire rings, dump station, flush toilets, electricity, and pay showers. Reservations are accepted with a deposit. Write R.D. 1, Box 312, Dingmans Ferry, PA 18328 (717–828–2266). Other public campgrounds are located near the park on both the Pennsylvania and New Jersey sides of the river. Four miles north of Water Gap in New Jersey, Worthington State Forest has campsites with tables, grills, and pit toilets (201–841–9575). Hiking, hunting, and fishing are also available in the park. Near the park's north end on New Jersey Highway 23, High Point State Park offers campsites with tables, grills, and flush toilets. Numerous private campgrounds are located nearby. East of Peters Valley on U.S. 206, Stokes State Forest provides campsites.

FISHING: Within the park, smallmouth bass and walleye are the most important sport species in the Delaware River. During spring, American shad migrate up the river in great numbers. Ice fishing is popular during winter months.

EISENHOWER NATIONAL HISTORIC SITE

c/o Gettysburg National Military Park
Gettysburg, PA 17325
(717) 334–1124

Eisenhower National Historic Site was authorized in 1969 and comprises 690 acres, including the farm and only home owned by General Dwight David Eisenhower and his wife, Mamie. The farm served as a retreat while Ike was president and became his retirement home in 1961. The park is located in south-central Pennsylvania, adjacent to Gettysburg National Military Park. Visitation to the site is only via the shuttle-bus service beginning at the Gettysburg Military Park visitor center.

Dwight Eisenhower moved to Pennsylvania from West Point in 1918 when he assumed his first command at Camp Colt in Gettysburg. Following World War II, while Eisenhower was serving as president of Columbia University, he and Mamie purchased a 189-acre farm on the edge of the famous Civil War battlefield at Gettysburg. Although unable to move here permanently until 1961 following his two terms as thirty-fourth president of the United States, Eisenhower did use the home as a retreat from his busy public life.

The original farmhouse was found to be a brick structure supported by a much older wooden home. Mamie had a new house built around a portion of the early house. Landscaping and construction were completed in 1955. Eisenhower inherited a dairy operation when he bought the farm, which he changed in favor of raising purebred black Angus cattle and, later, developing feeder cattle for sale. After Ike died in 1969, Mamie continued to live here until her death in 1979.

The historic site offers self-guiding tours of the farm. Visitors should obtain tickets for entrance to the site inside the National Park Service Visitor Center. Tickets are limited and allocated on a first-come basis. The shuttle bus (fee charged) leaves the visitor center for the historic site. Near the shuttle-bus arrival point at the site, a reception center contains exhibits of the Eisenhower family and life at Gettysburg. At the main home, park rangers provide brochures and information for a tour of the home. A tour of the home and grounds takes approximately one-and-one-half hours.

FACILITIES: Meals and lodging are available in Gettysburg. Restrooms and water are at the reception center and at the Gettysburg visitor center where the shuttle buses leave.

CAMPING: See camping section under Gettysburg National Military Park.

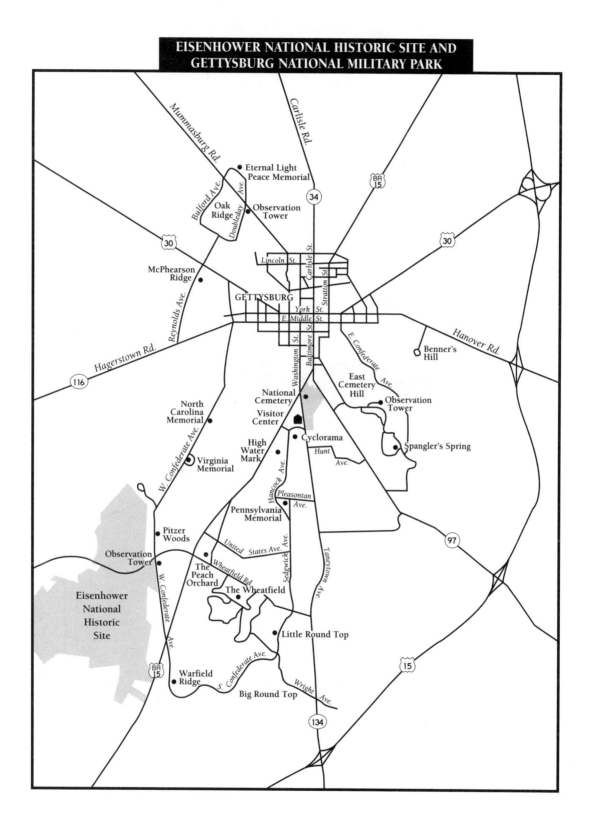

EISENHOWER NATIONAL HISTORIC SITE AND GETTYSBURG NATIONAL MILITARY PARK

Mummasburg Rd.

Carlisle Rd.

Eternal Light Peace Memorial

Bulford Ave.

Oak Ridge

Doubleday Ave.

Observation Tower

BR 15

34

30

30

McPhearson Ridge

Lincoln St.

Carlisle St.

GETTYSBURG

Stratton St.

York St.

E. Middle St.

Reynolds Ave.

Washington St.

Baltimore St.

Benner's Hill

Hanover Rd.

Hagerstown Rd.

E. Confederate Ave.

East Cemetery Hill

116

North Carolina Memorial

National Cemetery

Visitor Center

Observation Tower

W. Confederate Ave.

Virginia Memorial

High Water Mark

Cyclorama

Hunt Ave.

Spangler's Spring

Hancock Ave.

Pleasontan Ave.

Pennsylvania Memorial

Pitzer Woods

United States Ave.

Sedgwick Ave.

Taneytown Ave.

97

Observation Tower

W. Confederate Ave.

Wheatfield Rd.

The Peach Orchard

The Wheatfield

Eisenhower National Historic Site

Little Round Top

15

BR 15

Warfield Ridge

S. Confederate Ave.

Wright Ave.

Big Round Top

134

FORT NECESSITY NATIONAL BATTLEFIELD

1 Washington Way
Farmington, PA 15437
(412) 329–5512

Fort Necessity National Battlefield contains 900 acres and was established in 1931 to commemorate the site where, in 1754, Colonial troops commanded by Lieutenant Colonel George Washington were defeated in the opening battle of the French and Indian War. The park is located in southwestern Pennsylvania, 11 miles southeast of Uniontown via U.S. 40.

In April 1754, George Washington and a force of Virginians set out from Alexandria in an attempt to halt French expansion in North America. After defeating a small band of Frenchmen on Chestnut Ridge, Washington's troops built Fort Necessity and received reinforcements and additional supplies. On July 3, a force of 600 Frenchmen and 100 Indians attacked the fort, and by midnight, Washington had surrendered; he and his troops were permitted to withdraw

FORT NECESSITY NATIONAL BATTLEFIELD AND
FRIENDSHIP HILL NATIONAL HISTORIC SITE

To Pittsburg

Uniontown

Chalkhill

Masontown

Friendship Hill
National
Historic Site

Smithfield

Fort Necessity
National
Battlefield

Point Marion

PENNSYLVANIA
WEST VIRGINIA   MARYLAND

Morgantown

the following day. In 1755, another large British force under General Edward Braddock was again defeated by the French near present-day Pittsburgh. Braddock died during the retreat and was buried beneath the crude roadway.

A visitor center near the restored stockade is open daily from 8:30 A.M. to 5:00 P.M. except on Christmas Day. The visitor center offers exhibits and a slide program to help interpret the battle. Also available are self-guiding trails, living-history programs, and a picnic area. Nearby is Mount Washington Tavern, a restored stagecoach stop from the early 1800s that provided lodging and meals to travelers along the old National Road. The tavern is open daily from 8:30 A.M. to 5:00 P.M. The Braddock gravesite is open during daylight hours, year-round. Jumonville Glen, on nearby Chestnut Ridge, is open daily 10:00 A.M. to 5:00 P.M. from spring through autumn.

FACILITIES: No lodging or food service is available in the park, but both are in Uniontown. Restrooms and water are in the visitor center.

CAMPING: No camping is permitted at the battlefield. A short distance northeast, Ohiopyle State Park offers camping with tables, grills, flush toilets, showers, fishing, and boating.

FRIENDSHIP HILL NATIONAL HISTORIC SITE
R.D. 1, Box 149-A
Point Marion, PA 15474
(412) 725–9190

Friendship Hill National Historic site comprises 675 acres and was authorized in 1978 to preserve a thirty-five-room, stone-and-brick home on the Monongahela River that belonged to immigrant Albert Gallatin. Gallatin was secretary of the treasury under presidents Jefferson and Madison from 1801 to 1813. The site is located in southwestern Pennsylvania, 3 miles north of Point Marion along Pennsylvania Highway 166, about midway between Uniontown, Pennsylvania, and Morgantown, West Virginia.

Albert Gallatin first came to western Pennsylvania in the mid-1780s when the area was at the edge of a frontier. Gallatin was of the opinion that the Monongahela River would provide business opportunities as the areas to the west opened up and developed. In 1789, the brick house was begun. Nearly ten years later, a clapboard-sided, brick-and-log frame house was added. A large, square stone house was built in 1823. Although Gallatin called Friendship Hill his home for more than forty years, he was frequently required to take extended periods of leave to serve his country in the fields of finance, politics, diplomacy, and scholarship. While serving as secretary of treasury, Gallatin developed the concept of the National Road.

The park is open daily from 8:30 A.M. to 5:00 P.M. except on Christmas Day. A visitor center contains exhibits, and personnel to answer visitor questions. Guided tours of the house are given each day during summer, and brochures are available for self-guiding tours of the grounds. A number of trails are in the park. A twenty-minute loop trail passes the grave of Gallatin's first wife, while a 3.8-mile trail (2½ hours) follows the Monongahela River for nearly a mile, passing through a variety of meadows, woods, and streams.

FACILITIES: Restrooms and drinking water are available at the historic site. Restaurants are in Point Marion, while both food and lodging are in Uniontown and Morgantown.

CAMPING: No camping is permitted in the park. Coopers Rock State Forest, 10 miles east of Morgantown, West Virginia, offers campsites with tables, grills, flush toilets, showers, and fishing.

FISHING: The Monongahela River fronts the site for 2 miles. The best fishing, for walleye, bass, and catfish, is in the area just below Lock and Dam #7. Pennsylvania regulations apply.

GETTYSBURG NATIONAL MILITARY PARK
Gettysburg, PA 17325
(717) 334-1124

This famous 5,700-acre park was established in 1895 to memorialize a great 1863 Civil War battle in which a Confederate invasion of the North was repulsed. The park surrounds the city of Gettysburg in south-central Pennsylvania, 36 miles southeast from Pennsylvania's capital city Harrisburg via U.S. 15. Eisenhower National Historic Site is adjacent to Gettysburg National Military Park and could be visited in conjunction with a tour of Gettysburg. (See separate writeup on the Eisenhower site in this section.)

Subsequent to being turned back at Antietam in August 1862, Confederate General Robert E. Lee reorganized his Army of Northern Virginia and, in the spring of 1863, began a second invasion of the North. After being followed by Union forces under the command of General George Gordon Meade, the two sides clashed at Gettysburg early on July 1. Following a three-day battle in which 51,000 men were killed, wounded, or missing, the two armies marched away. With the repulse of the Confederate Army, the Battle of Gettysburg was over. The Confederate Army that staggered back to Virginia was physically and spiritually exhausted. Never again would Lee attempt an offensive operation of such magnitude.

The Park may be seen in a number of different ways. The first stop should be the National Park Service Visitor Center, which contains a Civil War Museum with numerous exhibits, a schedule of ranger-conducted walks and programs (mid-June through September), free brochures and information, and an Electric Map orientation program (fee charged). The map helps interpret the Battle of Gettysburg before you venture out into the field. The National Park Service Visitor Center offers several options for touring the battlefield: A free self-guided map of the 18-mile-long driving tour is available; individual visitors and bus groups may also hire a licensed guide for a two-hour conducted tour of the battlefield; and a self-guided taped tour can be purchased from the battlefield bookstore in the visitor center.

Adjacent to the visitor center, the Cyclorama Center offers a free twenty-minute-long film and presents the Cyclorama painting, a 360-by-26-foot original oil on canvas of Pickett's charge on the third day of the battle (fee charged).

Gettysburg National Military Park (opposite page)

For visitors interested in hiking, the High Water Mark Trail (¾ mile) begins at the Cyclorama and interprets the furious battle on July 3. The Soldier's National Cemetery Trail (1 mile) begins directly across from the visitor center and winds around the more than 6,000 veterans and their families that are buried here. The Big Round Top Loop Trail (1 mile) starts at the south end of the battlefield and tours the plants and geology of a Pennsylvania hardwood forest. Brochures for all these trails are available at the National Park Service Visitor Center. Bicycles can be used on all park roads. An 8-mile-long bridle trail is also available for those with horses.

FACILITIES: No food service or lodging is provided by the National Park Service, but both are readily available nearby, including across the road from the visitor center. Restrooms and water are provided at the visitor center, Cyclorama Center, and at various locations throughout the park.

CAMPING: No general camping is permitted in the park, although reservations may be made for organized youth group camping (April to October) by writing the superintendent. A number of private campgrounds are located near Gettysburg. Caledonia State Park, 15 miles west on U.S. 30, offers camping with tables, flush toilets, and showers. Corodus State Park, 20 miles east on highways 116 and 216, has similar facilities. The National Park Service operates Catoctin Mountain Park, 20 miles south of Gettysburg via U.S. 15 in Maryland. Catoctin is described in the Maryland chapter of this book.

HOPEWELL FURNACE NATIONAL HISTORIC SITE

2 Mark Bird Lane
Elverson, PA 19520
(610) 582–8773

Hopewell Furnace National Historic Site was authorized in 1938 and comprises 848 acres, including an iron-making community that has been restored to its appearance in the 1820–1840 period. The site is located in southeastern Pennsylvania, 5 miles south of Birdsboro via State Highway 345 or 10 miles northeast of the Morgantown interchange on the Pennsylvania Turnpike via State Highway 23 East and 345 North. Hopewell is 45 miles northwest of Philadelphia.

Hopewell Furnace was built on the headwaters of French Creek in 1771. Although England prohibited the manufacture of finished iron products by the colonists, the law was poorly enforced, and Hopewell began casting stove plates soon after its completion. Later, during the Revolutionary War, materials for armaments and ammunition were produced. The process used at Hopewell required iron ore, limestone, and hardwood forests—all of which were abundant here. In 1883, after producing more than 65,000 stoves, Hopewell was closed because the new iron-making technology made the charcoal process outdated.

The visitor center, open daily except Thanksgiving Day, Christmas Day, and New Year's Day, contains exhibits explaining the iron-making process and the furnace's history. A short slide program is also presented. From here, a self-guiding tour through the restored community visits numerous buildings, including a charcoal house, furnace, water wheel, blacksmith shop, tenant houses, and owner's house. Taped messages are at various locations along the trail, and park personnel provide limited living-history programs during the summer.

FACILITIES: No food or lodging is available in the site. Drinking water and modern restrooms are in the visitor center. Meals and lodging are in Reading, Pottstown, and Morgantown.

CAMPING: No camping is permitted at the site. Adjacent to Hopewell Furnace, French Creek State Park (201 sites) has shaded spaces with tables, grills, water, flush toilets, and showers. Ten cabins are available for rent. Picnicking, swimming, nature trails, and boating (electric or non-powered only) are also available (610–582–9680).

FISHING: In the state park, Hopewell Lake has northern pike, largemouth bass, walleye, and panfish; Scotts Run Lake contains brook trout and rainbow trout.

INDEPENDENCE NATIONAL HISTORICAL PARK
313 Walnut Street
Philadelphia, PA 19106
(215) 597–8974
(215) 597–1785 (TTY)

Independence National Historical Park was established in 1956 and comprises nearly forty-five acres, including many of the famous sites and structures associated with the American Revolution. The park is located in downtown Philadelphia with a visitor center at the corner of Third and Chestnut streets. A parking garage is located one block east of the visitor center on Second Street between Chestnut and Walnut streets. Four other areas operated by the National Park Service in Philadelphia are found on page 217.

Independence National Historical Park, Philadelphia, the home of American statesman Benjamin Franklin and birthplace of the United States, is as full of history as any city in the country. From Carpenter's Hall, where the First Continental Congress met in 1774 to address a declaration of rights to the king of England, to the first federally chartered bank, a number of historical structures are available for visitation in this first capital of the United States. Included among these are Independence Hall, where the Declaration of Independence was adopted and the U.S. Constitution was drafted; Congress Hall, where the U.S. Congress met from 1790 to 1800; Liberty Bell Pavilion, where the Liberty Bell is housed; Franklin Court, the site of Benjamin Franklin's home; the Second Bank of the United States, with documents, sculpture, the park's portrait collection, and talks; Todd House, where Dolley Madison lived; and Christ Church, where patriots and loyalists worshipped.

The visitor center at Third and Chestnut streets provides a twenty-eight-minute film and a variety of books and maps to guide visitors through the park. The National Park Service recommends that visitors with approximately half a day's time available to tour the park see the visitor center, Carpenter's Hall, Independence Hall, the Liberty Bell Pavilion, and Franklin Court. Those wishing to visit most of the sites should plan on spending at least a whole day in the city. Most park buildings are open daily from 9:00 A.M. to 5:00 P.M., with extended hours in summer. Free tickets for visitation to the Bishop White House and the Todd House are available at the visitor center.

The National Park Service is required to maintain these historical buildings in their original condition, which may create some difficulty for handicapped visitors. Only the visitor center and the Liberty Bell Pavilion are fully accessible to the handicapped. The first floors of Independence Hall, Congress Hall, and Old City Hall are accessible; Franklin Court and Graff House have limited accessibility. Wheelchairs are available for loan at the visitor center.

FACILITIES: Food and lodging are available in downtown Philadelphia. Water and restrooms are in the visitor center.

JOHNSTOWN FLOOD NATIONAL MEMORIAL

P.O. Box 355
St. Michael, PA 15951
(814) 495–4643

Johnstown Flood National Memorial comprises 164 acres and was authorized in 1964 to preserve the remains of the South Fork Dam, which collapsed in 1889 and caused the flooding of Johnstown with a loss of 2,209 lives. The park is located in southern Pennsylvania, 10 miles northeast of Johnstown near St. Michael on U.S. 219 and State Highway 869.

Heavy rains during May 30 and 31 of 1889 saturated the entire west-central section of Pennsylvania. The 30,000 residents of the Johnstown area were accustomed to spring floods and failed to heed warnings that the South Fork Dam was in danger of collapse. At approximately 3:10 P.M., the dam broke, and soon a 30- to 40-foot wall of water was traveling at up to 40 miles per hour down the narrow mountain valley. The result was the loss of 2,209 lives and $17 million in property damage; nearly everyone was left homeless.

A visitor center at the dam site, open daily from 8:30 A.M. to 5:00 P.M. (to 6:00 P.M. during summer), will help interpret events leading up to the disaster. Nearby are interpretive trails and demonstrations. South Fork Club clubhouse and cottages, a retreat for the rich, was spared by the flood and may be seen in St. Michael, a small town at the edge of the old lake bed. Johnstown Flood Museum at 304 Washington Street in Johnstown provides a number of excellent exhibits interpreting the flood. The museum is not affiliated with the National Park Service.

FACILITIES: No food or lodging is available at the memorial. Restrooms and water are at the visitor center. A picnic area with tables and grills is nearby. Meals and lodging are available in Johnstown.

CAMPING: No camping is permitted at the memorial. (See camping section under Allegheny Portage Railroad National Historic Site.)

PHILADELPHIA PARKS

In addition to Independence National Historical Park, which is discussed in detail under a separate heading in this section, the city of Philadelphia has several interesting historic sites. Visitors stopping in the downtown area should make an attempt to take in these other sites to enrich their sense of the history of this charming city.

Benjamin Franklin National Memorial (Twentieth and Benjamin Franklin Parkway; 215–448–1200): Located in a large hall adjoining the Franklin Institute, the seated statue of Benjamin Franklin was dedicated as a tribute to America's foremost inventor-statesman. Exhibits are located around the rotunda, and guides are on hand near the entrance. There is no fee to visit the memorial, but a fee is charged to enter the Franklin Institute Museum.

Edgar Allan Poe National Historic Site (532 North Seventh Street; 215–597–8780): the only surviving Philadelphia home of this famous American author who spent six productive years in the city. Poe lived in this home from 1842 or 1843 until 1844. Visitors may tour the home, where exhibits and an audiovisual program are available.

Gloria Dei (Old Swedes') Church National Historic Site (Delaware Avenue and Swanson Street; 215–389–1513): The present structure, constructed between 1698 and 1700, is on the site of an earlier log church built by Swedish settlers in 1677. This is the oldest surviving church in Pennsylvania and the second-oldest Swedish church in the United States. Gloria Dei contains numerous historic items and continues to serve an Episcopal parish.

Thaddeus Kosciuszko National Memorial (301 Pine Street, 215–597–9618): This park area was authorized in 1972 to preserve the home of a Polish military engineer who served with American forces during the Revolutionary War. Kosciuszko designed and constructed defense works, including those that were crucial to the American victory at Saratoga. Kosciuszko resided here during the winter of 1797–98. The outside and second floor of the building have been restored to their 1798 appearances.

PHILADELPHIA PARKS

← Race Street

To Franklin National Monument 12 Blocks

Elfreth's Alley

Arch Street

Free Quaker Meeting House

Christ Church Cemetery

Christ Church

Judge Lewis Quadrangle

Market Street Houses

Market Street

Declaration House

Seventh Street

Liberty Bell Pavilion

Franklin Court

Second Street

Front Street

Pemberton House Museum Shop

Old City Hall

Second Bank of the U.S.

New Hall

First Bank of the U.S.

Chestnut Street

Congress Hall →

Liberty Hall

Visitor Center

Independence Hall

Philosophical Hall

Carpenter's Hall

Philadelphia Exchange

Parking Garage

City Tavern

Independence Square

Todd House →

Bishop White House

Walnut Street

Washington Square

Rose Garden

Saint Joseph's Church

Dock Street

Locust Street

Mattis Street

Eighth Street

Seventh Street

Sixth Street

Fifth Street

Magnolia Garden

Fourth Street

Third Street

← *To Mikueh Israel Cemetery*

Spruce Street

Thaddeus Kosciuszko National Memorial

STEAMTOWN NATIONAL HISTORIC SITE

150 South Washington Avenue
Scranton, PA 18503
(717) 340–5200

Steamtown National Historic Site comprises forty-four acres and was authorized in 1986 to restore and preserve a former major railroad yard and to interpret the story of early-twentieth-century steam railroading in America. The site is in the town of Scranton in northeastern Pennsylvania.

The Lackawanna & Western Railroad was chartered in 1849 to haul iron from furnaces in Scranton to market. The railroad began operating in 1851, then merged with the Cobb's Gap Railroad a few years later to form the Delaware, Lackawanna & Western Railroad. The line grew to include branches to New York City, Lake Erie, Lake Ontario, and the interiors of New York and eastern Pennsylvania. One of the line's selling points to passengers was that the railroad used cleaner-burning anthracite coal that produced much less soot than the coal burned by competing railroads. The DL&W remained busy hauling military freight and coal during World War II, but after the war much of this business dried up. In 1960, the railroad was forced to merge with the Erie Railroad.

The Delaware Lackawanna & Western facility includes the roundhouse, switchyard, steam locomotives, and passenger, freight, and work cars. Visitors can see the new visitor center, theater, and history and technology museums. The history museum highlights the people and history of the United States from the early 1800s to modern times. The technology museum highlights technological changes and advances through the years. Included in the technology museum is a working HO scale model railroad layout that represents DL&W's Scranton yard. There are frequent tours of the roundhouse, where locomotives receive routine maintenance, and of shops where crews restore rolling stock. Train rides are offered from late spring through November. Call ahead for time schedule, reservations, and rate information. The park is open daily from 9:00 A.M. to 5:00 P.M., except Thanksgiving, Christmas, and New Year's days.

FACILITIES: Drinking water and restrooms are at the site. Food and lodging are nearby. For local visitor information contact Pennsylvania's Northeast Territory Visitors Bureau (1–800–22–WELCOME).

UPPER DELAWARE SCENIC & RECREATIONAL RIVER

R.R. #2, Box 2428
Beach Lake, PA 18405
(717) 685–4871

Upper Delaware Scenic & Recreational River was authorized in 1978 and includes a 73-mile stretch of a free-flowing river between Hancock and Sparrow Bush, New York. The river is located in northeastern Pennsylvania and southern New York, where it forms the border between the two states. New York Highway 97 follows the river for nearly its full length from Port Jervis to Hancock. Most land along the river is privately owned.

The Upper Delaware's initial residents relied on the river for transportation, which consisted primarily of canoes used by both frontiersmen and Indians. Larger boats eventually replaced canoes until, in the 1820s, coal was being shipped by boat from Pennsylvania to New York. Coal transportation involved use of a canal in conjunction with the river to connect Pennsylvania's anthracite coal mines to New York City. The canal started at Honesdale, Pennsylvania, where it followed the Lackawaxen River to the Delaware River. It then paralleled the Delaware to Port Jervis, where the canal cut cross-country to the Hudson River at Rondout. Initially, canal boats crossed the Delaware by means of rope ferry. This was updated in the late 1840s when a water aqueduct was built between Lackawaxen, Pennsylvania, and Minisink Ford, New York. During the 1850s, the canal transported a million tons of cargo annually.

The National Park Service's information center on Main Street in Narrowsburg, New York, is open daily from 9:00 A.M. to 4:30 P.M. (914–252–3947). Here, visitors will find maps, publications, and a scale model of the Roebling Delaware Aqueduct. Kiosks providing information, emergency first aid, and boating safety are located at boating access points at Damascus, Pennsylvania; Skinners Falls, New York; Narrowsburg, New York; Ten Mile River, New York; and Lackawaxen, Pennsylvania. One of the area's most interesting features is the Roebling Delaware Aqueduct at Minisink Ford. The aqueduct, the nation's oldest wire suspension bridge, was constructed by John Roebling, who later designed the Brooklyn Bridge. The aqueduct's purpose was to permit canal boats to cross over the Delaware River. Following abandonment of the canal in 1898, the aqueduct was purchased and converted to a bridge for trucks and cars. Rangers are stationed in the aqueduct's former tollhouse in Minisink Ford, while walks are offered periodically on weekends.

The National Park Service operates the Zane Grey Museum in Lackawaxen. Zane Grey, the "Father of the Western Novel," resided in Lackawaxen for thirteen years beginning in 1905. While here, Grey first achieved success as a writer and established his place as one of America's most popular authors. *Riders of the Purple Sage,* written in Lackawaxen, is one of his most noted works.

A major activity of visitors is to canoe the river. A number of firms offer boat rentals and the pickup and return of canoes and individuals at various points along the river. A directory of canoe liveries, boat rentals, and campgrounds is available at the visitor center or by mail from headquarters.

FACILITIES: Food and lodging are available in towns along the river. The Narrowsburg Information Center is handicap-accessible with restrooms.

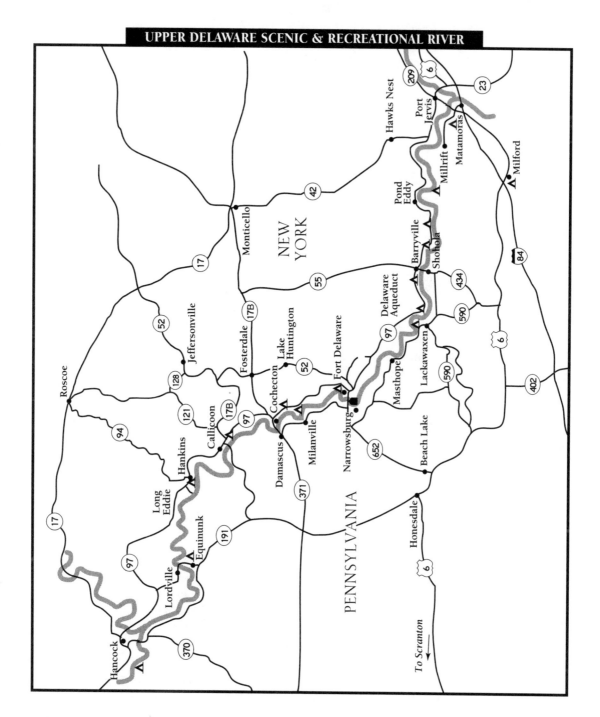

CAMPING: No camping is provided by the National Park Service. Private campgrounds are in various locations along the river.

FISHING: The river provides good fishing for brook, brown, and rainbow trout, smallmouth bass, and walleye. During May and June, American shad may spawn in deep pools. A license from either New York or Pennsylvania is sufficient for boat fishing or fishing from either shore.

VALLEY FORGE NATIONAL HISTORICAL PARK

Valley Forge, PA 19482
(610) 783–1077

Valley Forge National Historical Park comprises about 3,600 acres and was authorized in 1976 to commemorate the site of the 1777–78 winter encampment of George Washington and the Continental Army. The park's eastern entrance is approximately 18 miles northwest of Philadelphia via Interstate 76 (Schuylkill Expressway) and Route 422. When approaching from the Pennsylvania Turnpike, take exit 24 through the tollbooth and turn right on North Gulph Road.

On December 19, 1777, George Washington brought his ragged army of approximately 12,000 men to spend the winter at Valley Forge. The soldiers were short of food, supplies, and clothing, and many died in spite of the fact that no battles were fought here. Fortifications and log huts were built, and the army was rigorously drilled by General Frederick von Steuben. By the time spring had come, the Continental Army was well on its way to becoming a disciplined and skilled force.

A very nice visitor center at the east entrance contains exhibits and personnel to help interpret this historic area. The visitor center bookstore offers a wide range of publications. Valley Forge is a fee area, and admission is charged at Washington's Headquarters. A number of paved roads lead past extensive remains and reconstructions of major forts, lines of earthworks, reconstructed huts, monuments, and markers. Also of interest are Washington's Headquarters, the Grand Parade Ground where troops were drilled, and the National Memorial Arch. A paved trail for bicyclers, joggers, and walkers follows the tour route. Bus tours operate from the visitor center May through October, and tapes and tape players may be rented for use in private cars during those months.

FACILITIES: No lodging is available in the park, but hotels and motels can be found nearby. Restrooms are located at the visitor center and at other points in the park. Picnic areas are at Varnum's, Wayne's Woods, and Betzwood.

CAMPING: No camping is permitted in the park. A relatively nice campground operated by the local YMCA is a short distance northwest of Valley Forge in Phoenixville via State Route 23. The campsites have tables, grills, flush toilets, showers, electric hookups, and an indoor swimming pool. Approximately 25 miles northwest via state routes 23 and 345, French Creek State Park offers a nice campground. (For more information on this campground, see the camping section under Hopewell Furnace National Historic Site.) Other campground information is available at the visitor center.

FISHING: Fishing is permitted at Valley Forge National Historical Park in both the Valley Creek and the Schuylkill River. A state license is required. For more information contact a park ranger.

VALLEY FORGE NATIONAL HISTORICAL PARK

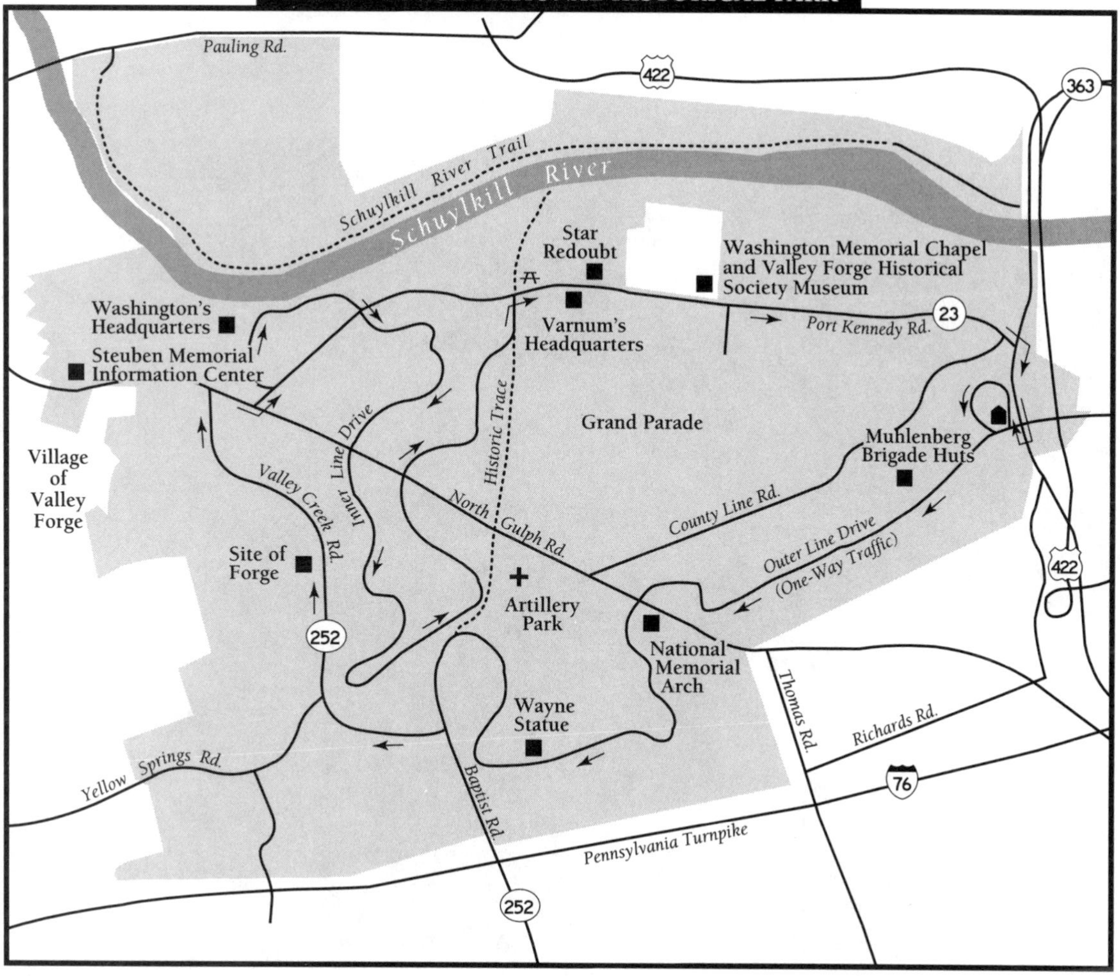

Pauling Rd.
422
363
Schuylkill River Trail
Schuylkill River
Star Redoubt
Washington Memorial Chapel and Valley Forge Historical Society Museum
Washington's Headquarters
Varnum's Headquarters
Port Kennedy Rd.
23
Steuben Memorial Information Center
Grand Parade
Muhlenberg Brigade Huts
Village of Valley Forge
Inner Line Drive
Historic Trace
Valley Creek Rd.
North Gulph Rd.
County Line Rd.
Outer Line Drive (One-Way Traffic)
422
Site of Forge
Artillery Park
252
National Memorial Arch
Thomas Rd.
Wayne Statue
Richards Rd.
Yellow Springs Rd.
Baptist Rd.
76
Pennsylvania Turnpike
252

Valley Forge National HIstorical Park

PUERTO RICO

TOURIST INFORMATION
(800) 223–6530

SAN JUAN NATIONAL HISTORIC SITE
Calle Norzagaray–Fort San Cristobal
Viejo San Juan, Puerto Rico 00901–2094
(787) 729–6960
Fax: (787) 729–6665
email: saju-administration@nps.gov

The world-famous castles and walls of Old San Juan, begun by the Spanish in the sixteenth century, are today protected by San Juan National Historic Site. Three and a half miles of walls and seventy-five acres of massive fortifications make up this World Heritage Site, which became part of the National Park Service in 1949. Forts El Morro and San Cristobal can be reached by auto turning right on Calle Norzagaray at Plaza Colon off Avenida Munoz Rivera. From the international airport or Isla Verde tourist hotel zone, follow Highway 26 west. It merges into Highway 25 at the historic San Antonio Bridge. Look for signs marked SAN JUAN or VIEJO SAN JUAN along the road. Continue on Highway 25 past the capitol building on your left; Fort San Cristobal covers the hillside to your right. Parking in the historic zone is extremely limited.

In Spanish Puerto Rico means "excellent harbor" and the sheltered deep-water anchorage found in San Juan Bay has been important to the history of this Caribbean island since Columbus discovered and named it in 1493. Spanish troops began to fortify this port city in the

1530s to protect its crucial shipping lanes to rich colonies in Mexico and Central America. To prevent the English, Dutch, and French from seizing Puerto Rico and using it as a base from which to attack Spanish shipping, fort building went on here for more than 350 years. Its peak came in the late 1700s, when the walls completely surrounding the city boasted more than 450 cannons.

After the wars of independence in Latin America in the early 1800s, there were no Spanish colonies left on the "Spanish Main," as the mainland of South and Central America was then called. Only the islands of Cuba and Puerto Rico remained loyal, remnants of a once vast domain. In 1898 a revolution in Cuba and the landing of American troops on Puerto Rico during the Spanish-American War ended the empire started 400 years earlier by Columbus.

The face of colonial Spain in the tropical Americas is still seen by walking among the historic homes, churches and plazas of Old San Juan. The original fortified city is an area seven by seven blocks, ringed by battlements and bastions that connect the two giant fortresses: El Morro, on the western tip of the islet, which broods over the entrance to the harbor from the sea; and Castillo de San Cristobal, which towers over the northeast shoulder of the city near Plaza Colon. Information is available from rangers on duty at the entrances of both fortresses. Tours and a twenty-seven-minute-long video in both English and Spanish are offered daily. Many visitors enjoy the forty-five-minute audiocassette tape self-tour of El Morro.

No parking is available at either El Morro or on nearby streets of the western sector of Old San Juan. San Cristobal has a small parking lot (seventeen cars) because of the steep hillside and huge eighteenth-century walls. Use the public parking at La Puntilla and the free shuttle trams to move about the historic city. Built to a human scale, Old San Juan is best explored by walking; a hat and good walking shoes are a must.

FACILITIES: No facilities are provided by the National Park Service. Food and lodging are available in Old San Juan.

RHODE ISLAND

STATE TOURIST INFORMATION
(800) 556–2484

ROGER WILLIAMS NATIONAL MEMORIAL
282 North Main Street
Providence, RI 02903
(401) 528–5385

This four-and-one-half-acre park was established in 1965 to memorialize the founder of Rhode Island and pioneer of religious freedom. The memorial is located in downtown Providence, between North Main Street (one-way north) and Canal Street (one-way south) at the corner of Smith Street (Route 44). From Interstate 95, exit on Charles Street when traveling south or take the State Offices exit when driving north.

Roger Williams sailed from London in 1630 after becoming frustrated in England with the king's supremacy in church and spiritual matters. Equally unhappy in Massachusetts, Williams was banished from the Bay Colony; subsequently, in 1636, he founded with his small band of followers what is now the city of Providence. The new colony grew and prospered and was one of the first in the world to set forth in clear terms the principle that men should be permitted freedom of religious belief and that the state should govern "only in civil things." In 1676, most of Providence, including Williams's homestead, was destroyed in King Philip's War. In 1683, Roger Williams was buried in a simple ceremony.

A visitor center, housed in a renovated eighteenth-century structure, is open daily from 8:00 A.M. to 4:30 P.M. daily in summer and Monday through Friday in winter. Exhibits and a three-

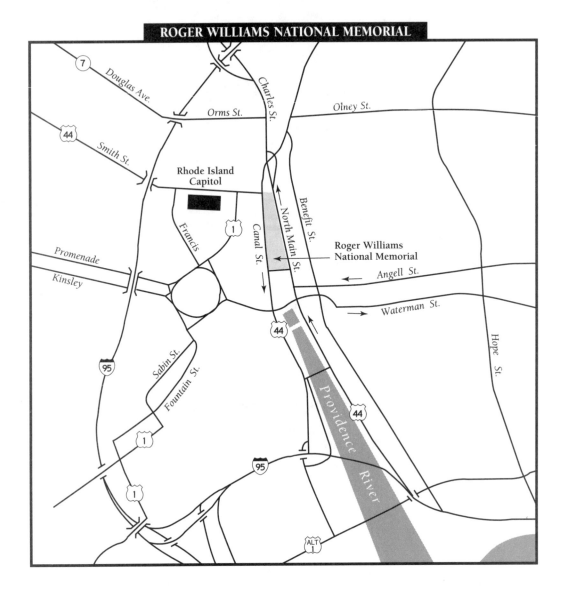

minute slide presentation are available. The center is closed on Thanksgiving, Christmas, and New Year's Day. Free parking is available in the memorial's lot on Canal Street. The Hahn Memorial on the grounds marks the site of the spring once used by the Williams family. Within walking distance of the memorial are a number of points of interest, including the Old State House and the first Baptist church in America.

FACILITIES: Restrooms and water are available in the visitor center. Food service can be found near the memorial.

CAMPING: No camping is permitted at the memorial. Casimir Pulaski Memorial State Park, 20 miles northwest via U.S. 44, offers camping.

TOURO SYNAGOGUE NATIONAL HISTORIC SITE

85 Touro Street
Newport, RI 02840
(401) 847–4794

This affiliated area of the National Park Service was designated a national historic site in 1946 to help preserve an outstanding example of colonial religious architecture. The synagogue is in downtown Newport, Rhode Island, on Touro Street. From Newport Bridge, exit south on Farewell Street and merge left on Thames before turning east on Touro.

Ground was broken for Touro Synagogue in 1759, and four years later the dedication was conducted by Rev. Isaac Touro. The synagogue was designed by well-known colonial architect Pete Harrison and constructed with financial assistance from the Jewish congregation in New York City. With the new synagogue and a previously acquired cemetery (one block up from the synagogue), one of the earliest Jewish communities in what would soon become the United States could perform the three essential functions of Jewish communal life: worship, religious instruction of the children, and burial in sanctified ground.

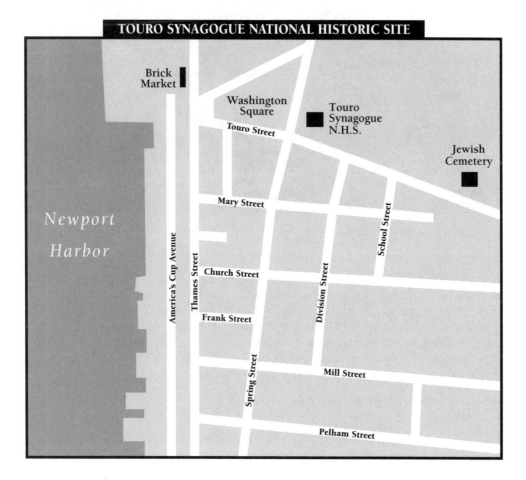

Touro Synagogue National Historic Park

Touro Synagogue is open daily for tours except Saturdays and Jewish holidays. Tours begin every half hour with the last tour one-half hour before closing. Hours are 10:00 A.M. to 4:00 P.M. from the July Fourth weekend through Labor Day. From Labor Day through October 15, and from Memorial Day to July Fourth, hours are 11:00 A.M. to 3:00 P.M. Sunday, and 1:00 P.M. to 2:00 P.M. Monday through Friday. Hours the remainder of the year are 1:00 P.M. to 3:00 P.M. Sunday, and 2:00 P.M. by appointment Monday through Friday. Services are Friday at 6:00 P.M. (7:00 P.M. in summer) and Saturday morning at 9:00 A.M.

FACILITIES: No food or lodging is available at the site, but a major commercial area is located on Thames Street a few blocks away.

CAMPING: No camping is permitted at the site, and although private campgrounds are located in the Newport area, they are generally expensive.

SOUTH CAROLINA

STATE TOURIST INFORMATION
(800) 872–3505

CHARLES PINCKNEY NATIONAL HISTORIC SITE
c/o Fort Sumter National Monument
1214 Middle Street
Sullivans Island, SC 29482
(803) 881–5516

Charles Pinckney National Historic Site comprises twenty-eight acres of a once-proud 715-acre plantation. It was authorized in 1988 to interpret the life of Charles Pinckney, a distinguished public servant in the early years of the nation and one of the principal framers of the Constitution. The site also preserves part of Pinckney's plantation, Snee Farm. The historic site is located 6 miles east of Charleston, South Carolina, within the city limits of Mt. Pleasant, South Carolina. It is approximately ½ mile north of U.S. 17 on Long Point Road.

Charles Pinckney (1757–1824) was educated in Charleston and elected to the South Carolina legislature when he was 22 years old. He served as an officer in the American Revolution, and in 1878 he served as a delegate to the Constitution Convention in Philadelphia. He addressed the convention more than one hundred times and offered a draft of a new constitution. At least twenty-four points he proposed in that draft survived to become part of the U.S. Constitution. He later served as a member of the state General Assembly, U.S. Senator, Minister (ambassador) to Spain, member of the U.S. House of Representatives, and served four terms as governor of South Carolina.

Charles Pinckney inherited Snee Farm from his father, who had purchased the plantation in 1754. The farm was originally part of a 1698 royal grant. A working plantation, rice, indigo, cotton, and vegetables were grown on Snee Farm for nearly 250 years. Today the visitor center is located in a rare example of a one-and-one-half-story low-country cottage built in 1828 of cypress and pine. The site is open Thursday through Monday, except Christmas Day, from 9:00 A.M. to 5:00 P.M.

FACILITIES: Full facilities including food and lodging are available near the historic site.

CONGAREE SWAMP NATIONAL MONUMENT
200 Caroline Sims Road
Hopkins, SC 29061
(803) 776–4396

Congaree Swamp National Monument, authorized by Congress in 1976, preserves 22,200 acres of the last significant tract of old-growth bottomland hardwood forest in the United States. Congaree Swamp is in south-central South Carolina, about 20 miles southeast of Columbia. From Columbia, take SC 48 (Bluff Road) and follow the signs.

Congaree Swamp National Monument, a naturalist's paradise, is a forested floodplain of record-size trees in a river-bottom environment once typical of the colonial South. On June 30, 1983, the park was designated an International Biosphere Reserve. Twenty miles of hiking trails range in length from 1 to almost 11 miles. Two $^2/_3$-mile boardwalks are available for walking (one is wheelchair-accessible). One boardwalk is usually above water even during flooding conditions. A two-hour guided walk is offered every Saturday at 1:30 P.M. Cedar Creek provides an 18-mile canoe trail through the swamp.

A visitor contact station is a short distance inside the monument entrance. Visitors may pick up information here. The station is open daily from 8:30 A.M. to 5:00 P.M., except Christmas. Long pants, long-sleeved shirts, sneakers or boots, maps, compass, first aid kit, and insect repellent are recommended.

FACILITIES: No food or lodging is available in the monument, but both are found in Columbia.

CAMPING: Primitive camping is allowed in the monument by permit only. Open fires are prohibited except in the Bluff campsite. Poinsett State Park (east of the monument on Highway 261) and Sesquicentennial State Park (northwest of the monument on U.S. 1) have campgrounds with tables, grills, water, flush toilets, showers, electrical hookups, swimming, and fishing. Both state parks are located on South Carolina state highway maps. Directions are available at the visitor contact station.

FISHING: Fishing includes catches of bass, bream, and catfish. A South Carolina license is required. Federal regulations prohibit the use of minnows, fish eggs, or amphibians as bait.

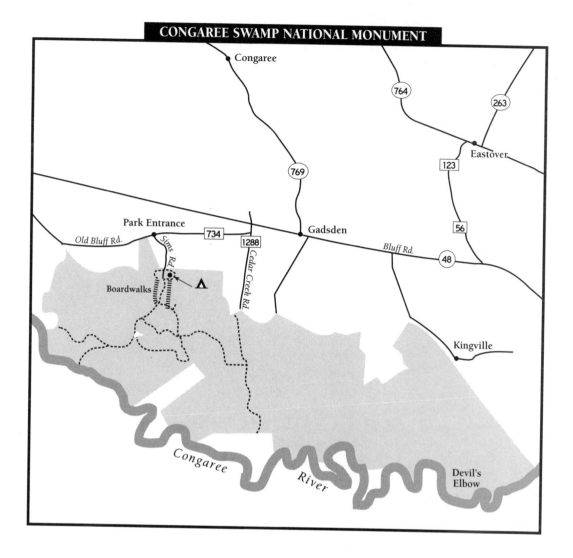

COWPENS NATIONAL BATTLEFIELD

P.O. Box 308
Chesnee, SC 29323
(864) 461–2828

Cowpens National Battlefield comprises 842 acres and was established as a national battlefield site in 1929 to commemorate a decisive victory by American forces in the Revolutionary War. The battlefield is located on U.S. Highway 11, 10 miles northwest of Gaffney and 2 miles east of Chesnee, South Carolina.

To protect British outposts in the Carolinas from the American army, Lord Cornwallis sent Lieutenant Colonel Banastre Tarleton after an American detachment led by Brigadier General Daniel Morgan. On January 17, 1781, a successful stand by Morgan's troops at the Cowpens resulted in a rout of the British forces and an important American patriot victory in the South. During the one-hour battle, the British incurred losses approaching 80 percent of their forces (110 dead, more than 200 wounded, and 500 captured). American losses were much lighter, with only twelve dead and sixty wounded.

The park's visitor center, ½ mile inside the entrance, contains museum exhibits, an excellent slide presentation, and a battlefield map display. The only charge is for admission to the presentation, *Daybreak at the Cowpens,* which is shown on the hour. A self-guiding trail (1¼ miles, forty-five minutes) to battlefield sites begins behind the visitor center. The trail is level and has benches. A cassette describing the battle may be rented or purchased to take along on the walk. A one-way, 3-mile auto-tour road circles the battlefield. The park is open daily from 9:00 A.M. until 5:00 P.M. except Thanksgiving Day, Christmas Day, and New Year's Day. The tour road and picnic facility close at 4:30 P.M.

FACILITIES: Food and lodging can be found in Gaffney and Spartanburg. A picnic area with water, toilets, tables, and a group shelter is at the far end of the park's auto-tour road. Water, restrooms, and a soft-drink machine are in the visitor center.

CAMPING: No camping is permitted at the park. A state park with camping facilities is adjacent to Kings Mountain National Military Park, 30 miles east of Cowpens. A privately owned campground is 12 miles from the park.

FORT SUMTER NATIONAL MONUMENT

1214 Middle Street
Sullivans Island, SC 29482
(803) 883–3123

This 189-acre monument was authorized in 1948 to memorialize the site of the first engagement of the Civil War. The park also includes Fort Moultrie, the scene of a patriot victory in 1776. Fort Sumter is located in Charleston Harbor and can be reached only by boat. Tour boats leave from the Charleston City Marina on Lockwood Drive, just south of U.S. 17, and from Patriots Point in Mt. Pleasant. (For schedules call 803–722–1691.)

Construction of five-sided Fort Sumter commenced in 1829 as one part of a series of coastal fortifications. The fort, designed for 135 guns, was nearly complete in time for the Confederate shelling, which began at 4:30 A.M. on April 12, 1861. On April 14, following the surrender of the fort, Federal troops were allowed to evacuate. For the next four years, Fort Sumter remained a Confederate stronghold. The fort was abandoned in February 1865 with the approach of Sherman's army.

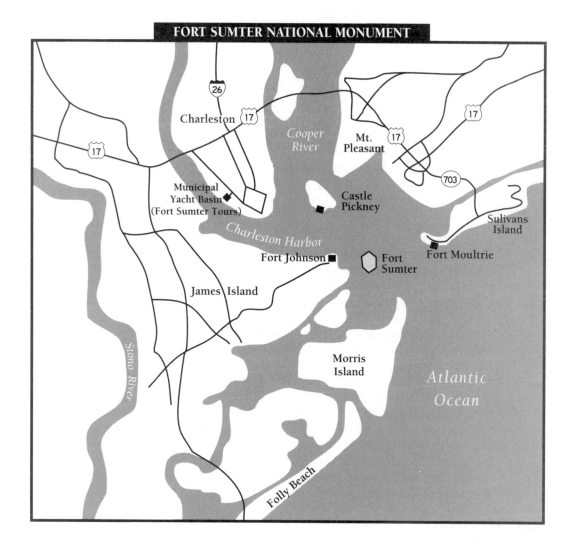

FORT SUMTER NATIONAL MONUMENT

Fort Sumter is open daily from 9:00 A.M. to 6:00 P.M. from April 1 to Labor Day and shorter periods the rest of the year (closed Christmas). Park personnel are on duty, and a museum is located inside the fort. Brochures are available for a self-guiding tour. Across Charleston Harbor, Fort Moultrie is the site of a fortification that saw service from the Revolutionary War to World War II. This restored fort is open for self-guiding tours from 9:00 A.M. to 5:00 P.M. This fort is also closed on Christmas Day. A visitor center providing audiovisual presentations is located on Middle Street opposite the fort.

FACILITIES: No food or lodging is available in the monument, but both can be found nearby.

HISTORIC CAMDEN

P.O. Box 710
Camden, SC 29020
(803) 432–9841

Historic Camden comprises ninety-eight acres and was authorized as an affiliated area of the National Park Service in 1982 to assist in restoration and interpretation of this colonial village, established in the mid-1730s. Historic Camden is in central South Carolina, about 30 miles northeast of Columbia via either Interstate 20 or U.S. 1.

Fredricksburg Township (the original name of the Camden area) was laid out during the winter of 1731–32 as a result of instructions from King George II to locate a township "on the River Watery." By the time the current name was adopted in 1768 in honor of Lord Camden, a British Parliament champion of colonial rights, the settlement had become an inland center of population and trade.

Camden was occupied by British troops following the fall of Charleston in 1780. British General Cornwallis established military posts at several interior locations in the state, including Camden. The British fortified the town with a stockade wall and six small forts around the perimeter. Although the British successfully defended the town against American forces, heavy losses caused the British to evacuate, burning the fortifications as they left.

Historic Camden includes six buildings and period structures that have been reconstructed or moved to this location. The Cunningham House (circa 1840) at the end of the parking lot serves as tour headquarters. Adjacent to the museum center, the original town site offers archaeological findings and reconstructions. This includes a partial reconstruction of the town wall, the reconstructed foundation of the powder magazine, and the reconstructed home of Camden's founder. Historic Camden is open daily except major holidays. Guided tours (fee charged) are offered from 10:00 A.M. to 4:00 P.M. (1:00 P.M. Sundays). Free self-guided tours are available daily (except as noted above) from 10:00 A.M. to 5:00 P.M. A museum shop is open from 10:00 A.M. to 5:00 P.M.

FACILITIES: Food and lodging are available in Camden.

CAMPING: No camping is permitted at Historic Camden. Sesquicentennial State Park between Camden and Columbia on U.S. 1 offers full camping facilities including hookups. Lee State Park, east of Bishopville, offers similar facilities.

KINGS MOUNTAIN NATIONAL MILITARY PARK

P.O. Box 40
Kings Mountain, NC 28086
(919) 936–7921

Kings Mountain National Military Park contains nearly 4,000 acres and was established in 1931 to commemorate the site where American frontiersmen defeated a British force on October 7, 1780, at a critical point during the American Revolution. The park is located in north-central South Carolina—close to the state line—between Spartanburg, South Carolina, and Charlotte, North Carolina, via Interstate 85.

Five years after the beginning of the American Revolution, England turned its attention toward conquering the South. As part of this effort, Major Patrick Ferguson was charged by General Cornwallis with building the Loyalists into a strong Carolina militia. After recruiting several thousand Carolinians, Ferguson headed north with an ultimate objective of carrying the war into Virginia. However, on October 7, he and more than 1,100 men were attacked and defeated while camped on Kings Mountain. The American victory delayed Cornwallis's plan and permitted the Continental Army to organize a new offensive in the South.

The park's beautiful visitor center contains historical exhibits and a film to help interpret the battle. From here, a paved 1½-mile self-guiding battlefield trail (forty-five minutes to one hour with some steep grades) leads around the battlefield ridge and to the military park's chief features. A variety of monuments and interpretive signs are scattered along the trail.

FACILITIES: No food or lodging is available in the park, but both can be found in the towns of Gaffney, York, and Spartanburg, South Carolina, and Kings Mountain, North Carolina. Restrooms and water are in the visitor center.

CAMPING: Only primitive backpack camping is permitted in the park. South Carolina's Kings Mountain State Park is adjacent to the military park and offers a campground with tables, water, flush toilets, showers, a dump station, laundry, store, and swimming (864–222–3209).

FISHING: Fishing is not available in the military park. Fishing access is in adjacent Kings Mountain State Park.

NINETY SIX NATIONAL HISTORIC SITE

P.O. Box 496
Ninety Six, SC 29666
(864) 543–4068

Ninety Six National Historic Site comprises 989 acres and was authorized in 1976 to memorialize the site of an important colonial trading village and Revolutionary War stronghold held briefly by the British. The historic site is located in western South Carolina, 9 miles east of Greenwood and 2 miles south of the town of Ninety Six on State Highway 248.

The first store at Ninety Six, named because it lay 96 miles down a major trail from an important Cherokee village, was opened about 1752. A fort built near the trading post withstood two Indian attacks before the Cherokees made peace in 1761. Soon, the area began to grow, and in 1769, Ninety Six was established as the seat of a judicial district. After the English seized control of South Carolina in 1780, Ninety Six became a major military post and recruiting depot and was occupied by British or Loyalist forces. An earthen star-shaped fort constructed by the Loyalists was the object of a major siege by Patriots under the command of Nathanael Greene in 1781. Although the fort was never captured by the Patriots, the Loyalists eventually withdrew to Charleston.

The site is open 8:00 A.M. to 5:00 P.M. daily except Thanksgiving, Christmas, and New Year's Day. A visitor center contains museum exhibits to help interpret the history of Ninety Six. A mile-long (one hour) interpretive trail takes visitors by the earthen fort abandoned by the British, reconstructed earthwork embankments of the old fortifications, and through the town site of old Ninety Six. The hike provides a nice leisurely walk, and numerous interpretive signs are along the way. Benches are located in shaded areas along the trail.

FACILITIES: A soft-drink machine and restrooms are at the administration building, and drinking water is in the visitor center. Food and lodging are in the town of Greenwood and food only is in the town of Ninety Six.

CAMPING: No camping is permitted in the park. Nine miles north of the historic site on Lake Greenwood (north on 248, right on 34, left on 702), Greenwood State Park offers tables, water, flush toilets, showers, electrical hookups, swimming, and fishing. Many of the one hundred sites are on the water, and a boat ramp is available.

FISHING: Fishing is available on a seasonal basis at the site. A South Carolina license is required.

TENNESSEE

STATE TOURIST INFORMATION
(615) 741–2158

ANDREW JOHNSON NATIONAL HISTORIC SITE

P.O. Box 1088
Greeneville, TN 37744
(423) 638–3551

Andrew Johnson National Historic Site, which comprises seventeen acres, was authorized in 1935 to preserve the home, tailor shop, and burial site of the seventeenth president of the United States. The site is located in northeastern Tennessee in the town of Greeneville, 29 miles southwest of Johnson City via U.S. 11E.

In 1826, when he was seventeen years old, Andrew Johnson and his family moved to Greeneville, where he soon established himself as a successful tailor. After his first venture into politics in 1829, he progressed to five terms as U.S. Representative, governor of Tennessee, and U.S. Senator. An opponent of secession, he became military governor of Tennessee during the Civil War and ran as Lincoln's vice-president in 1864. Upon Lincoln's assassination in April 1865, he began a stormy career as United States president.

During Andrew Johnson's term in the White House, he alienated Congress to the point that it instituted its own Civil War reconstruction program. Additional problems resulted in Johnson's being impeached by the House, with only a single vote keeping him from being judged guilty and removed from office by the Senate. After serving as president, Johnson

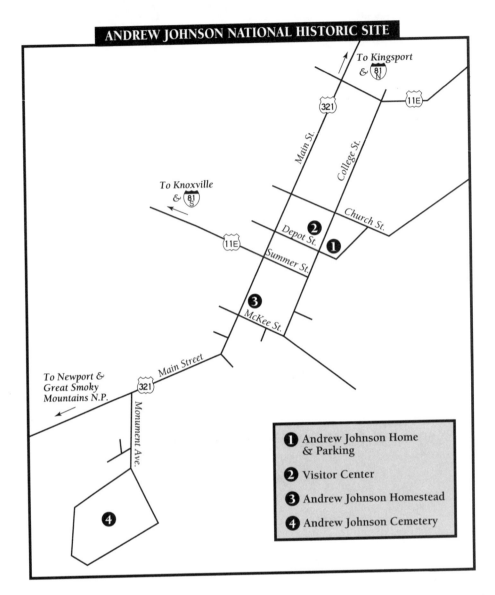

returned to Greeneville. He was elected to the U.S. Senate in 1875 and died six months later, on July 31, 1875.

The historic site is open daily except Thanksgiving, Christmas, and New Year's Day from 9:00 A.M. to 5:00 P.M. The visitor center houses a museum, bookstore, and Johnson's tailor shop at the corner of Depot and College streets. Across the street is the early home in which Johnson lived from the 1830s until 1851. In 1851 Johnson purchased and moved into the Homestead located on Main Street. The Homestead, restored to its 1869 appearance, is fully furnished with Johnson family belongings. The Homestead is open to visitors by guided tour only (fee charged). Andrew Johnson is buried in the Andrew Johnson National Cemetery, located one block south of West Main Street at the end of Monument Avenue.

FACILITIES: Food and lodging are available in the town of Greeneville.

CAMPING: No camping is permitted in the park. National Forest Service campgrounds are located southeast of Greeneville.

Andrew Johnson National Historic Site

BIG SOUTH FORK NATIONAL RIVER
AND RECREATION AREA

Route 3, Box 401
Oneida, TN 37841
(615) 879–3625

Big South Fork National River and Recreation Area, which will eventually encompass over 123,000 acres, was authorized in 1974 to preserve an area of the Cumberland Plateau that contains scenic gorges and valleys with a wide range of unique natural and historical features. The park is located in northeastern Tennessee and southeastern Kentucky, with main access via Leatherwood Ford Road, Tennessee 297, connecting Oneida and Jamestown, Tennessee. U.S. 27 follows the park's eastern border.

Big South Fork National River and Recreation Area is an effort by the federal government to protect the Big South Fork River and its major tributaries as natural and free-flowing streams while developing the adjacent plateau area for its full recreational potential. The area now contains lush vegetation, where homesteads, mines, logging camps, and roads once dotted the landscape. Flowing through the center of the area is the Big South Fork of the Cumberland River, which is fed by the Clear Fork and New rivers. Immediately adjacent to the Big South Fork is Historic Rugby, a restored 1880s settlement originally built for sons of British gentry; the Daniel Boone National Forest; Pickett State Park; and the Sgt. York Gristmill and Gravesite, near Pall Mall, Tennessee.

One of the major recreational activities in the Big South Fork is to float the river, where visitors find everything from a tame, slow-moving stream to bubbling, churning rapids. Hiking, mountain biking, and horseback riding, also popular recreational activities, offer access to the heart of the recreation area, where one may find scenic overlooks, huge sandstone arches, chimney rocks, abundant wildlife, or peaceful solitude. For those driving, Devil's Jump or Yahoo Falls in Kentucky and East Rim in Tennessee each provide access to gorge overlooks. Leatherwood Ford provides convenient river access.

A visitor center at the Bandy Creek Campground in Tennessee, offering exhibits and information, is open daily from 8:00 A.M. to 4:30 P.M. The Blue Heron Mining Community nine miles west of Stearns, Kentucky, offers a look at life in a company coal-mining town. Access to Blue Heron is by car or via the Big South Fork Scenic Railway (about 40 minutes one way by train).

FACILITIES: Rustic lodging including water, bunk beds, toilets, and kitchens, are available at Charit Creek Lodge, a park concessioner. Charit Creek is accessible by foot or horseback. Reservations are recommended. Write Charit Creek Lodge, 250 Lonesome Valley Road, Sevierville, TN 37862 (615–429–5704). Groceries, food, and lodging are available in surrounding towns. Hospitals are in Oneida and Jamestown.

CAMPING: The Bandy Creek Campground (180 sites), located off Highway 297, provides water and electrical hookups, tables, grills, hot showers, flush toilets, and a swimming pool. Other established campgrounds are at Blue Heron and Pickett State Park. Backcountry camping is permitted throughout the park.

FISHING/HUNTING: Fishing and hunting are permitted in accordance with state and federal regulations throughout most of the recreation area. An appropriate state license is required. Hunting and fishing licenses may be purchased in surrounding towns.

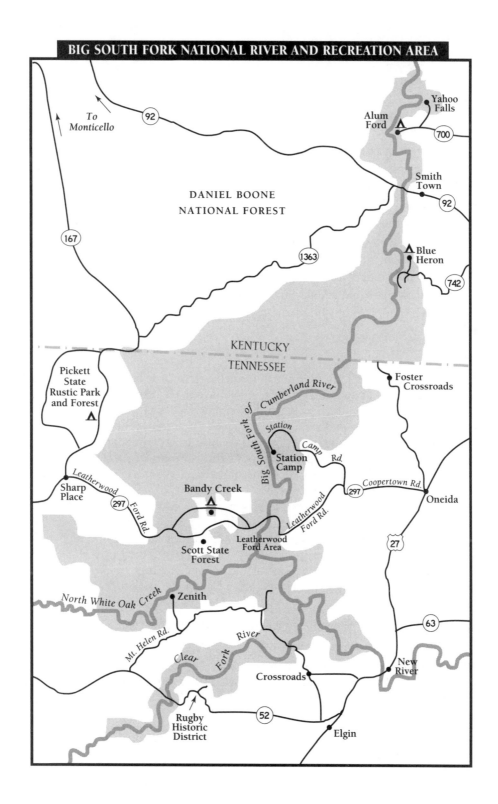

BIG SOUTH FORK NATIONAL RIVER AND RECREATION AREA

To Monticello

92

DANIEL BOONE
NATIONAL FOREST

167

1363

Alum Ford

700

Yahoo Falls

Smith Town

92

Blue Heron

742

KENTUCKY

TENNESSEE

Foster Crossroads

Pickett State Rustic Park and Forest

Big South Fork of Cumberland River

Station

Station Camp

Camp Rd.

Coopertown Rd.

297

Oneida

Leatherwood

Sharp Place

297

Ford Rd.

Bandy Creek

Leatherwood Ford Rd.

Leatherwood Ford Area

27

Scott State Forest

North White Oak Creek

Zenith

63

Mt. Helen Rd.

Clear Fork River

Crossroads

New River

52

Rugby Historic District

Elgin

FORT DONELSON NATIONAL BATTLEFIELD

P.O. Box 434
Dover, TN 37058
(615) 232–5706

Fort Donelson National Battlefield comprises 544 acres and was established in 1928 to commemorate the site of the first major victory for the Union in the Civil War. The victory gave an obscure brigadier general—Ulysses Grant—the acclaim he needed to become one of the most important forces in the war. The story involved both army and naval action in the struggle to control the Confederate-built earthworks on the Cumberland River. The park protected the remains of Fort Donelson proper, the water batteries that repulsed the Union fleet, and almost 3 miles of rifle pits. Today, the park includes the building where the surrender took place and several hundred acres of land where the troops maneuvered. The park is located in northern Tennessee, on the west side of the town of Dover, on U.S. 79.

After months of attempting to break through Confederate defense lines, Union forces captured Fort Henry and moved on to Fort Donelson in February 1862. Confederate guns were able to drive off Union gunboats on the Cumberland River, but superior Union forces under the command of Ulysses Grant surrounded the fort and forced the surrender of nearly 13,000 Confederate troops on February 16. The victory opened the heartland of the South to Federal invasion.

The park visitor center is open daily (except Christmas) from 8:00 A.M. to 4:30 P.M. It offers information, a ten-minute slide program, a museum, and an interpretive leaflet for a 6-mile self-guiding auto tour of the fort and the battlefield.

Within the fort walls there are reproductions of soldiers' cabins, which are used in the summer to demonstrate Confederate military life. Rifle demonstrations also take place during the summer. Artillery pieces representative of the Confederate armament are positioned along the rifle pits and exhibited at the lower river battery. The exterior of the Dover Hotel where General Simon Buncker surrendered to General U.S. Grant has been restored. Fort Donelson National Cemetery adjoins the park and is under National Park Service administration. The grounds close at sundown.

FACILITIES: Food and lodging are available in Dover. Restrooms and water are in the visitor center.

CAMPING: No camping is permitted in the park. The Tennessee Valley Authority's Land Between the Lakes offers full camping facilities, including electric and water hookups, showers, and a dump station at Piney Campground, 9 miles west of Fort Donelson on Highway 79. Paris Landing State Park provides similar facilities 4 miles farther west.

FISHING: Fishing is permitted in the Cumberland River with a valid license. Catches include bass, catfish, and crappie.

GREAT SMOKY MOUNTAINS NATIONAL PARK

Gatlinburg, TN 37738
(615) 436–1200

Great Smoky Mountains National Park was established in 1934 to preserve more than 520,000 acres of unspoiled forests on the loftiest range east of South Dakota's Black Hills. The park is located along the Tennessee–North Carolina border, with main access via Newfound Gap Road, which bisects the park and connects Gatlinburg, Tennessee, and Cherokee, North Carolina.

Although the Great Smoky Mountains (named for the smokelike haze that is often present in this area) usually reach their peak of beauty around the middle of October, they offer outstanding scenery and outdoor activities year-round. More than 800 miles of horse and foot trails wind through the park, and paved roads provide access to some of the more popular locations. At Cades Cove, an 11-mile-loop road leads past pioneer homesteads and small frame churches, where early mountain people lived. Newfound Gap Road winds through the high mountains and provides access to a side road that climbs to Clingmans Dome and an observation tower with outstanding vistas of the park.

Self-guiding trails are scattered throughout the area, and park interpreters present talks and conduct walks during summer months. Activity schedules are available at visitor centers, ranger stations, and campgrounds.

When entering from Cherokee, North Carolina, stop at the Oconaluftee Visitor Center for exhibits and a pioneer farmstead. Nearby is an operating water-powered mill for grinding corn. From the Gatlinburg, Tennessee, entrance, Sugarlands Visitor Center has exhibits, video programs, and park information.

FACILITIES: LeConte Lodge, which can be reached only via an all-day hike, offers several cabins from late March to late October. For reservations (which are necessary), write LeConte Lodge, Gatlinburg, TN 37738 (423–429–5704). A campground store is at Cades Cove. Saddle horses may be rented at Cades Cove, Smokemont, Dudley Creek, Deep Creek, and Two Mile Branch.

CAMPING: Developed campgrounds with cold running water, fire grills, tables, flush toilets (no showers), and sanitary stations are at Balsam Mountain (forty-five sites, no dump station), Cosby (174 sites, three group camps), Deep Creek (122 sites, three group camps), Cades Cove (161 sites, four group camps), Elkmont (218 sites, four group camps), Smokemont (140 sites, three group camps), Abrams Creek (sixteen sites), Big Creek (twelve sites), and Cataloochee (twenty-seven sites, three group camps).

There is a camping limit of seven days between May 15 and November 1. Reservations are required from May 1 through October 31 at Cades Cove, Elkmont, and Smokemont. For reservations, call 1–800–365–CAMP.

FISHING: Smallmouth and rock bass and brook, brown, and rainbow trout inhabit the 600 miles of fishing streams in the park. Bass live at lower elevations. Fishing regulations require a 7-inch minimum size and set a daily limit of five fish, except for rock bass, which has no size limit and a 20-per-day possession limit. The brook trout is a protected species and possession is prohibited. A Tennessee or North Carolina license is required to fish all open waters within the park.

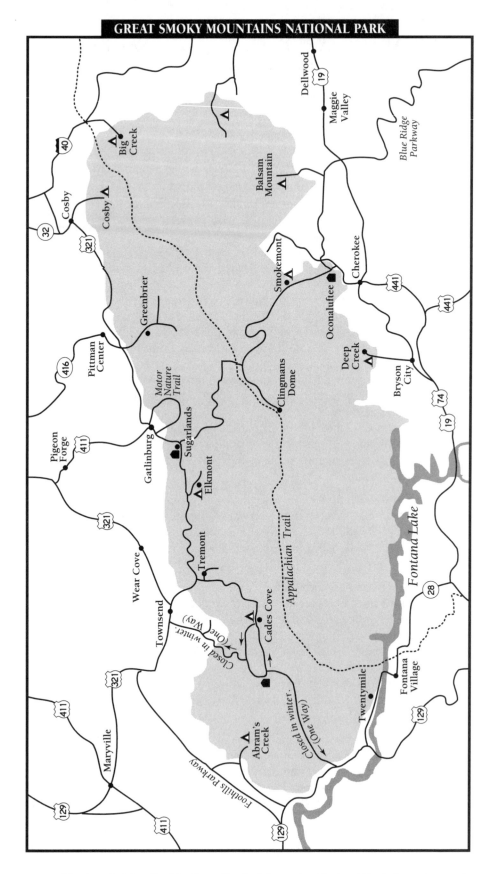

The Appalachian Trail in Great Smoky Mountains National Park (opposite page)

OBED WILD AND SCENIC RIVER

P.O. Box 429
Wartburg, TN 37887
(615) 346–6294

Obed Wild and Scenic River, which comprises 5,057 acres, was authorized in 1976 to preserve some of the most rugged and scenic country in the Southeast. The river is located in eastern Tennessee, with major access via Interstate 40.

The primary attraction of this park is the clean, clear waters of the Obed River and its principal tributaries, Clear Creek and Daddy's Creek. The area is rich in plant life and provides a habitat for forty-one identified species of mammals and 138 species of birds. The 45-mile section of the Obed system offers recreational activities in the form of white-water canoeing, kayaking, rafting, tubing, swimming, wading, hiking, rock climbing, and nature study. There are a limited number of access points to the rivers. A free park brochure includes a map of the area.

The Obed's stream system has cut 200- to 500-foot gorges in the area's sandstone. These gorges cut through a variety of soil environments that produce vastly different vegetation, including blooming plants and hardwood trees. Float trips are best during the rainy season, from December through April, when the rivers are full. Commercial raft trips are available (contact the park for information). A visitor center is located in Wartburg, Tennessee.

FACILITIES: There are currently no federal facilities within the authorized park area. The area's major town, Wartburg, offers most visitor facilities.

CAMPING: No developed campgrounds are within the park boundaries, but primitive camping is permitted along the river or at access sites. A developed campground is available at Cumberland Mountain State Park, 8 miles south of Crossville. Primitive camping is also available at Frozenhead State Natural Area, 2 miles from Wartburg near State Highway 62.

FISHING: These rivers support populations of smallmouth, rock and largemouth bass, catfish, bluegill, and carp. A Tennessee license is required.

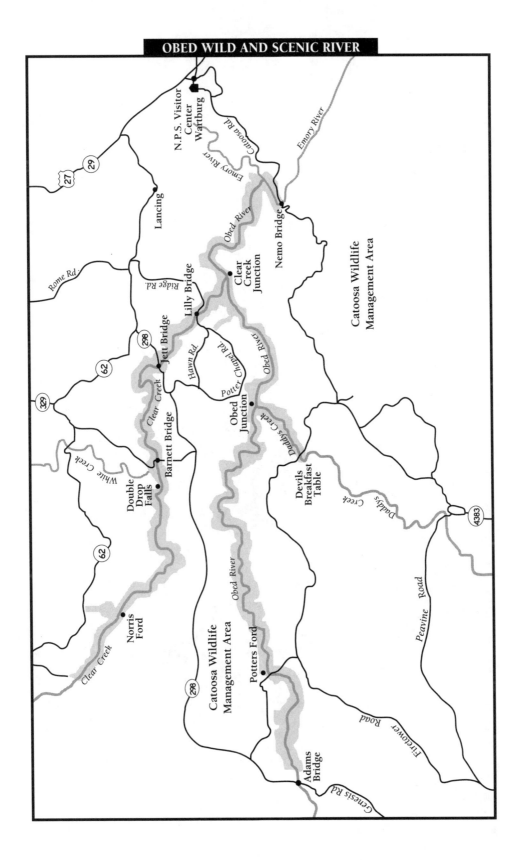

OBED WILD AND SCENIC RIVER

N.P.S. Visitor Center
Wartburg

Catoosa Rd.

Emory River

Emory River

29

27

Lancing

Obed River

Nemo Bridge

Catoosa Wildlife
Management Area

Rome Rd.

Ridge Rd.

Lilly Bridge

Clear Creek
Junction

298

Jett Bridge

62

Hawn Rd.

Potter Chapel Rd.

Obed River

329

Clear Creek

Barnett Bridge

Obed
Junction

Daddys Creek

Double
Drop
Falls

White Creek

Devils
Breakfast
Table

Daddys Creek

4383

62

Obed River

Peavine   Road

Norris
Ford

Catoosa Wildlife
Management Area

Potters Ford

298

Clear Creek

Firetower Road

Adams
Bridge

Genesis Rd.

SHILOH NATIONAL MILITARY PARK

P.O. Box 61
Shiloh, TN 38376
(901) 689–5275

Shiloh, which contains 3,996 acres, was established in 1894 to commemorate the site of a bitter 1862 Civil War battle. The park is located in southern Tennessee, 105 miles east of Memphis. It is 23 miles north of Corinth, Mississippi, via Mississippi 2 and Tennessee 22.

After capturing Fort Henry and Fort Donelson, Ulysses S. Grant sailed with 40,000 Union troops to Pittsburg Landing to wait until General D. C. Buell's Army of the Ohio joined him. Confederate General A. Sidney Johnson decided to launch an attack before the two armies could unite. The offensive was unsuccessful, and the following day the combined Union armies of more than 55,000 men were able to drive the 37,000 Confederate troops back to Corinth. The next month, the Union forces captured both Corinth and Memphis.

The park's visitor center near Pittsburg Landing is open daily (except Christmas) and offers a twenty-five-minute film. Visitors may view artifacts and exhibits, obtain information on the park, and pick up leaflets for a self-guiding tour. Troop location markers are placed throughout the park, and prehistoric Indian mounds are near the river. Thirty-two thousand Civil War veterans are buried in Shiloh National Cemetery.

FACILITIES: Restrooms and drinking water are in the visitor center. Meals and lodging are available in the towns of Adamsville and Savannah.

CAMPING: No camping is permitted in the park. Pickwick Landing State Park, 14 miles southeast via State Highways 22 and 57, offers full camping facilities (including a swimming pool). A Tennessee Valley Authority campground is across Pickwick Dam from the state park.

Obed Wild and Scenic River (opposite page)

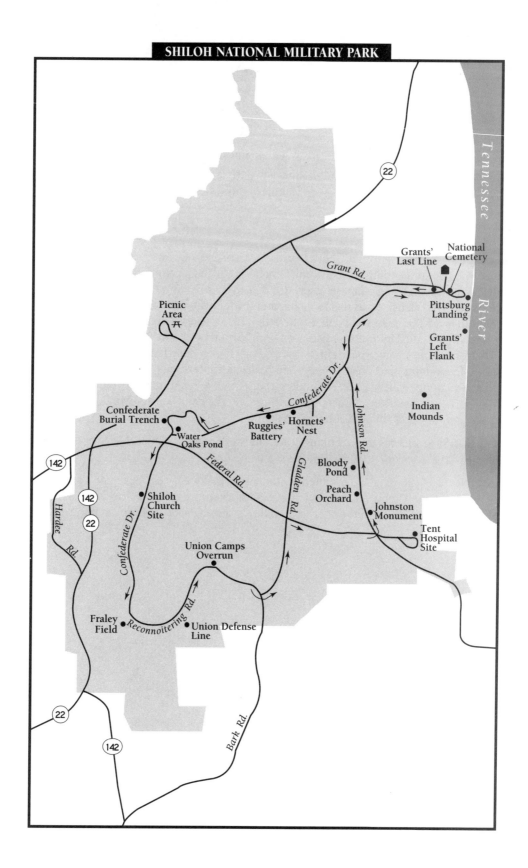

SHILOH NATIONAL MILITARY PARK

Tennessee River

22

Grant Rd.

Grants' Last Line

National Cemetery

Pittsburg Landing

Picnic Area

Grants' Left Flank

Confederate Dr.

Indian Mounds

Confederate Burial Trench

Ruggies' Battery

Hornets' Nest

Johnson Rd.

Water Oaks Pond

142

Federal Rd.

Bloody Pond

142

Gladden Rd.

Peach Orchard

22

Shiloh Church Site

Johnston Monument

Hardee Rd.

Confederate Dr.

Tent Hospital Site

Union Camps Overrun

Fraley Field

Reconnoitering Rd.

Union Defense Line

22

142

Bark Rd.

STONES RIVER NATIONAL BATTLEFIELD

3501 Old Nashville Highway
Murfreesboro, TN 37129
(615) 893–9501

Stones River, which comprises 450 acres, was established in 1927 to memorialize a fierce 1862–63 Civil War battle that ended with 23,000 casualties and both sides claiming victory. The park is located in central Tennessee, 28 miles southeast of Nashville in the northwest corner of the town of Murfreesboro.

After capturing Forts Henry and Donelson and occupying Nashville, 45,000 Union troops set out in late 1862 to sweep a force of 38,000 Confederates from the Murfreesboro area. The battle ended inconclusively, but within days the Confederates retreated 40 miles to Tullahoma, Tennessee, and Union forces occupied Murfreesboro. In early 1863, Union troops constructed Fortress Rosecrans, one of the largest earthen forts of the Civil War, from which they supplied the army in its drive to Chattanooga.

The park is open daily except Christmas from 8:00 A.M. to 5:00 P.M. A visitor center near the entrance has a museum, an audiovisual program, and folders for a self-guiding tour through the battlefield. Stops are identified by numbered markers, and short trails and exhibits help to interpret the events that occurred at each site. A trail and exhibits interpret the remains of Fortress Rosecrans, located at Old Fort Park. Only 3,000 feet of the original 14,000 feet of earthworks remain. During summer months on weekends, living-history programs are offered.

FACILITIES: Food and lodging are not available in the park, but nearly all facilities can be found in nearby Murfreesboro. Restrooms and drinking water are in the visitor center.

CAMPING: No camping is permitted in the park. Several state parks with camping facilities are within 30 miles.

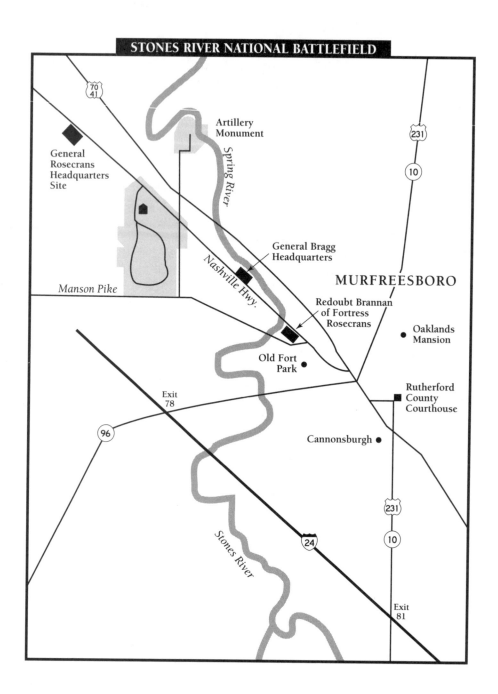

Artillery
Monument

General
Rosecrans
Headquarters
Site

Spring River

Manson Pike

Nashville Hwy.

General Bragg
Headquarters

MURFREESBORO

Redoubt Brannan
of Fortress
Rosecrans

Oaklands
Mansion

Old Fort
Park

Exit
78

Rutherford
County
Courthouse

96

Cannonsburgh

231

10

Stones River

24

Exit
81

VIRGINIA

STATE TOURIST INFORMATION
(800) 847–4882

APPOMATTOX COURT HOUSE NATIONAL HISTORICAL PARK
P.O. Box 218
Appomattox, VA 24522
(804) 352–8987

Appomattox Court House National Historical Park comprises 1,325 acres and was authorized by act of Congress August 3, 1925, as Appomattox Court House National Monument. Its designation was changed to a national historical park in 1954. The park commemorates and preserves the site where Robert E. Lee surrendered to Ulysses S. Grant on April 9, 1865. The site is located in south-central Virginia, 20 miles east of Lynchburg. It is on State Highway 24, |3 miles northeast of the town of Appomattox.

After having his escape blocked by Federal troops, General Robert E. Lee decided to surrender his tired and starving Army of Northern Virginia at Appomattox Court House. On April 9, 1865, the two generals met in the home of Wilmer McLean and agreed upon terms. On April 12, the Confederates surrendered their rifles and began the journey home.

The park's main attractions are in the village of Appomattox Court House, which has been largely restored to its 1865 appearance. A visitor center located in the reconstructed courthouse building provides an information desk, exhibits, and an illustrated slide program. Other buildings open to the public include McLean House, where the surrender took place; Meeks

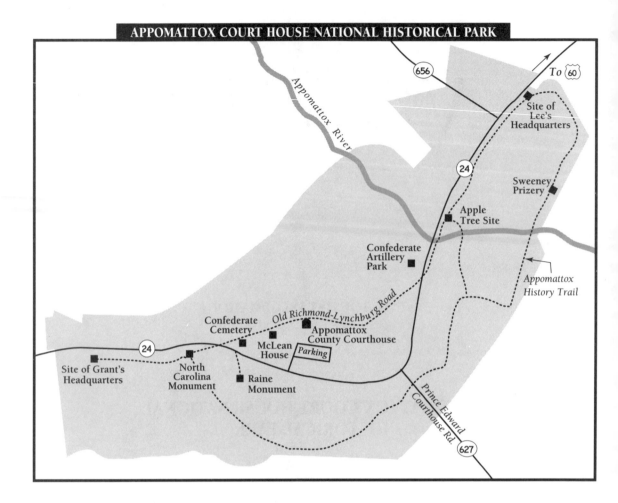

General Store; Woodson Law Office; Clover Hill Tavern, built in 1819 and the village's oldest structure; and the county jail. All except the McLean House, which is reconstructed, have been restored to their appearance during the period of the surrender. West of the village is a Confederate cemetery, while northeast is the site of Lee's headquarters. A 5-mile-long hiking trail connects all of the park's sites, and living-history interpretations are given periodically.

FACILITIES: No lodging or food service is available in the park. Restrooms with access for the handicapped are located in the old servants' quarters. Motels, restaurants, and stores are in the town of Appomattox, 3 miles southwest.

CAMPING: No camping is permitted in the park. Holliday Lake State Park is 12½ miles northeast via state highways 24, 626, 640, and 692. Turn left on Highway 24 leaving the historical park and then right on 626 and follow the signs. Here, campers will find sixty-one sites (no hookups), flush toilets, showers, a dump station, and a 150-acre lake offering boat rentals, swimming, and fishing. Several miles of trails are available for hikers (804–248–6308).

FISHING: While fishing is permitted (state license required) in the Appomattox River, which flows through the historical park, catches are minimal. Better fishing is available at Holliday Lake, which is stocked with bass, bluegill, and crappie.

ARLINGTON HOUSE, THE ROBERT E. LEE MEMORIAL

c/o George Washington Memorial Parkway
Turkey Run Park
McLean, VA 22101
(703) 557–0613

This twenty-eight-acre park was authorized in 1925 to preserve the antebellum home of the Custis and Lee families. The house is located in northeastern Virginia, across the Arlington Memorial Bridge from Washington, D.C. It may be reached by walking from the Arlington Cemetery Visitors Center or by taking the concessioner-operated tourmobiles.

Arlington House was constructed over a fifteen-year period beginning in 1802 by George Washington Parke Custis, the adopted son of George Washington. He planned the house as a collection point for Washington heirlooms and entertained many distinguished people here. In 1831, Custis's only surviving child, Mary, married Robert E. Lee in this house, which was eventually left to her at her father's death. Although the Lees enjoyed the house, they found it necessary to abandon Arlington soon after the beginning of the Civil War. The property was confiscated by the Federal government in 1862 and two years later became the site for a national cemetery.

The house is open for self-guiding tours 9:30 A.M. to 6 :00 P.M. April through September and from 9:30 A.M. to 4:30 P.M. October through March. Park guides are on duty, and a free leaflet explaining the history of each room is available at the entrance. In Arlington National Cemetery surrounding the house, visitors may wish to walk to President John F. Kennedy's gravesite and the Tomb of the Unknown Soldier.

FACILITIES: No snack bars, restaurants or lodging are at the site or in Arlington National Cemetery.

Appomattox Court House National Historical Park (next two pages)

BOOKER T. WASHINGTON NATIONAL MONUMENT

Route 3, Box 310
Hardy, VA 24101
(703) 721–2094

Booker T. Washington National Monument comprises 224 acres and was authorized in 1956 to preserve the birthplace and early childhood home of this famous black leader and educator. The park is located in southern Virginia, 20 miles southeast of Roanoke via state highways 220 and 122.

On this small plantation, Booker T. Washington was born into slavery on April 5, 1856. After being declared free nine years later, he left with his mother, brother, and sister for West Virginia. Booker later was graduated from Hampton Institute, a school for ex-slaves, and in 1881, established Tuskegee Institute in Tuskegee, Alabama. From an initial enrollment of thirty and a beginning salary budget of $2,000, Washington led the school through a period of growth that resulted in a campus of 1,500 students with a $2 million endowment. The respected educator and leader died on November 14, 1915.

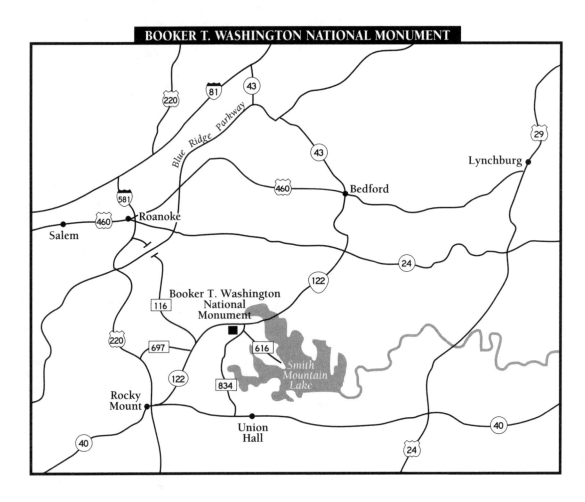

Booker T. Washington National Monument

The park's visitor center and grounds are open daily from 8:30 A.M. to 5:00 P.M. except Thanksgiving Day, Christmas Day, and New Year's Day. The monument is being restored as a nineteenth-century tobacco farm, and although none of the original buildings are still standing, several have been reconstructed to help visitors visualize what life was like when Booker T. Washington lived here. A ¼-mile-long self-guiding trail with audio messages leads through a farm complete with crops and farm animals. Park interpreters are in period dress from mid-June to Labor Day. The Jack-O-Lantern Branch Trail is a 1½-mile meandering walk through park fields and forests. A trail map and guide are available at the visitor center. An entrance fee is charged of visitors who are seventeen to sixty-one years of age.

FACILITIES: No food service or lodging is available. Restrooms and drinking water are in the visitor center. A shaded picnic area with tables only is on the park grounds. Meals and lodging are in Bedford, Roanoke, and Rocky Mount.

CAMPING: No camping is permitted on the monument grounds. Roanoke Mountain Campground on the Blue Ridge Parkway is 19 miles northwest of the monument via highways 122 and 116. This campground, operated by the National Park Service, provides tables, grills, water, and flush toilets but no hookups. Private campgrounds are closer; directions are available from personnel at the monument.

COLONIAL NATIONAL HISTORICAL PARK; JAMESTOWN NATIONAL HISTORIC SITE

P.O. Box 210
Yorktown, VA 23690
(804) 898–3400

Colonial National Monument was authorized in 1930 (redesignated a national historical park in 1936) to preserve a variety of historical areas within its 9,320 acres. Included are the following: Jamestown National Historic Site, the site of the first permanent English settlement in America; Yorktown Battlefield, scene of the last major battle of the Revolutionary War; and the Colonial Parkway, a 23-mile scenic parkway passing by the town of Williamsburg.

Colonial National Historical Park tells the story of our country's early history. Founded in 1607, Jamestown was the first successful English colony in North America. Although it did not become a very large town, Jamestown did serve as the principal town and seat of government of Virginia for ninety-two years.

A tour of Jamestown begins at the visitor center, which contains exhibits and a theater program to help explain the town's history. A walking tour leads through ruins of the old town site, although the Old Church Tower is the only seventeenth-century structure remaining above ground. Three- and 5-mile loop roads provide access to the rest of the island. Near the entrance, at the reconstructed glasshouse, craftsmen demonstrate the art of glass blowing. An admission is charged for entrance to Jamestown.

At the end of Colonial Parkway is the Yorktown Battlefield, scene of a 1781 military siege that proved to be the culminating battle of the American Revolution. A visitor center provides exhibits and a theater program on the battle that produced the surrender of 8,000 British troops to an allied American and French force under the command of General George Washington. A self-guided auto tour (auto tapes available in the visitor center) begins at the center and circles points of interest on the battlefield, encampment areas, and the old town. The Moore House, where negotiations for the surrender took place, is open for tours daily during the summer and on weekends during spring and fall.

FACILITIES: Antiques and handicrafts are sold by concessioners in Yorktown. A cafeteria is located near Jamestown at Jamestown Settlement. Food and lodging are available at Williamsburg and Yorktown. Restrooms are in both visitor centers, and a picnic area is in Yorktown. Marinas are located at Jamestown on the James River and at Gloucester Point on the York River. Boats may not be launched from the Colonial Parkway.

CAMPING: No camping is permitted in the park, but private campgrounds are located in the area. A city park in Newport News provides campsites with tables, grills, water, showers, electrical hookups, and laundry facilities. The campground is off Route 143 near the intersection of Fort Eustis and Jefferson Avenue (804–887–5381).

FISHING: Fishing is available at various locations along the Colonial Parkway.

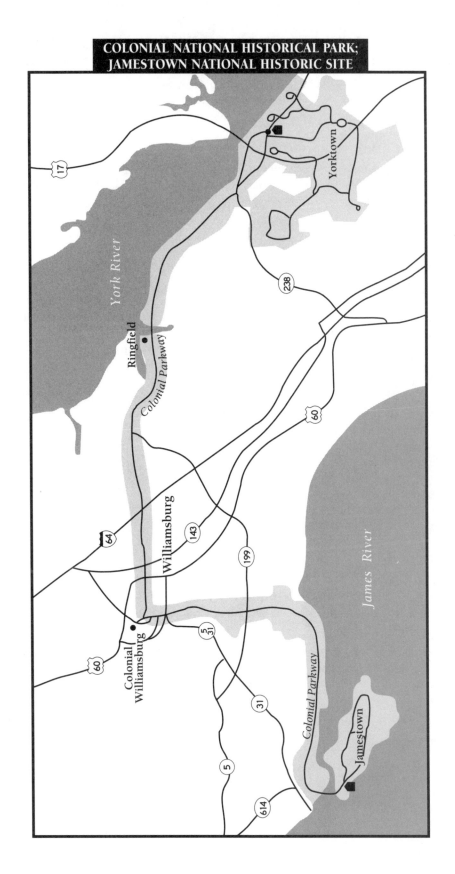

COLONIAL NATIONAL HISTORICAL PARK;
JAMESTOWN NATIONAL HISTORIC SITE

York River

Yorktown

17

238

Ringfield

Colonial Parkway

60

64

Williamsburg

143

199

60

5
31

Colonial Williamsburg

31

Colonial Parkway

James River

5

Jamestown

614

FREDERICKSBURG AND SPOTSYLVANIA COUNTY BATTLEFIELDS MEMORIAL NATIONAL MILITARY PARK

120 Chatham Lane
Fredericksburg, VA 22405
(703) 373–4461

This 5,909-acre park was established in 1927 to preserve portions of four major Civil War battlefields: Fredericksburg, Chancellorsville, Wilderness, and Spotsylvania Court House. The widely scattered park is located in northeastern Virginia, in seven units in the city of Fredericksburg and four surrounding counties.

After Lee's army was stopped at Antietam in September 1862, Union forces were again ready to move southward. The first two battles—Fredericksburg in December of 1862 and Chancellorsville in May of 1863—ended in Confederate victories, resulting in a change of Union command. After another unsuccessful push by Robert E. Lee into the North was halted at Gettysburg, Union forces again marched south, where they were to engage the Confederates at the Wilderness and Spotsylvania Court House. Unable to break through Lee's front, Ulysses S. Grant sidestepped southeast toward Richmond, where more bloody fighting would eventually result in Confederate surrender.

The military park consists of four battlefields and three historic buildings. The main visitor center, on U.S. 1 in Fredericksburg, contains exhibits and information to help interpret the park. Nearby, Fredericksburg National Cemetery contains the remains of more than 15,000 Federal soldiers who died in the Civil War. A second visitor center and museum is at the Chancellorsville Battlefield. Both centers contain schedules of various programs that are available throughout the park. Handicapped visitors are encouraged to use Chancellorsville Visitor Center, which is fully accessible.

"Stonewall" Jackson Shrine, located south on Interstate 95 and east on Highway 606, preserves the scene of the famous Confederate's death on May 10, 1863. Chatham, an eighteenth-century mansion used extensively by Union forces during the war, is open daily. Old Salem Church provided the focal point for a bloody battle during the Chancellorsville campaign. Interpretive hiking trails are available at each of the four battlefields.

FACILITIES: No food or lodging is provided by the Park Service. Restrooms are in each visitor center, and picnic facilities are at each of the four battlefields and at Chatham and the "Stonewall" Jackson Shrine.

CAMPING: No camping is permitted in the park. Prince William Forest Park, 23 miles north of Fredericksburg on Interstate 95, offers 120 sites with tables, grills, water, and flush toilets.

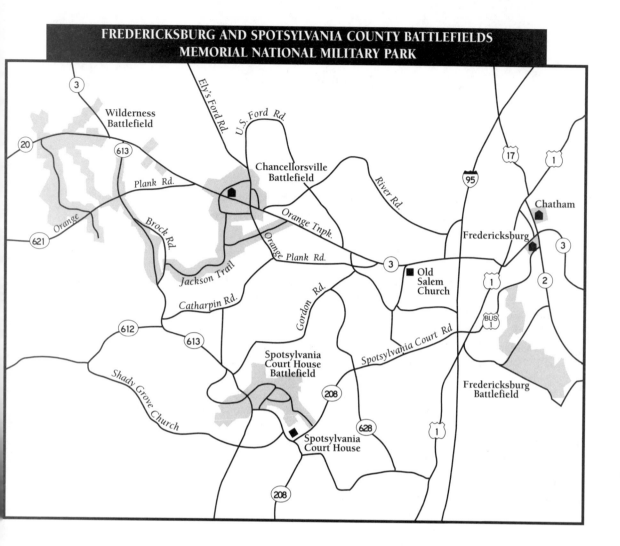

FREDERICKSBURG AND SPOTSYLVANIA COUNTY BATTLEFIELDS MEMORIAL NATIONAL MILITARY PARK

Wilderness Battlefield

Ely's Ford Rd.

U.S. Ford Rd.

Chancellorsville Battlefield

River Rd.

Plank Rd.

Orange

Brock Rd.

Orange Tnpk.

Chatham

Fredericksburg

Orange Plank Rd.

Old Salem Church

Jackson Trail

Gordon Rd.

Catharpin Rd.

Spotsylvania Court House Battlefield

Spotsylvania Court Rd

Fredericksburg Battlefield

Shady Grove Church

Spotsylvania Court House

BUS 1

GEORGE WASHINGTON BIRTHPLACE NATIONAL MONUMENT

Rural Route #1, Box 717
Washington's Birthplace, VA 22575
(804) 224–1732

George Washington Birthplace National Monument comprises 538 acres of some of the most beautiful land in the National Park Service. The monument was established in 1930 to memorialize the birthplace of the first U.S. president. It is located in eastern Virginia, 38 miles southeast of Fredericksburg via state highways 3 and 204.

It was here that Augustine Washington bought Popes Creek Plantation in 1718. It was a 150-acre farm with a 25-foot by 16-foot brick home and outbuildings. He doubled the size of the house between 1722–26. His son, George, was born on February 22, 1732. Young George spent his first three and a half years at Popes Creek before his father moved the family in 1735 to what later was known as Mount Vernon. The Popes Creek home accidentally burned down in 1779 and was never rebuilt at this site.

The monument is open from 9:00 A.M. to 5:00 P.M. daily except Christmas Day and New Year's Day. A visitor center near the parking lot provides interpretive exhibits and a film on Washington's life here. Although only an outline of the foundation of the birthplace site is visible, a memorial association has constructed and furnished a typical home of the moderately wealthy of the period. Outbuildings surround the home, and a beautiful view of Popes Creek and the more-distant Potomac River surround the monument. Park rangers are in period dress and provide demonstrations of colonial life.

FACILITIES: No food or lodging is available at the monument. Both are in Fredericksburg, Montross, and Colonial Beach. Restrooms, a gift shop, vending machines, and drinking water are in the visitor center. Restrooms and drinking water are also in a beautiful picnic area a short drive from the birthplace site.

CAMPING: No camping is permitted in the park. Westmoreland State Park offers a shaded campground with tables, grills, water, flush toilets, showers, fishing, swimming (both river and a large pool), and boating. The park is approximately 6½ miles southeast of the monument on Highway 3 (804–493–8821).

FISHING: Fishing is permitted from the picnic area (designated area only) or in the Potomac River within the park. Catches include perch, bluefish, and catfish; a Virginia license is required.

GEORGE WASHINGTON MEMORIAL PARKWAY

Turkey Run Park
McLean, VA 22101
(703) 557–3635

This 7,142-acre parkway links many landmarks in the life of George Washington. It is primarily located in northeastern Virginia, where it connects Great Falls with Mount Vernon along the Potomac River. A smaller section on the Maryland side connects Great Falls with Chain Bridge.

At the same time that George Washington Memorial Parkway preserves scenery along the Potomac River, it connects a number of areas important in the life of America's first president. At the parkway's southern terminus, Washington's home of Mount Vernon is now managed by a nonprofit association that opens the house for daily tours from 9:00 A.M. to 5:00 P.M., March through September, and from 9:00 A.M. to 4:00 P.M., October through February (703–780–2000). Driving north, the parkway passes through Alexandria, Washington's hometown, and Washington, D.C., the nation's capital, which he founded. At the parkway's northern end, Great Falls Park (703–759–2915) contains the ruins of engineer George Washington's Patowmack Canal.

Additional places of interest along the parkway include Fort Hunt, where batteries guarded the approach to Washington in the late 1800s; Dyke Marsh, which contains a variety of aquatic plants and birds; Jones Point Lighthouse, where a small beacon warned of sandbars from 1836 to 1925; Theodore Roosevelt Island, an eighty-eight-acre wooded island sanctuary in the Potomac River commemorating the twenty-sixth president of the United States (see separate writeup under District of Columbia); Fort Marcy, a Civil War earthwork defense fort; the Clara Barton House, the thirty-eight-room home of the founder of the American Red Cross and, for seven years, the headquarters of that organization (see separate writeup under Maryland); and Glen Echo Park, an arts and cultural center with a 1921 Dentzel carousel. These are but a few of the places of interest along the George Washington Memorial Parkway.

FACILITIES: No lodging is provided by the National Park Service, although both are available nearby. The Mount Vernon Inn near the Mount Vernon entrance gate serves breakfast, lunch, and dinner. The Potowmack Landing Restaurant at Dainderfield Island and the snack bar at Columbia Island Marina offer food services to visitors. Public restrooms are available at Belle Haven, Columbia Island Marina, Fort Hunt, Theodore Roosevelt Island, and Turkey Run Park.

CAMPING: No camping is provided by the National Park Service, but public campgrounds are in the area. (See the camping section under Greenbelt Park, Maryland.)

FISHING: Fishing from the bank is permitted; a valid license is required. Bass, carp, catfish, and perch are possible catches.

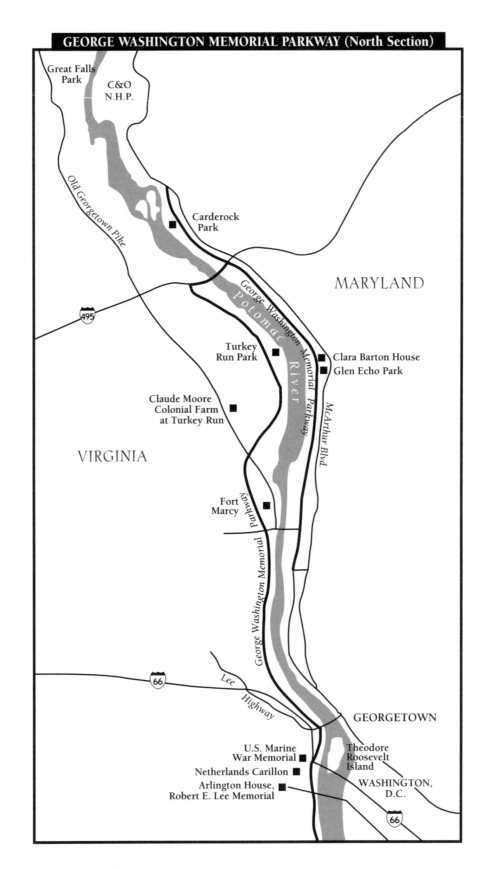

GEORGE WASHINGTON MEMORIAL PARKWAY (North Section)

Great Falls Park

C&O N.H.P.

Old Georgetown Pike

Carderock Park

MARYLAND

George Washington Memorial Parkway

Potomac River

495

Turkey Run Park

Clara Barton House

Glen Echo Park

McArthur Blvd.

Claude Moore Colonial Farm at Turkey Run

VIRGINIA

Fort Marcy

George Washington Memorial Parkway

66

Lee Highway

GEORGETOWN

U.S. Marine War Memorial

Theodore Roosevelt Island

Netherlands Carillon

Arlington House, Robert E. Lee Memorial

WASHINGTON, D.C.

66

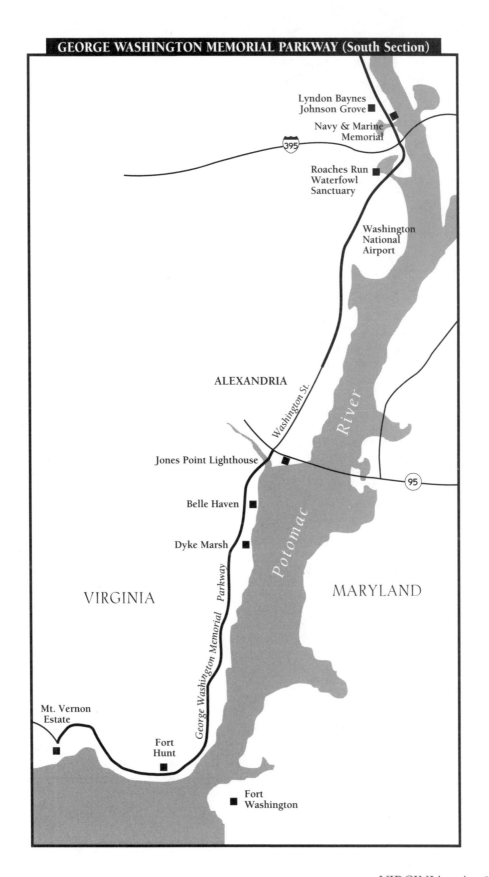

Lyndon Baynes
Johnson Grove

Navy & Marine
Memorial

395

Roaches Run
Waterfowl
Sanctuary

Washington
National
Airport

ALEXANDRIA

Washington St.

River

Jones Point Lighthouse

95

Belle Haven

Potomac

Dyke Marsh

VIRGINIA

George Washington Memorial Parkway

MARYLAND

Mt. Vernon
Estate

Fort
Hunt

Fort
Washington

GREEN SPRINGS HISTORIC DISTRICT

c/o Fredericksburg and Spotsylvania County
Battlefields Memorial National Military Park
120 Chatham Lane
Fredericksburg, VA 22405
(703) 373–4461

Green Springs Historic District is an area of structures representing a wide variety of architectural styles. The Green Springs area comprises approximately 14,000 acres, and in 1977, the secretary of the interior agreed to accept preservation easements of nearly half the district's area. The historic district is located in central Virginia, in Louisa County.

Green Springs Historic District is an area where early-American architecture is concentrated among fine rural manor houses and related buildings in a pristine landscape. The district was declared a Virginia Historic Landmark and nominated to the National Register of Historic Places in 1973. One year later, the district was declared a National Historic Landmark. The Green Springs area is cooperatively managed by the National Park Service, the Commonwealth of Virginia, and Historic Green Springs, Inc. The latter is reached at P.O. 515, Gordonsville, VA 22942.

Buildings in the district range from farmhouses to large plantations. Thirty-five buildings constructed from the early to mid-1700s to the early 1900s are considered to be architecturally significant. All thirty-five structures are privately owned, and none are open to the public.

FACILITIES: Food and lodging are available in a number of communities around the Green Springs area, including Gordonsville.

CAMPING: Private campgrounds are near Gordonsville and Louisa.

MAGGIE L. WALKER NATIONAL HISTORIC SITE

c/o Richmond National Battlefield Park
3215 East Broad Street
Richmond, VA 23223
(804) 226–1981

Maggie L. Walker National Historic Site comprises approximately one-and-one-quarter acres and was authorized in 1978 to commemorate the life and achievements of the first woman bank founder and president, Maggie Lena Walker (1866–1934). This African-American woman earned unusual success in finance and business through self-determination and leadership, building success within the African-American community locally and nationally. The site is in Richmond at 110½ East Leigh Street in Jackson Ward, a National Historic District.

Maggie Lena Walker began her professional career as a schoolteacher, but she achieved her extraordinary mark on society with the Independent Order of St. Luke, a fraternal organization that provided financial aid to its members in sickness and a proper burial at death. She joined the society at age fourteen. In 1899, at age thirty-three, Walker assumed leadership of the Order and reoriented its management to be financially sound and profitable. Walker, in association with the Order, established a newspaper, a department store, and a bank, where depositors were urged to "save their nickels and watch them turn into dollars." The bank opened in 1903 as the St. Luke Penny Savings Bank, with Walker as president. It continues in operation today as the Consolidated Bank and Trust Company. Walker's stewardship of the bank and the Order, and her lifelong commitment to uplift the African-American community, provided a great legacy.

The site at 10½ East Leigh Street was Maggie Lena Walker's residence from 1904 until her death in 1934 and remained in the Walker family until acquisition by the National Park Service. Walker and four generations of her family shared this Victorian-era structure, which she expanded to accommodate her needs. The house contains many items belonging to the Walker family and has been restored to its 1930 appearance.

The historic site is open Wednesday through Sunday, 9:00 A.M. to 5:00 P.M., except Thanksgiving, Christmas, and New Year's Day. Reservations for groups of five or more are required. Admission is free.

FACILITIES: Restrooms are available. Food and lodging can be found in Richmond.

CAMPING: See the camping section under Richmond National Battlefield Park (Virginia).

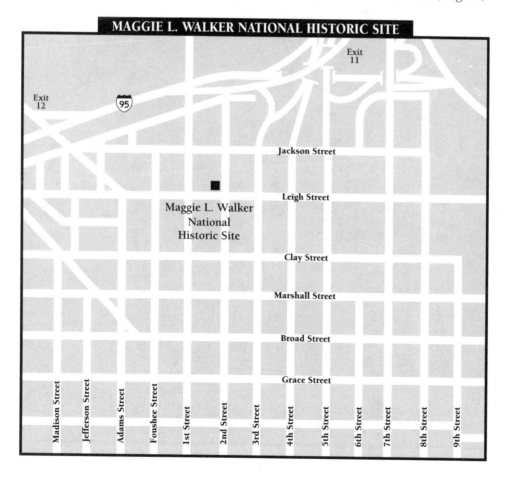

MAGGIE L. WALKER NATIONAL HISTORIC SITE

MANASSAS NATIONAL BATTLEFIELD PARK

6511 Sudley Road
Manassas, VA 22110
(703) 361–1339
(703) 361–7075 (TDD)

Manassas National Battlefield Park comprises 5,100 acres and was designated in 1940 to commemorate the site of two important Civil War battles. The battlefield is located in northern Virginia, 26 miles southwest of Washington, D.C., via U.S. 29 or Interstate 66. The visitor center is on State Highway 234 (Sudley Road), 1 mile north of the interchange with Interstate 66 (exit 47).

The first battle of Manassas (also known as Bull Run), on July 21, 1861, was the initial major confrontation between opposing armies in the Civil War. This clash of 18,000 men on each side resulted in a Confederate victory as the Union army was routed back to Washington. The battle made it evident to both sides the war would be long and bloody. Thirteen months later, on

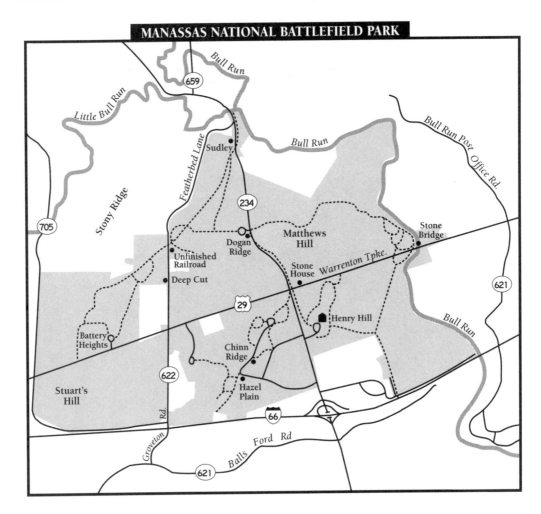

August 28–30, 1862, a second and much larger battle at Manassas proved equally disastrous to Union forces and gave Robert E. Lee the opportunity to carry the war north into Maryland.

The park visitor center, housing a museum and audiovisual orientation program, is open daily except Christmas from 8:30 A.M. to 5:00 P.M. (to 6:00 P.M. mid-June through Labor Day). A 1-mile-long self-guided walking tour of Henry Hill, site of the first battle, begins here. A 1.4-mile trail at Stone Bridge and a 0.6-mile trail at Sudley Springs also cover areas associated with first Manassas battle. A 12-mile driving tour is required to view the more extensive second Manassas battlefield. Maps are available at the visitor center and at a new visitor contact station on Stuart's Hill scheduled to open in mid-June 1996.

FACILITIES: Restrooms and drinking water are at the visitor center. The park maintains a picnic area but, no food service or lodging is available in the park. Restaurants and lodging are situated nearby on State Highway 234 in Manassas.

CAMPING: No camping is permitted on the battlefield. Bull Run Regional Park, approximately 2 miles southeast of the visitor center, offers camping (150 sites) with tables, grills, water, showers, flush toilets, and electric hookups.

FISHING: Angling for bass, catfish and other species in Bull Run is permitted; a Virginia fishing license is required.

PETERSBURG NATIONAL BATTLEFIELD
P.O. Box 549
Petersburg, VA 23804
(804) 732–3531

Petersburg National Battlefield comprises 2,735 acres and was established as a national military park in 1926 (name changed to a national battlefield in 1962) to commemorate the site of a ten-month Civil War campaign in which the Union army attempted to seize the railroad center supplying Richmond and Lee's army. The main unit of the battlefield is located in southeastern Virginia, just east of the city of Petersburg via State Highway 36. Also included in the battlefield are outlying forts southwest of the city, the City Point Unit in the city of Hopewell, Virginia, and the Five Forks Unit in Dinwiddie County.

After failing to capture Richmond by direct attack, Ulysses S. Grant and the Union army decided to move farther south and attempt to cut off Robert E. Lee's railroad supply lines. Early assaults against the Confederate line failed, and Grant was forced to settle down to a siege that was to last nearly ten months and take the lives of 70,000 Americans.

During the lengthy battle at Petersburg, Grant selected City Point, a strategic location at the junction of two rivers within easy water communication of Fort Monroe and Washington, D.C., as his headquarters. This location became the logistical and communication center for the Union forces until Grant disbanded the headquarters and moved closer to the front for the final campaign of the war. Lee had placed a large Confederate force at Five Forks under the command of General George Pickett, but the force was put out of action by Union troops who were then able to cut off the rail supply line to Petersburg. On the night of April 2, 1865, Lee evac-

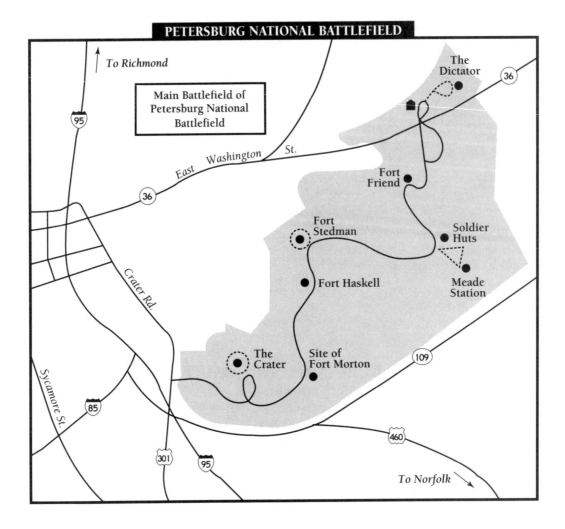

uated Petersburg and moved toward Appomattox, where his final surrender was to occur a week later.

The visitor center contains exhibits, a seventeen-minute map presentation that is conducted every half hour, and a schedule of programs taking place throughout the park in summer months. Programs include cannon firings, mortar demonstrations, and reenactments of camp life. Visitors may also obtain maps for a self-guiding auto tour of the battlefield. A number of the tour's stops provide short interpretive walking trails. An auto-tape tour is available for purchase.

FACILITIES: No food service or lodging is available in the park, but both can be found nearby. Restrooms and drinking water are in the visitor center.

CAMPING: No camping is permitted on the battlefield grounds. Campsites are available in Pocahontas State Forest and Park, northwest of Petersburg via Interstate 95 and State Highway 10.

PRINCE WILLIAM FOREST PARK

18100 Park Headquarters Road
Triangle, VA 22172
(703) 221–7181

A sanctuary for native plants and animals in rapidly urbanizing northern Virginia, Prince William Forest Park protects more than 17,000 acres of Piedmont forest in the Quantico Creek watershed and is the largest national park area within the Washington, D.C., metropolitan area. Rustic cabins built by the Civilian Conservation Corps are now listed on the National Register of Historic Places and are used by group campers. The park provides a place to hike, picnic, camp, and fish, with 37 miles of trails. several lakes, and two picnic areas. The park entrance is about 35 miles south of Washington, D.C., via Interstate 95, 1/4 mile off exit 619 West.

Prince William Forest Park is primarily used as a recreational retreat from the urban Washington area. This land was temporarily ruined following extensive tree cutting and farming by early pioneers so that, by the late 1800s, most of the farms had been abandoned. The result is an extensively forested watershed.

Numerous activities are available to park visitors. Bicycle riding is permitted on all roads (including fire roads), and 35 miles of trails and fire roads are accessible to hikers. Major trails are marked, and self-guiding trails, exhibits, conducted walks, and talks are available at various areas of the park. Information may be obtained at the park visitor center.

FACILITIES: Cabins are available for rental April through October (703–221–4706). No food service is available in the park. Restrooms are located at both picnic areas, Turkey Run Ridge Nature Center, and Oak Ridge Campground.

CAMPING: Oak Ridge (seventy-nine spaces), the major campground, is 6 miles from the park entrance. It is open year-round (two-week limit per year) and provides flush toilets, tables, water, and paved parking slips. The Travel Trailer Village (seventy-six spaces) is a concessioner-operated campground with hookups, showers, and a laundry, located off Virginia Highway 234 North. For information, write Prince William Travel Trailer Village, 16058 Dumfries Road, Dumfries, VA 22026 (703–221–2474). For organized groups, Turkey Run Ridge group camping area is open all year by reservation only and has tables, fireplaces, and flush toilets. Chopawamsic Backcountry Campground is primitive, and permits are required. Cabin camps with cabins, a central kitchen–dining hall, and a washhouse may be reserved by organized groups during the camping season. More information may be obtained by writing or calling the park (703–221–7181) from 8 30 A.M. to 5:00 P.M.

FISHING: Native fishes such as bass, bluegill, perch, pickerel, and catfish are available in several park lakes and ponds. A Virginia license and artificial bait are required.

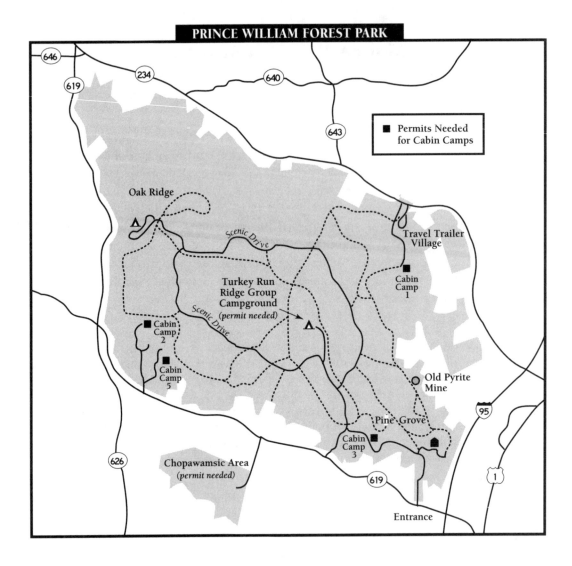

Map labels:
646, 619, 234, 640, 643
Permits Needed for Cabin Camps
Oak Ridge
Scenic Drive
Travel Trailer Village
Cabin Camp 1
Turkey Run Ridge Group Campground *(permit needed)*
Scenic Drive
Cabin Camp 2
Cabin Camp 5
Old Pyrite Mine
95
Pine Grove
Cabin Camp 3
626
Chopawamsic Area *(permit needed)*
619
1
Entrance

RED HILL PATRICK HENRY NATIONAL MEMORIAL
Brookneal, VA 24528
(804) 376–2044

Red Hill Patrick Henry National Memorial comprises 117 acres and was authorized in 1986 to honor the life of this famous Virginia legislator, revolutionary patriot, and orator who made Red Hill his last home. Red Hill is also Patrick Henry's burial place. The memorial is in south central Virginia, 35 miles southeast of Lynchburg via U.S. Highway 501.

Patrick Henry was born in Studley, Virginia, on May 29, 1736. This patriot is best known for his revolutionary oratory, especially a 1775 speech at Richmond's St. John's Church during the Second Virginia Convention when he stated, "I know not what course others may take, but as for me, give me liberty or give me death." Following the Revolutionary War, he continued his public service by working on the Bill of Rights and being elected Virginia's first governor. After serving five terms as governor, he retired to Red Hill in 1794, where he practiced law until his death in 1799.

Red Hill is an eighteenth-century plantation with Patrick Henry's original law office and his reconstructed home, kitchen, carriage house, cook's cabin, stable, and cemetery. The main house was destroyed by fire in 1919 and has been reconstructed on its original foundation. The memorial's visitor center is in the museum, where visitors will find Patrick Henry artifacts and a sixteen-minute videotape. Red Hill is open daily from 9:00 A.M. to 5:00 P.M. (4:00 P.M. from November through March). The memorial is closed on Thanksgiving, Christmas, and New Year's Day.

FACILITIES: Restrooms and drinking water are available in the museum. Food and lodging are in Brookneal.

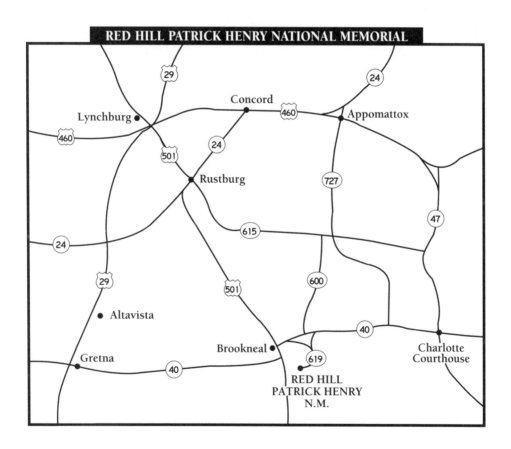

RICHMOND NATIONAL BATTLEFIELD PARK

3215 East Broad Street
Richmond, VA 23223
(804) 226–1981

Richmond National Battlefield Park was authorized in 1936 to commemorate the battlefields around the Confederate capital of Richmond. The park's 769 acres are in and around the city of Richmond, Virginia, as ten separate sites in three counties.

The city of Richmond served as a political, medical, manufacturing, and supply center for the South; it also was an important symbol of the Confederacy. For these reasons, Union forces launched repeated major drives toward the city and the Confederate army that was defending it. Two of the drives, the Seven Days Campaign in 1862 and Ulysses S. Grant's campaign of 1864, are particularly significant. Richmond withstood all attacks until Grant's successful siege of Petersburg forced Robert E. Lee's army to retreat from Richmond on April 2, 1865. The city fell the next day, and the final collapse of the Confederacy soon followed.

The park's main visitor center, on the site of Chimborazo Hospital at 3215 East Broad Street in Richmond, offers exhibits, audiovisual programs, and a brochure with a map that outlines a self-guided battlefields tour. Visitors will also find a schedule of living-history programs and special events during the summer. Smaller welcome stations with exhibits are located at Cold Harbor and Fort Harrison; these are staffed seasonally. Hiking trails are at Gaines' Mill, Chickahominy Bluff, Fort Harrison, Fort Brady, and Drewry's Bluff. Interpretive facilities with audio stations and/or signs are at each park site.

FACILITIES: No food service or lodging is provided in park areas, although both are available nearby. Restrooms and water are in each of the visitor centers. Picnic facilities exist only at Fort Harrison and Cold Harbor.

CAMPING: No camping is permitted in the park. Pocahontas State Park and Forest, a short distance southwest of Richmond via highways 10 and 655, provides camping with tables, grills, water, flush toilets, a dump station, swimming, and fishing.

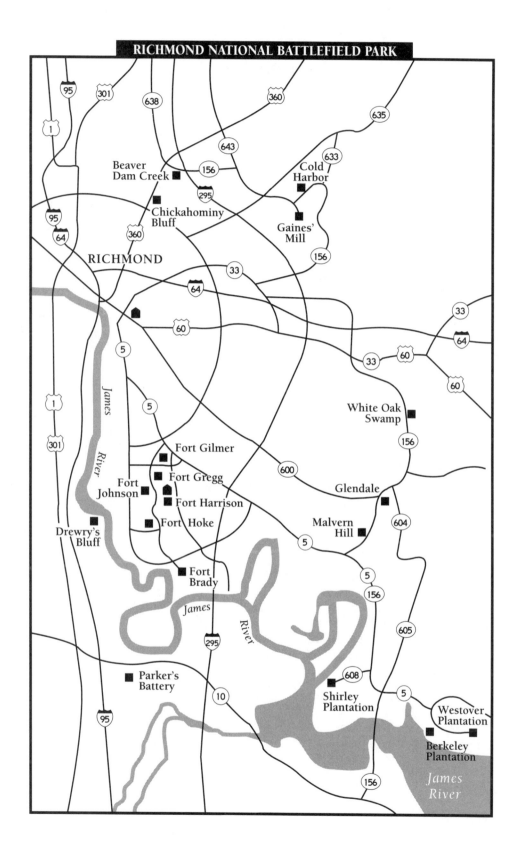

SHENANDOAH NATIONAL PARK

Route 4, Box 348
Luray, VA 22835
(703) 999–2229

Shenandoah National Park was established in 1935 and comprises 195,000 acres along an 80-mile stretch of the Blue Ridge Mountains. The drive along the ridge of mountains provides visitors with splendid vistas of the Shenandoah Valley and the Piedmont. The park is located in northern Virginia, with the northern entrance approximately 60 miles west of Washington, D.C.

Shenandoah National Park lies astride the Blue Ridge Mountains, which form the eastern boundary of the Appalachian Range. To the west, the Shenandoah River flows northeastward between the Blue Ridge and Allegheny mountains. To the east is the rolling Piedmont country.

Main access to the park's features is along 105-mile Skyline Drive, which winds along much of the crest of the range. Numerous pullouts are provided for viewing the spectacular scenery. Visitor centers with exhibits, audiovisual programs, and maps are at Dickey Ridge near the north entrance and at Big Meadows, 51 miles south. The Dickey Ridge Visitor Center is open daily (9:00 A.M. to 5:00 P.M.) from late spring through mid-November. The Byrd Visitor Center at Big Meadows is open daily (9:00 A.M. to 5:00 P.M.) late spring through mid-November. At these centers and at the entrance stations, visitors may obtain a guide to activities and a guide map to features along Skyline Drive. Naturalist programs, including hikes, demonstrations, and evening campfire talks, are provided at several locations during summer months and less frequently during spring and fall.

FACILITIES: Food service is available at Elkwallow, Thornton Gap, Skyland, Big Meadows, and Loft Mountain. Service stations and camper-supply stores are at various points along the drive. Overnight accommodations are at Big Meadows, Lewis Mountain, and Skyland. For information or reservations, write ARAMARK Virginia Sky-Line Company, P.O. Box 727, Luray, VA 22835 (703–743–5108 or 1–800–999–4714).

CAMPING: Campgrounds with tables, grills, flush toilets, and water are at Big Meadows (230 sites, dump station, showers, laundry, store, and wagon rides), Lewis Mountain (thirty-one sites), Loft Mountain (221 sites, dump station, laundry, showers, and store), and Dundo Youth Group Camp (seven group sites, pit toilets; reservations required). All but Big Meadows are open from May to October. Big Meadows opens earlier, closes in mid-November, and is on a reservation system (1–800–365–2267). Although Big Meadows is generally the first to be filled, it is also the most noisy and congested. The nicest campground is probably at Loft Mountain.

FISHING: Angling is limited to trout fishing with artificial lures in the more than one hundred miles of streams contained in the park. No person may keep more than six trout per day or have more than six trout in possession. A Virginia license is required.

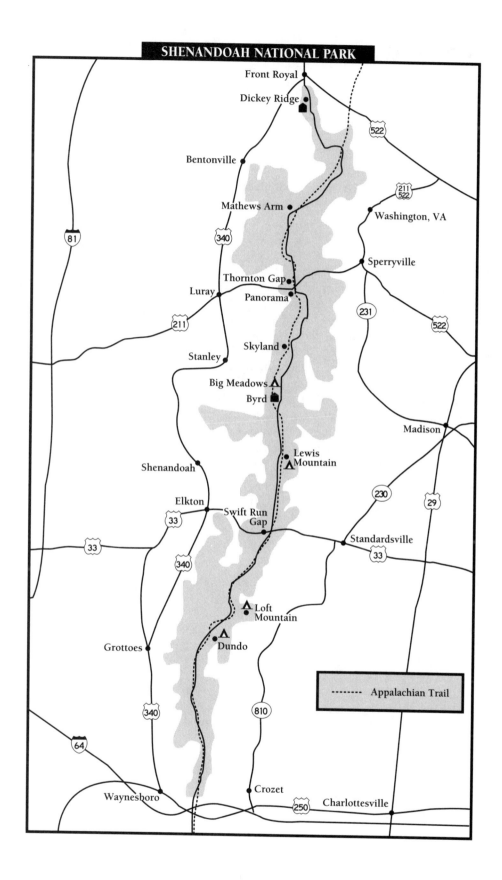

SHENANDOAH NATIONAL PARK

Front Royal

Dickey Ridge

522

Bentonville

211
522

Mathews Arm

Washington, VA

340

Sperryville

Thornton Gap

Luray

Panorama

231

211

522

Skyland

Stanley

Big Meadows

Byrd

Madison

Lewis
Mountain

Shenandoah

230

29

Elkton

Swift Run
Gap

33

Standardsville

33

340

33

Loft
Mountain

340

Dundo

Grottoes

- - - - - Appalachian Trail

810

64

Waynesboro

Crozet

250

Charlottesville

WOLF TRAP FARM PARK FOR THE PERFORMING ARTS

1551 Trap Road
Vienna, VA 22182
(703) 255–1800
(703) 255–1820 (TDD)

This 117-acre park was authorized in 1966 to establish the first national park for the performing arts. The park is located in Vienna, Virginia, approximately 15 miles (thirty minutes) west of Washington, D.C. From Route 7, turn left on Towlston Road to Wolf Trap.

Wolf Trap Farm Park was created through Mrs. Catherine Filene Shouse's gift of farmland and funds for construction of a performing arts center. Wolf Trap is a unique joint venture between the United States government and the private, nonprofit Wolf Trap Foundation. Wolf Trap Farm Park is administered and managed by the National Park Service, which also has technical and operational responsibilities for the Filene Center. The Wolf Trap Foundation is responsible by cooperative agreement for selecting and funding Filene Center programming, providing publicity and promotion of the Filene Center, and operating the box office. A full range of artistic performances is offered during the summer months.

The National Park Service operates an interpretive program during the summer in the rustic Theatre-in-the-Woods. Programs for children and adults are offered free of charge during July and August and include puppet shows, dance, mime, and instrumentalists. A wide variety of free lectures, in-depth discussions, and performance previews are also offered (reservations required). For reservations and information about these activities, call (703) 255–1827/8.

FACILITIES: A nonprofit gift shop is open one hour prior to performances. A dining pavilion offers food service beginning two hours prior to each performance. Snack bars are also available. Picnicking is permitted in the park, but sites are limited.

VIRGIN ISLANDS

BUCK ISLAND REEF NATIONAL MONUMENT

P.O. Box 160
Christiansted, St. Croix, VI 00820
(809) 773–1460

Buck Island Reef National Monument comprises 880 acres and was established in 1961 to protect one of the finest marine gardens in the Caribbean. The monument is located a short distance off the island of St. Croix and may be reached by boat from Christiansted.

Beginning in the 1750s, Buck Island was used for agriculture, pasturage, and lumbering. The extensive lumber cutting of the 1800s and overgrazing by goats ended in the 1950s, however, and the island started returning to its natural state of tropical vegetation. While the island itself is impressive, it is the water surrounding the island that contains the major attractions.

Licensed boats on St. Croix may be hired for a visit to Buck Island. The skippers will have snorkeling equipment that can be used in the beautiful lagoon just off the island (visitors should bring their own lunch). Arrow markers and signs on the ocean floor guide snorkelers along the Buck Island Reef Nature Trail (about thirty minutes). A primitive hiking trail on the island provides access to the tropical vegetation.

FACILITIES: No food or lodging is available on the island. The Park Service provides picnic tables, grills, a small house for changing clothes, a sheltered pavilion, and restrooms. Meals and lodging are available in Christiansted.

CAMPING: No camping is permitted on the island.

FISHING: Fishing is allowed in the salt water surrounding the island. Spearguns are prohibited within the park.

CHRISTIANSTED NATIONAL HISTORIC SITE

P.O. Box 160
Christiansted, St. Croix, VI 00820
(809) 773–1460

Christiansted National Historic Site contains seven acres and was designated part of the National Park Service in 1952 to commemorate colonial development of the Virgin Islands and to preserve eighteenth- and nineteenth-century structures in this former capital of the Dutch West Indies. The park is located in downtown Christiansted on St. Croix.

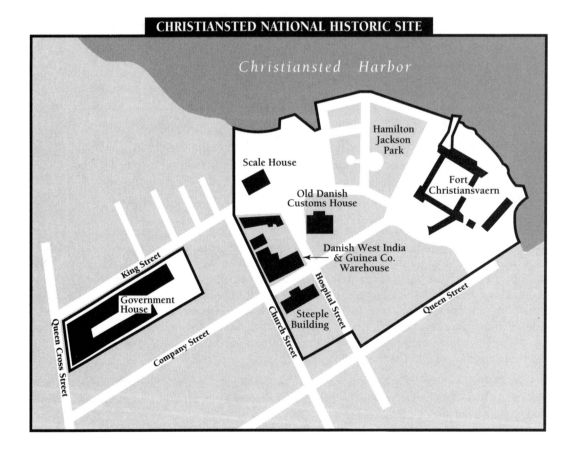

In 1733, the Danish West Indian & Guinea Company bought St. Croix to develop its flatlands for sugar production. By 1750, most of the island was under cultivation, which brought on a flow of great wealth throughout the early nineteenth-century. A drop in sugar prices beginning in 1820 combined with emancipation of slaves in 1848 helped bring an end to the prosperity. The island was purchased by the United States in 1917 to prevent Germany from establishing a submarine base in the area.

National Park Service headquarters, located in Fort Christiansvaern, a Danish fort completed in 1749, is open seven days a week from 8:00 A.M. to 5:00 P.M. Here visitors may obtain information and a folder for a self-guiding tour of the historic area. In addition to the fort, the site contains five other historic buildings. These include the Old Danish Customs House, where the government collected taxes due on goods; Scalehouse, where imports and exports were weighed; Government House, which served as the governor's residence; Danish West Indian & Guinea Company Warehouse, which housed provisions, offices, and personnel; and Steeple Building, which was built originally as a church and later served as a bakery, hospital, and school. A museum is located in Steeple Building.

FACILITIES: No food or lodging is provided by the National Park Service, but both can be found nearby in the town of Christiansted.

VIRGIN ISLANDS NATIONAL PARK

6310 Estate Nazareth
St. Thomas, VI 00802
(809) 776–6201

Virgin Islands National Park was authorized in 1956 to preserve nearly 14,700 acres of tropical island and water that include quiet coves, blue-green waters, and white sandy beaches fringed by lush green hills. The park is located on St. John Island and may be reached via daily ferry across Pillsbury Sound from Red Hook, St. Thomas. Visitors can fly to Charlotte Amalie, St. Thomas, where taxis run to Red Hook.

St. John Island, a former home for Indians, pirates, and planters, is also a land of tropical seas and beautiful coral reefs where temperatures rarely climb above 98 degrees Fahrenheit or fall below 65. Cruz Bay Visitor Center on St. John is open daily 8:00 A.M. to 4:30 P.M. and provides exhibits, maps, and a schedule of park activities including hikes, programs, and guided snorkel trips. Self-guiding trails are at Annaberg, Cinnamon Bay, and Reef Bay. An underwater trail with exhibits for snorkelers is at Trunk Bay. Lifeguards are on duty daily at Trunk Bay, and snorkel equipment may be rented there as well as at Cinnamon Bay.

A 15-mile tour by auto or taxi via Centerline Road and North Shore Road includes beautiful scenery and outstanding beaches. Native-guided taxi tours of the park are operated from Cruz Bay; rental vehicles are also available here. Points of interest in the park include the partially restored ruins of the Annaberg sugar mill factory complex, ancient petroglyphs, and ruins of the Reef Bay sugar mill.

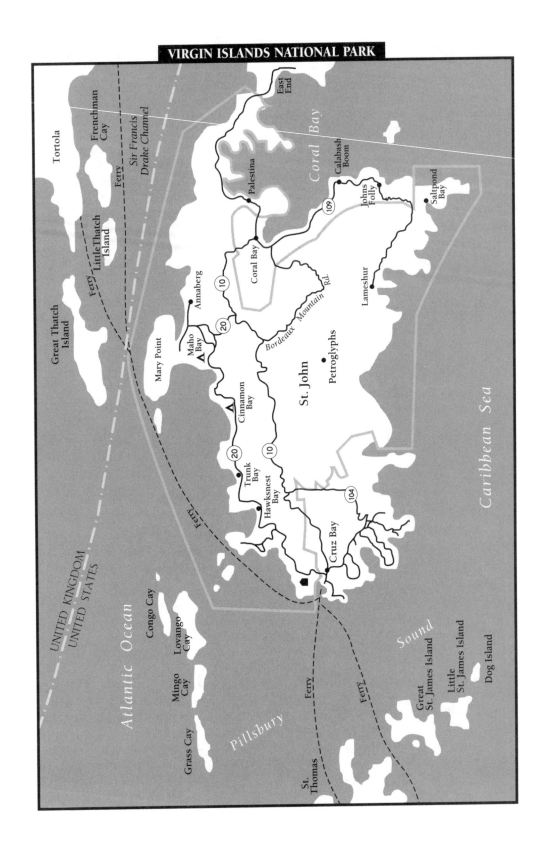

FACILITIES: Cinnamon Bay campground has forty cottages and forty equipped tents. Bare tent sites are available as well. Equipment includes cots, linen, utensils, and stove. Food, fuel, ice, and charcoal are sold at a small store nearby. For reservations or information, write Cinnamon Bay Campground, P.O. Box 720, Cruz Bay, St. John, VI 00831 (809–776–6330 or 800–539–9998). Restaurants are in Cruz Bay, and meals may be purchased in Cinnamon Bay. Sandwiches and drinks are available at Trunk Bay.

CAMPING: See the facilities section above.

FISHING: Waters surrounding the island contain such saltwater sport fish as tarpon, barracuda, jacks, bonito, and bonefish. Fishing includes deep-sea trolling and angling in shallower reef and inshore waters. Boats for deep-sea fishing, drift fishing, or shoreline trolling may be chartered on the island. No spearfishing is permitted in the park.

Bluestone National Scenic River

WEST VIRGINIA

STATE TOURIST INFORMATION
(800) 225–5982

BLUESTONE NATIONAL SCENIC RIVER
104 Main Street
P.O. Box 246
Glen Jean, WV 25846
(304) 465–0508

Bluestone National Scenic River, encompassing 4,268 acres, was authorized as part of the National Park Service in 1988 to preserve an 11-mile section of the free-flowing Bluestone River. Access to the river is through Bluestone and Pipestem state parks off State Route 20 south of Hinton, West Virginia.

The Bluestone River begins on East River Mountain and flows 77 miles to its confluence with the New River at Bluestone Lake. The 11-mile section of the Bluestone River (named for the deep blue limestone streambed) that is preserved as a national scenic river begins at the river's entry into Pipestem State Park and extends to Bluestone Lake. The ancient river has cut a gorge to depths of up to 1,200 feet. The rough terrain of this region has generally inhibited human habitation to produce a scenic, unspoiled area where visitors will find opportunities for fishing, hiking, boating, and enjoying nature. The scenic river is open year-round.

Some of the finest views of the Bluestone are in Pipestem State Park, where there is an overlook along the rim road. Viewpoints of the river are also at the Canyon Rim Center and the Main Lodge. An aerial tram operates from April through October from Canyon Rim to Mountain Creek Lodge. For hikers, an 8-mile trail that once served as a road for wagons and automobiles follows the river from Mountain Creek Lodge to Bluestone State Park.

FACILITIES: There are no federal facilities within the boundaries of the national scenic river. Mountain Creek Lodge within Pipestem State Park operates from April through October.

CAMPING: No camping is permitted within the boundaries of Bluestone National Scenic River. Pipestem State Park has eighty sites with flush toilets, showers, and full hookups. Bluestone State Park has eighty-five sites with flush toilets, showers, and electrical hookups.

FISHING: The Bluestone offers fishing for smallmouth bass, panfish, and catfish. A West Virginia license is required.

GAULEY RIVER NATIONAL RECREATION AREA

104 Main Street
P.O. Box 246
Glen Jean, WV 25846
(304) 465–0508

Gauley River National Recreation Area comprises 10,300 acres and was authorized in 1988 to preserve portions of two of the finest white-water rivers in the eastern United States. The area is in central West Virginia between Summersville and Fayetteville. Vehicle access is from State Route 129 at Summersville Dam, from Woods Ferry Road (four-wheel-drive only), and from Swiss Road off State Route 39.

Gauley River National Recreation Area includes 25 miles of the Gauley River and 6 miles of the Meadow River. The Gauley River is one of the best white-water boating rivers in the East. The scenic gorges and valleys within and near the recreation area provide a wide variety of natural and cultural activities.

The Gauley River drops twenty–six feet per mile through a gorge with an average depth of 500 feet. More than one hundred rapids, huge volumes of water, and spectacular scenery make this one of the world's finest rivers for rafting. The upper section of the river is most demanding. White-water rafting is available for about four weeks in September and October when the Summersville reservoir is lowered to make room for winter and early spring rains.

FACILITIES: Food and lodging are available nearby.

CAMPING: No camping facilities are provided by the National Park Service. Camping is available nearby at Babcock State Park (304–438–6205), which has fifty sites with flush toilets and showers. Summersville Lake (304–872–3412), operated by the U.S. Army Corps of Engineers, has 110 sites with flush toilets and showers.

FISHING: Both rivers provide excellent fishing. A West Virginia license is required.

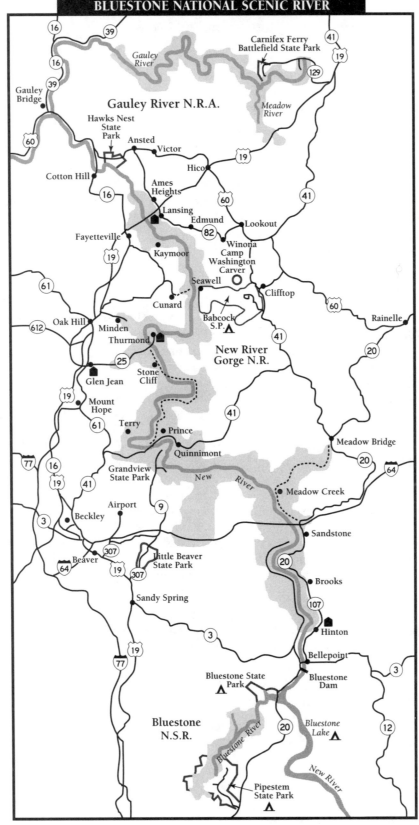

Carnifex Ferry
Battlefield State Park

Gauley
River

Gauley River N.R.A.

Meadow
River

Gauley
Bridge

Hawks Nest
State
Park

Ansted

Victor

Cotton Hill

Hico

Ames
Heights

Lansing

Edmund

Lookout

Fayetteville

Kaymoor

Winona
Camp
Washington
Carver

Seawell

Clifftop

Rainelle

Oak Hill

Minden

Cunard

Babcock
S.P.

New River
Gorge N.R.

Thurmond

Stone
Cliff

Glen Jean

Mount
Hope

Terry

Prince

Quinnimont

Meadow Bridge

Grandview
State Park

New   River

Airport

Beckley

Meadow Creek

Sandstone

Beaver

Little Beaver
State Park

Brooks

Sandy Spring

Hinton

Bellepoint

Bluestone State
Park

Bluestone
Dam

Bluestone
N.S.R.

Bluestone
Lake

Bluestone River

New River

Pipestem
State Park

HARPERS FERRY NATIONAL HISTORICAL PARK

P.O. Box 65
Harpers Ferry, WV 25425
(304) 535–6223

Harpers Ferry National Historical Park, located at the scenic confluence of the Shenandoah and Potomac rivers, comprises about 2,500 acres. Authorized as a national monument in 1944, the are was declared a National Historical Park in 1963. Today the park has a variety of exhibits, interpretive programs and hiking trails exploring the park's six Paths Through History: industry; John Brown; Civil War; African-American history (particularly Storer College); natural history; and transportation. The park is approximately 65 miles northwest of Washington, D.C.; 20 miles southwest of Frederick, Maryland, via US 340. Signs along US 340 direct visitors to the visitor center and parking facility by turning at the signal light on US 340.

The strategic location of Harpers Ferry resulted in its early settlement so that, by the mid-1800s, the town had a population of approximately 3,000. The area was given a shot in the arm in the 1790s when President Washington urged establishment of a national armory here. The later arrival of the railroad and the C&O Canal speeded things along. Unfortunately, the combination of the Civil War (the town changed hands many times during the conflict) and a series of severe floods in the late 1800s resulted in abandonment of the area by many of its citizens.

One famous visitor to Harpers Ferry in 1859 was John Brown. Brown planned to free slaves by force and establish a free-Negro stronghold. His initial attack came at Harpers Ferry, a town with an arsenal of armaments in a location near the Mason-Dixon line. Brown and his twenty-one men captured the armory, which, in turn, was later stormed by troops led by Colonel Robert E. Lee. Brown was subsequently hanged for murder, treason, and slave insurrection. The building where Brown and his men sought refuge is part of the park and open for visitation.

The park area has restored buildings including a blacksmith shop, confectionary, dry-goods store, provost marshal's office, clothing store, jewelry store, and homes. An information center containing exhibits is open daily from 8:30 A.M. until 5:00 P.M. Park museums explain the six themes of Harpers Ferry National Historical Park: industry, John Brown, Civil War, natural history, transportation, and African-American history. Activities available include audiovisual presentations, guided walks, living-history programs, hiking trails, and self-guiding tours.

FACILITIES: No lodging is provided by the National Park Service. Visitors enter Harpers Ferry National Historical Park through the park's new visitor center at the Cavalier Heights District. Shuttle buses transport visitors to other areas of the park. Private restaurants are located a few blocks from the Lower Town District. Restrooms are next to the visitor center.

CAMPING: No camping is permitted in the historical park. Private campgrounds are nearby. Gambrill State Park (Maryland), 6 miles northwest of Frederick on Highway 40, offers camping with tables, grills, water, flush toilets, showers, and fishing (310–473–8360).

FISHING: Fishing is permitted in the Shenandoah and Potomac rivers, which border the park. Catches include bass, catfish, crappie, and pike. An appropriate state license is required.

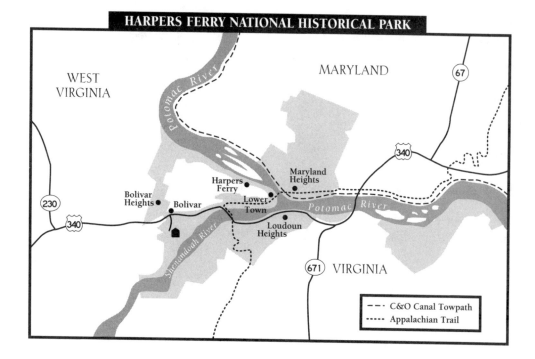

NEW RIVER GORGE NATIONAL RIVER

104 Main Street
P.O. Box 246
Glen Jean, WV 25846
(304) 465–0508

New River Gorge National River was authorized in 1978 and comprises 62,000 acres along a rugged, white-water river running northward through deep canyons. The river is located in south-central West Virginia, between the towns of Hinton and Fayetteville. The nearest large town is Beckley.

This area of West Virginia that was once known for its coal mines, timbering, and railroads contains one of North America's oldest rivers. The 53-mile segment of the river corridor between Hinton and Fayetteville provides visitors with an abundance of natural, scenic, historic, and recreational features. Many miles of hiking, mountain biking, and horseback trails are available. The New River offers excellent white-water rafting. A list of commercial outfitters offering guide service is available from the park office.

Park headquarters is located in Glen Jean. Five visitor centers—Canyon Rim Visitor Center on U.S. 19 near Fayetteville, Hinton Visitor Center at State Route 3 By-Pass in Hinton, and Grandview Visitor Center located 5 miles north of Interstate 64 on Route 9—have exhibits, photos of the park, and a schedule of activities. The Canyon Rim Visitor Center is open year-round, while the visitor centers at Hinton and Grandview are open seasonally and on weekends year-round. Glen Jean Bank Visitor Center and Thurmond Depot are open seasonally.

FACILITIES: Water and restrooms are at each visitor center. Picnic areas are at Canyon Rim and Grandview visitor centers. Food and lodging are found in nearby communities.

CAMPING: Only primitive camping areas are provided by the National Park Service. Toward the northern end of the river, Babcock State Park offers campsites with tables, grills, water, flush toilets, and showers. At the park's southern end, 9 miles south of Hinton on Highway 20, Bluestone State Park and Pipestem State Park have similar facilities. Private campgrounds are near Fayetteville and Hinton.

FISHING: Fishing is excellent, with stocked brown and rainbow trout in some of the tributary streams, the New River is known for its catfish, crappie, pike, smallmouth bass, and walleye fishing. A West Virginia license is required for warm-water fish. If fishing for trout, a state trout stamp is required in addition to the regular fishing license.

This site is shown on the map on page 291.

WISCONSIN

STATE TOURIST INFORMATION
(800) 432–8747

APOSTLE ISLANDS NATIONAL LAKESHORE
Route 1, Box 4
Old Courthouse Building
Bayfield, WI 54814
(715) 779–3397

Apostle Islands National Lakeshore, established in 1970, comprises 69,372 acres containing twenty-one islands and 12 miles of shoreline along the south side of Lake Superior. In 1986, Long Island became the twenty-first island to become part of the national lakeshore. The park is located on and near the Bayfield Peninsula in northern Wisconsin, approximately 77 miles northeast of Duluth, Minnesota. A concessioner provides excursion boat service to and among the islands from Bayfield and Little Sand Bay in the summer.

The twenty-two Apostle Islands (all but one are within the park) are products of a million-year period when ice intermittently covered this region. As the glaciers receded, meltwater began to fill the basin that would eventually become Lake Superior. Evidence of earlier lake levels (old beachlines and cliffs) can still be seen on some of the islands.

By the early 1900s this area was booming, and Bayfield was a center for loggers, fishermen, shippers, and tourists. Beginning in the early 1930s, however, the combination of a bad economy and a region laid bare by fire and ax sent the area into decline. The vegetation has now returned, and the lighthouses, quarries, and fishing camps are open to the public.

The park's information office and visitor center in Bayfield is open daily except during winter months when it may close on weekends. It contains exhibits, interpretive literature, and an audiovisual program. The information station at Little Sand Bay contains exhibits on the region's history and current recreational activities, including tours of a restored historical fishing operation. The center is 3 miles north of Bayfield in the Red Cliff Indian Reservation.

Boating is one of the most popular activities in the area. Boat-ramp facilities are in Red Cliff, Bayfield, Cornucopia, and Little Sand Bay. Public docks are at Sand Island, South Twin Island,

Little Sand Bay, Rocky Island, Manitou Island, Stockton Island, Oak Island, Basswood Island, Outer Island, Otter Island, Raspberry Island, and Devils Island. Marinas (with boat-storage facilities) are in the Bayfield–Madeline Island area. Sea kayaks have become a very popular means of transportation among the Apostle Islands. Sailboat and sea kayak rentals and chartered fishing trips are available in Bayfield. For those without boats, daily excursion trips leave from Bayfield in summer.

The best way to see some of the more remote islands is by foot. More than 50 miles of hiking trails are maintained on the islands by the National Park Service. Stockton, the Apostles' largest island, has 14½ miles of trails. During summer, park rangers on Stockton guide nature walks and present evening programs. Rangers are also stationed on Manitou Island to conduct tours of the historic commercial fishing camp and on Raspberry Island to conduct tours of the island's light station (one of six in the national lakeshore).

FACILITIES: No overnight accommodations are provided in the park, but motels are available in Bayfield, Washburn, Cornucopia, and Ashland, and on Madeline Island.

CAMPING: Camping is allowed on eighteen islands. Permits are required for camping and are available at the visitor stations. Group campsites (for use by seven or more campers) may be reserved in advance. All other camping is available on a first-come basis. A variety of public and private campgrounds are in the surrounding communities and Chequamegon National Forest. Red Cliff Indian Reservation offers modern campgrounds near Red Cliff. Be sure to boil Lake Superior water before drinking or using for cooking.

FISHING: The area aroung Apostle Islands is one of the best fish-producing habitats in Lake Superior. Sports fishing for lake, brown, and rainbow trout and for introduced species of slamon is good. Streams on the peninsula are popular for rainbow and brown trout. A Wisconsin license is required.

ICE AGE NATIONAL SCENIC TRAIL; ICE AGE NATIONAL SCIENTIFIC RESERVE

Wisconsin Department of Natural Resources
P.O. Box 7921
Madison, WI 53707
(608) 266–2181

The first national scientific reserve in the National Park Service, authorized in 1964, contains 50,000 acres of nationally significant features of continental glaciation. Ice Age National Scientific Reserve is jointly administered by the National Park Service and the State of Wisconsin. It consists of nine detached units located throughout Wisconsin. Ice Age National Scenic Trail is partially developed along its planned 1,000-mile length.

As recently as 12,000 years ago, Wisconsin—along with much of the rest of the northern United States—was covered by the last of at least four major glacial advances. During these periods, falling snow did not melt but accumulated and changed to ice under its own pressure.

As the masses of ice moved southward, they leveled hills, filled valleys, and moved billions of tons of materials over the land. In Wisconsin, evidence of these huge glaciers is still clearly seen. Features known as drumlins, kames, eskers, moraines, kettles, and lake plains are preserved in the reserve.

Ice Age National Scientific Reserve consists of nine separate units located across the state, from Lake Michigan in the east to the St. Croix River on the Minnesota border. Four of these are state parks or forests (Kettle Moraine State Forest and Devil's Lake, Mill Bluff, and Interstate parks), and one (Horicon) is a state wildlife area. The remaining four areas are not yet developed.

Kettle Moraine contains an interpretive center, many miles of hiking trails, and regularly scheduled naturalist programs. Interstate Park and Devil's Lake also have extensive interpretive programs and facilities.

Ice Age National Scenic Trail was established in 1980. Approximately 160 miles of the 1,000-mile trail have been certified by the National Park Service with routed wooden signs and yellow-paint blazes providing distance and directional information. Most parts of the trail crossing public land are completed, while portions crossing private land await development. For information on state sections, write Wisconsin Department of Natural Resources, Box 7921, Madison, WI 53707. For information on other sections, write Ice Age National Scenic Trail, National Park Service, 700 Ray-O-Vac Drive, Madison, WI 53711.

FACILITIES: Although lodging is not available in the Ice Age units, it is available in nearby communities. Food service is available seasonally at Devil's Lake.

CAMPING: Camping is available in the Kettle Moraine, Devil's Lake, Interstate, and Mils Bluff units.

FISHING: Fishing is available in or near a number of the units, and a Wisconsin license is required.

ST. CROIX NATIONAL SCENIC RIVERWAY
P.O. Box 708
St. Croix Falls, WI 54024
(715) 483–3284

The St. Croix National Scenic Riverways was established between 1968 and 1972 to preserve approximately 250 miles of riverways that show little evidence of disturbance by man. The park begins near the sources of the St. Croix and Namekagon rivers in northern Wisconsin and follows the border between Wisconsin and Minnesota.

Thousands of years ago, this region of the United States was leveled by glacial ice flowing down from the north. As the climate warmed and the glacier melted, much of the resulting water used the St. Croix basin as an escape. The scraping of the advancing ice sheet combined with the later water runoff exposed ancient rocks and volcanic formations that are visible along the rivers.

The French were the first Europeans to venture into this region. Here they found the Dakota and Chippewa tribes living in an area rich in both plant and wildlife. The St. Croix valley became an abundant source of beaver pelts for Europe until the early 1800s. Today, much of the riverway cuts through second-growth hardwood forests.

Although the St. Croix and Lower St. Croix were initially established as two park areas, they now constitute a single riverway. The St. Croix section consists of 102 miles of the St. Croix River and 98 miles of its Namekagon tributary (see map). The Lower St. Croix carries the park an additional 52 miles from Taylors Falls to the Mississippi. The main visitor center and headquarters is at St. Croix Falls, and information stations are open in the summer near the towns of Grantsburg and Trego, Wisconsin. The visitor center in Stillwater, Minnesota is open year-round.

Canoeing the rivers is one of the park's most popular activities. During late summer and fall, the water level is generally low and the lower sections of the river provide the best trips. A listing of the numerous canoe outfitters located along the riverway may be obtained by writing the park superintendent. Most visitors find that 10–20 miles of paddling downstream is a full day. The Lower St. Croix is popular for power-boating, water-skiing, and house-boating. State parks along this part of the riverway provide camping, picnicking, nature hikes, and interpretive exhibits.

FACILITIES: No food service or lodging is provided by the Park Service. Overnight accommodations and supplies are in nearby communities.

CAMPING: A number of primitive campgrounds are located along the riverway. Campgrounds with vault toilets and water are at Howell Landing and Earl Park. Several state parks along the riverway maintain developed campgrounds.

FISHING: Bass, muskellunge, and walleye pike are in the rivers, and the Namekagon is noted for brown, brook, and rainbow trout. A license is required. Where the river forms a boundary between the two states, a license from either is valid while fishing from a boat.

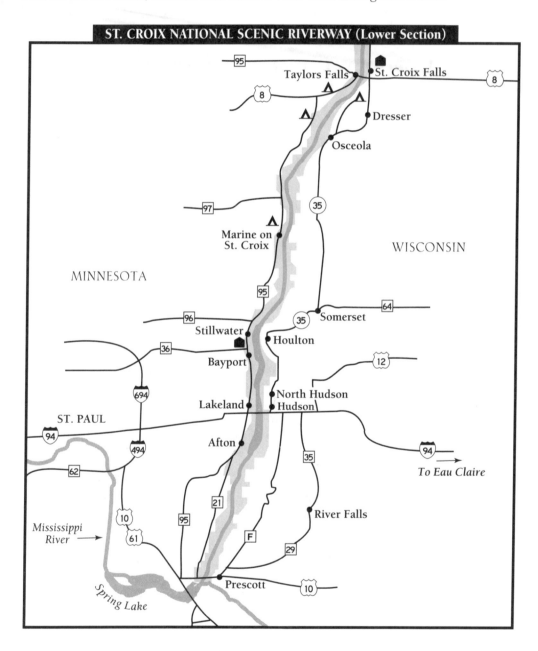

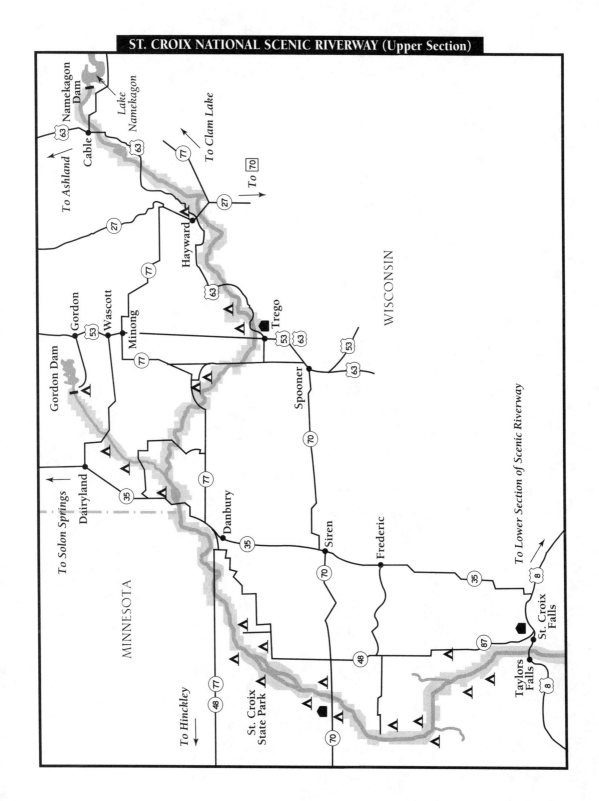

ST. CROIX NATIONAL SCENIC RIVERWAY (Upper Section)

NATIONAL PARK AREAS FACILITIES AND ACTIVITIES CHART

This chart presents current information on visitor services in the areas described in this book. Generally, the services listed are those in the parks themselves. Additional services are usually available in nearby cities. Parks permitting activities such as horseback riding or boating do not necessarily rent equipment. Many parks curtail service in their off-seasons. A few park areas are not listed here because they do not have visitor services regulated by the National Park Service.

St. Croix National Scenic Riverway (opposite page)

	Entrance Fee	Visitor Center	Museum/Exhibit	NPS Guided Tour	Self-guiding Tour/Trail	Guide for Hire	Picnic Area	Campground	Group Campsite	Backcountry Use Permits	Hiking	Mountain Climbing	Horseback Riding	Swimming	Bathhouse	Boating	Boat Rental	Boat Ramp	Fishing	Hunting	Off-road Vehicle Trail	Bicycle Trail	Snowmobile Route	Cross-country Ski Trail	Cabin Rental	Hotel, Motel, Lodge	Groceries, Ice	Restaurant, Snacks	Campsites	Handicap Access Restrooms	Handicap Access Visitor Center
ALABAMA																															
Horseshoe Bend Natl. Military Park, 11288 Horseshoe Bend Rd., Daviston, AL 36256	●	●	●		●		●				●																			●	●
Little River Canyon National Preserve, 2201 E. Gault Ave. North, Fort Payne, AL 35967											●					●		●	●	●	●								●		
Russell Cave Natl. Monument, 3729 County Rd. 98, Bridgeport, AL 35740		●	●	●	●		●				●																			●	●
Tuskegee Institute Natl. Historic Site, P.O. Drawer 10, Tuskegee, AL 36088		●	●	●	●																									●	●
CONNECTICUT																															
Weir Farm National Historic Site, 735 Nod Hill Rd., Wilton, CT 06897		●	●																												
DISTRICT OF COLUMBIA																															
Constitution Gardens, c/o NCP – Central, 900 Ohio Dr., SW, Washington, DC 20242		●		●																											
Ford's Theatre Natl. Historic Site, c/o NCP – Central, 900 Ohio Dr., SW, Washington, DC 20020		●	●	●																									●		
Frederick Douglas Natl. Historic Site, 1411 W St., SE, Washington, DC 20020		●	●	●		●															●										
John F. Kennedy Center for the Performing Arts, Natl. Park Service, 2700 F St., NW, Washington, DC 20566		●	●	●																							●	●			
Lincoln Memorial, c/o NCP – Central, 900 Ohio Dr, SW, Washington, DC 20242		●		●	●		●																							●	●
Lyndon B. Johnson Mem. Grove on the Potomac, c/o G. W. Mem. Pkwy., Turkey Run Park, McLean, VA 22101							●				●		●			●			●							●	●			●	●
Rock Creek Park, 5000 Glover Rd., NW, Washington, DC 20015		●		●			●				●		●						●		●								●	●	●
Theodore Roosevelt Island, c/o G.W. Mem., Turkey Run Park, McLean, VA 22101			●	●							●																				
Thomas Jefferson Memorial and Tidal Basin, c/o NCP – Central, 900 Ohio Dr., SW, Washington, DC 20242		●	●	●																									●		
Vietnam Veterans Memorial, c/o NCP – Central, 900 Ohio Dr., SW, Washington, DC 20242		●		●																										●	●
Washington Monument, c/o NCP – Central, 900 Ohio Dr., SW, Washington, DC 20242		●	●	●																	●						●		●	●	●
White House, c/o NCR, National Park Service, 1100 Ohio Dr., SW, Washington, DC 20242		●	●	●																										●	●
FLORIDA																															
Big Cypress Natl. Preserve, Star Route, HCR 61, Ochopee, FL 33943		●	●	●	●		●	●		●	●					●		●	●	●	●								●	●	●
Biscayne Natl. Park, P.O.Box 1369, Homestead, FL 33090		●	●	●	●		●									●		●	●							●			●	●	●
Canaveral Natl. Seashore, 308 Julia St., Titusville FL 32780	●	●	●	●	●		●							●		●		●	●		●						●		●	●	●
Castillo de San Marcos Natl. Monument, 1 Castillo Dr., St. Augustine, FL 32084	●	●	●	●	●																										
DeSoto Natl. Memorial P.O. Box 15390, Bradenton, FL 34280	●	●	●	●	●		●																								
Dry Tortugas National Park, c/o Everglades Natl. Park, P.O. Box 6208, Key West, FL 33041			●		●		●	●								●			●										●	●	●
Everglades Natl. Park, P. O. Box 279, Homestead, FL 33030	●	●	●	●	●		●	●								●	●		●		●	●				●	●		●	●	●
Fort Caroline Natl. Memorial, 12713 Fort Caroline Rd., Jacksonville, FL 32225		●	●	●	●		●																							●	●

FLORIDA (continued)

Fort Matanzas Natl. Monument, c/o Castillo de San Marcos NM, 1 Castillo Dr., St. Augustine, FL 32084

Gulf Islands Natl. Seashore, 1801 Gulf Breeze Parkway, Gulf Breeze, FL, 32561 (See also Miss.)

Timucuan Ecological and Historical Preserve, 12713 Fort Caroline Rd., Jacksonville, FL 32225

GEORGIA

Andersonville Natl. Historic Site, Rt. 1, Box 800, Andersonville, GA 31711

Chattahoochee River Natl. Recreation Area, 1978 Island Ford Parkway, Atlanta, GA 30350

Chickamauga and Chattanooga Natl. Military Park (Ga., Tenn.), P.O. Box 2128, Fort Oglethorpe, GA 30742

Cumberland Island Natl. Seashore, P.O. Box 806, St. Marys, GA 31558

Fort Frederica Natl. Monument, Rt. 9, Box 286C, St. Simons Island, GA 31522

Fort Pulaski Natl. Monument, Box 30757, Savannah, GA 31410

Jimmy Carter National Historic Site, Plains, GA 31780

Kennesaw Mountain Natl. Battlefield Park, 900 Kennesaw Mountain Dr., Kennesaw, GA 30152

Martin Luther King, Jr., Natl. Historic Site, 522 Auburn Ave., NE, Atlanta, GA 30312

Ocmulgee Natl. Monument, 1207 Emery Highway, Macon, GA 31201

ILLINOIS

Illinois and Michigan Canal National Heritage Corridor, 15709 S. Independence Blvd., Lockport, IL 60441

Lincoln Home Natl. Historic Site, 413 S. Eighth St., Springfield, IL 62701

INDIANA

George Rogers Clark Natl. Historical Park, 401 S. Second St., Vincennes, IN 47591

Indiana Dunes Natl. Lakeshore, 1100 N. Mineral Springs Rd., Porter, IN 46304

Lincoln Boyhood Natl. Memorial, P.O. Box 1816, Lincoln City, IN 47552

KENTUCKY

Abraham Lincoln Birthplace Natl. Historic Site, 2995 Lincoln Farm Rd., Hodgenville, KY 42748

Cumberland Gap Natl. Historical Park (Ky., Tenn., Va.), P.O. Box 1848, Middlesboro, KY 40965

Mammoth Cave Natl. Park, Mammoth Cave, KY 42259

MAINE

Acadia Natl. Park, P.O. Box 177, Bar Harbor, ME 04609

Roosevelt Campobello International Park, P.O. Box 97, Lubec, ME 04652

Saint Croix Island International Historic Site, c/o Acadia Natl. Park, P.O. Box 177, Bar Harbor, ME 04609

	Entrance Fee	Visitor Center	Museum/Exhibit	NPS Guided Tour	Self-guiding Tour/Trail	Guide for Hire	Picnic Area	Campground	Group Campsite	Backcountry Use Permits	Hiking	Mountain Climbing	Horseback Riding	Swimming	Bathhouse	Boating	Boat Rental	Boat Ramp	Fishing	Hunting	Off-road Vehicle Trail	Bicycle Trail	Snowmobile Route	Cross-country Ski Trail	Cabin Rental	Hotel, Motel, Lodge	Groceries, Ice	Restaurant, Snacks	Handicap Access: Campsites	Handicap Access: Restrooms	Handicap Access: Visitor Center
	●	●	●	●	●	●	●	●	●	●	●	●	●	●	●	●	●	●	●	●	●	●	●	●	●	●	●	●	●	●	●
MARYLAND																															
Antietam Natl. Battlefield, Box 158, Sharpsburg, MD 21782	●	●	●		●				●		●								●			●							●	●	●
Assateague Island Natl. Seashore (Md., Va.), 7206 Seashore Ln., Berlin, MD 21811	●	●	●	●	●		●	●	●	●	●			●	●	●			●	●	●								●	●	●
Catoctin Mountain Park, 6602 Foxville Rd., Thurmont, MD 21788		●	●	●	●		●	●	●		●	●							●					●	●				●	●	●
Chesapeake and Ohio Canal Natl. Historical Park (Md., W.Va., D.C.), P.O. Box 4, Sharpsburg, MD 21782		●	●	●	●		●	●	●		●		●			●	●	●	●			●						●		●	●
Clara Barton Natl. Historic Site, 5801 Oxford Rd., Glen Echo, MD 20812		●	●	●	●																	●									
Fort McHenry Natl. Monument and Historic Shrine, end of E. Fort Avenue, Baltimore, MD 21230-5393	●	●	●	●	●		●																							●	●
Fort Washington Park, NCP – East, 1900 Anacostia Dr., SE, Washington, DC 20020	●	●	●	●	●		●				●								●			●									
Greenbelt Park, 6565 Greenbelt Rd., Greenbelt, MD 20770				●	●		●	●	●		●																		●	●	
Hampton Natl. Historic Site, 535 Hampton Ln., Towson, MD 21204		●	●	●	●																							●			●
Piscataway Park, c/o NCP – East, 1900 Anacostia Dr., SE, Washington, DC 20019							●				●								●										●		
Thomas Stone Natl. Historic Site, 6655 Rose Hill Rd., Port Tobacco, MD 20677		●	●	●	●		●				●																			●	●
MASSACHUSETTS																															
Adams Natl. Historic Site, P.O. Box 531, Quincy, MA 02269-0531	●		●	●																											
Boston Natl. Historic Park, Charleston Navy Yard, Boston, MA 02129		●	●	●	●		●																					●		●	●
Cape Cod Natl. Seashore, 99 Marconi Site Rd., Wellfleet, MA 02667	●	●	●	●	●	●	●			●	●		●	●	●				●	●	●	●				●		●		●	●
Frederick Law Olmsted Natl. Historic Site, 99 Warren St., Brookline, MA 02146			●	●	●																										
John Fitzgerald Kennedy Natl. Historic Site, 83 Beals St., Brookline, MA 02146	●	●	●	●																											
Longfellow Natl. Historic Site, 105 Brattle St., Cambridge, MA 02138	●	●	●	●																											●
Lowell Natl. Historical Park, 67 Kirk St., Lowell, MA 01852		●	●	●	●		●									●		●	●							●	●	●		●	●
Minute Man Natl. Historical Park, 174 Liberty St., Concord, MA 01742	●	●	●	●	●																									●	
Salem Maritime Natl. Historic Site, Custom House, 174 Derby St., Salem, MA 01970		●	●	●	●		●				●					●			●			●						●			
Saugus Iron Works Natl. Historic Site, 244 Central St., Saugus, MA 01906		●	●	●	●		●																							●	●
Springfield Armory Natl. Historic Site, 1 Armory Square, Springfield, MA 01105			●		●																									●	
MICHIGAN																															
Isle Royale Natl. Park, 800 E. Lakeshore Dr., Houghton, MI 49931		●		●	●		●	●	●	●	●			●		●	●		●						●	●	●	●		●	●
Pictured Rocks Natl. Lakeshore, P.O. Box 40, Munising, MI 49862		●	●		●		●	●		●	●			●		●		●	●	●			●	●					●	●	●
Sleeping Bear Dunes Natl. Lakeshore, 9922 Front St., Empire, MI 49630		●	●	●	●		●	●	●	●	●			●	●	●	●	●	●	●				●				●	●		●

MISSISSIPPI

Brices Cross Roads Natl. Battlefield Site, c/o Natchez Trace Parkway, R.R. 1, NT-143, Tupelo, MS 38801

Gulf Islands Natl. Seashore, 3500 Park Rd., Ocean Springs, MS 39564 (See also Fla.)

Natchez National Historic Park, P.O. Box 1208, Natchez, MS 39121

Natchez Trace Parkway (Miss., Ala., Tenn.), R.R. 1, NT-143, Tupelo, MS 38801

Tupelo Natl. Battlefield, c/o Natchez Trace Parkway, R.R. 1, NT-143, Tupelo, MS 38801

Vicksburg Natl. Military Park, 3201 Clay St., Vicksburg, MS 39180

NEW HAMPSHIRE

Saint-Gaudens Natl. Historic Site, R.R. 3, Box 73, Cornish, NH 03745-9704

NEW JERSEY

Edison Natl. Historic Site, Main St. and Lakeside Ave., West Orange, NJ 07052

Morristown Natl. Historical Park, Washington Place, Morristown, NJ 07960

Pinelands National Reserve, P.O. Box 7, New Lisbon, NJ 08064

NEW YORK

Castle Clinton Natl. Monument, c/o NPS, Manhattan Sites, 26 Wall St., New York, NY 10005

Eleanor Roosevelt Natl. Historic Site, 519 Albany Post Rd., Hyde Park, NY 12538

Federal Hall Natl. Memorial, c/o NPS, Manhattan Sites, 26 Wall St., New York, NY 10005

Fire Island Natl. Seashore, 120 Laurel St., Patchogue, NY 11772

Fort Stanwix Natl. Monument, 112 E. Park St., Rome, NY 13440

Gateway Natl. Recreation Area (N.Y., N.J.) Floyd Bennett Field, Bldg. 69, Brooklyn, NY 11234

General Grant Natl. Memorial, c/o NPS, 26 Wall St., New York, NY 10005

Hamilton Grange Natl. Memorial, c/o NPS, 26 Wall St., New York, NY 10005

Home of Franklin D. Roosevelt Natl. Historic Site, 519 Albany Post Rd., Hyde Park, NY 12538

Martin Van Buren Natl. Historic Site, P.O. Box 545, Rt. 9H, Kinderhook, NY 12106

Sagamore Hill Natl. Historic Site, 20 Sagamore Hill Rd., Oyster Bay, NY 11771-1899

Saint Paul's Church Natl. Historic Site, 897 S. Columbus Ave., Mount Vernon, NY 10550

Saratoga Natl. Historical Park, 648 Route 32, Stillwater, NY 12170

Statue of Liberty Natl. Monument (N.Y., N.J.), c/o NPS, 26 Wall St., New York, NY 10005

Theodore Roosevelt Birthplace Natl. Historic Site, c/o NPS, 26 Wall St., New York, NY 10005

Theodore Roosevelt Inaugural Natl. Historic Site, 641 Delaware Ave., Buffalo, NY 14202

Vanderbilt Mansion Natl. Historic Site, 249 Albany Post Rd., Hyde Park, NY 12538

Women's Rights Natl. Historical Park, P.O. Box 70, Seneca Falls, NY 13148

FACILITIES AND ACTIVITIES CHART

Columns (left to right): Entrance Fee · Visitor Center · Museum/Exhibit · NPS Guided Tour · Self-guiding Tour/Trail · Guide for Hire · Picnic Area · Campground · Group Campsite · Backcountry Use Permits · Hiking · Mountain Climbing · Horseback Riding · Swimming · Bathhouse · Boating · Boat Rental · Boat Ramp · Fishing · Hunting · Off-road Vehicle Trail · Bicycle Trail · Snowmobile Route · Cross-country Ski Trail · Cabin Rental · Hotel, Motel, Lodge · Groceries, Ice · Restaurant, Snacks · Campsites · Restrooms · Visitor Center (Handicap Access)

NORTH CAROLINA

- Blue Ridge Parkway (N.C., Va.), 1400 BB&T Building, Asheville, NC 28801
- Cape Hatteras Natl. Seashore, Rt. 1, Box 675, Manteo, NC 27954
- Cape Lookout Natl. Seashore, 131 Charles St., Harkers Island, NC 28531
- Carl Sandburg Home Natl. Historic Site, 1928 Little River Rd., Flat Rock, NC 28731
- Fort Raleigh Natl. Historic Site, Cape Hatteras Group, Rt. 1, Box 675, Manteo, NC 27954
- Guilford Courthouse Natl. Military Park, 2332 New Garden Rd., Greensboro, NC 27410
- Moores Creek Natl. Battlefield, P.O. Box 69, Currie, NC 28435
- Wright Brothers Natl. Memorial, Cape Hatteras Group, Rt. 1, Box 675, Manteo, NC 27954

OHIO

- Cuyahoga Valley Natl. Recreation Area, 15610 Vaughn Rd., Brecksville, OH 44141
- Dayton Aviation Heritage National Historic Park, P.O. Box 9280, Wright Bros. Station, Dayton, OH 45409
- Hopewell Culture National Historic Park, 16062 State Route 104, Chillicothe, OH 45601
- James A. Garfield Natl. Historic Site, Lawnfield, 8095 Mentor Ave., Mentor, OH 44060
- Perry's Victory and International Peace Memorial, P.O. Box 549, 93 Delaware Ave., Put-in-Bay, OH 43456
- William Howard Taft Natl. Historic Site, 2038 Auburn Ave., Cincinnati, OH 45219

PENNSYLVANIA

- Allegheny Portage Railroad Natl. Historic Site, P.O. Box 189, Cresson, PA 16630
- Delaware and Lehigh Navigation Canal National Heritage Corridor, 10 E. Church St., Bethlehem, PA 18018
- Delaware Natl. Scenic River, Delaware Water Gap Natl. Recreation Area (Pa., N.J.), Bushkill, PA 18324
- Edgar Allen Poe Natl. Historic Site, c/o Independence NHP, 313 Walnut St., Philadelphia, PA 19106
- Eisenhower Natl. Historic Site, Gettysburg, PA 17325
- Fort Necessity Natl. Battlefield, 1 Washington Way, Farmington, PA 15437
- Friendship Hill Natl. Historic Site, R.D. 1, Box 149-A, Point Marion, PA 15474
- Gettysburg Natl. Military Park, Gettysburg, PA 17325
- Hopewell Furnace Natl. Historic Site, 2 Mark Bird Lane, Elverson, PA 19520
- Independence Natl. Historical Park, 313 Walnut St., Philadelphia, PA 19106
- Johnstown Flood Natl. Memorial, P.O. Box 355, St. Michael, PA 15951
- Steamtrain Natl. Historic Site, 150 S. Washington Ave., Scranton, PA 18503
- Thaddeus Kosciuszko Natl. Memorial, c/o Independence NHP, 313 Walnut St., Philadelphia, PA 19106
- Upper Delaware Scenic and Recreational River (Pa., N.Y.), R.R.2, Box 2428, Beach Lake, PA 18405
- Valley Forge Natl. Historical Park, Valley Forge, PA 19482

PUERTO RICO

San Juan Natl. Historic Site, Calle Norzagaray–Fort San Cristóbal, Viejo San Juan, PR 0090–2094

RHODE ISLAND

Roger Williams Natl. Memorial, 282 N. Main St., Providence, RI 02903

SOUTH CAROLINA

Charles Pinckney Natl. Historic Site, c/o Ft. Sumter Natl. Mon., 1214 Middle St., Sullivans Island, SC 29482

Congaree Swamp Natl. Monument, 200 Caroline Sims Rd., Hopkins, SC 29061

Cowpens Natl. Battlefield, P.O. Box 308, Chesnee, SC 29323

Fort Sumter Natl. Monument, 1214 Middle St., Sullivans Island, SC 29482

Historic Camden, P.O. Box 710, Camden, SC 29020

Kings Mountain Natl. Military Park, P.O. Box 40, Kings Mountain, NC 28086

Ninety Six Natl. Historic Site, P.O. Box 496, Ninety Six, SC 29666

TENNESSEE

Andrew Johnson Natl. Historic Site, P.O. Box 1088, Greeneville, TN 37744

Big South Fork Natl. River and Recreation Area (Tenn., Ky.), Route 3, Box 401, Oneida, TN 37841

Fort Donelson Natl. Battlefield, P.O. Box 434, Dover, TN 37058-0434

Great Smoky Mountains Natl. Park (Tenn., N.C.), Gatlinburg, TN 37738

Obed Wild and Scenic River, P.O. Box 429, Wartburg, TN 37887

Shiloh Natl. Military Park, P.O. Box 61, Shiloh, TN 38376

Stones River Natl. Battlefield, 3501 Old Nashville Highway, Murfreesboro, TN 37129

VIRGINIA

Appomattox Court House Natl. Historical Park, P.O. Box 218, Appomattox, VA 24522

Arlington House, The Robert E. Lee Memorial, c/o G. W. Mem. Pkwy., Turkey Run Park, McLean, VA 22101

Booker T. Washington Natl. Monument, Rt. 3, Box 310, Hardy, VA 24101

Colonial Natl. Historical Park, P.O. Box 210, Yorktown, VA 23690

Fredericksburg and Spotsylvania Natl. Military Park, 120 Chatham Lane, Fredericksburg, VA 22405

George Washington Birthplace Natl. Monument, R.R. 1, Box 717, Washington's Birthplace, VA 22575

George Washington Memorial Parkway (Va., Md.), Turkey Run Park, McLean, VA 22101

Jamestown Natl. Historic Site, P.O. Box 210, Yorktown, VA 23690

VIRGINIA (continued)

	Entrance Fee	Visitor Center	Museum/Exhibit	NPS Guided Tour	Self-guiding Tour/Trail	Guide for Hire	Picnic Area	Campground	Group Campsite	Backcountry Use Permits	Hiking	Mountain Climbing	Horseback Riding	Swimming	Bathhouse	Boating	Boat Rental	Boat Ramp	Fishing	Hunting	Off-road Vehicle Trail	Bicycle Trail	Snowmobile Route	Cross-country Ski Trail	Cabin Rental	Hotel, Motel, Lodge	Groceries, Ice	Restaurant, Snacks	Campsites	Restrooms	Visitor Center (Handicap Access)
Maggie L. Walker Natl. Historic Site, c/o Richmond NBP, 3215 E. Broad St., Richmond, VA 23223		●	●																											●	●
Manassas Natl. Battlefield Park, 6511 Sudley Rd., VA 22110	●	●	●	●	●		●				●		●																	●	●
Petersburg Natl. Battlefield, P.O. Box 549, Rt. 36 East, Petersburg, VA 23804	●	●	●	●	●		●				●		●						●			●								●	●
Prince William Forest Park, 18100 Park Headquarters Rd., Triangle, VA 22172	●	●			●		●	●	●	●	●								●			●								●	●
Red Hill Patrick Henry Natl. Memorial, Brookneal, VA 24528		●	●		●		●																							●	
Richmond Natl. Battlefield Park, 3215 E. Broad St., Richmond, VA 23223		●	●		●		●				●																			●	●
Shenandoah Natl. Park, Rt. 4, Box 348, Luray, VA 22835	●	●	●	●	●		●	●	●	●	●		●						●					●	●	●	●	●	●	●	●
Wolf Trap Farm Park for the Performing Arts, 1551 Trap Rd., Vienna, VA 22180	●	●					●																							●	●

VIRGIN ISLANDS

	Entrance Fee	Visitor Center	Museum/Exhibit	NPS Guided Tour	Self-guiding Tour/Trail	Guide for Hire	Picnic Area	Campground	Group Campsite	Backcountry Use Permits	Hiking	Mountain Climbing	Horseback Riding	Swimming	Bathhouse	Boating	Boat Rental	Boat Ramp	Fishing	Hunting	Off-road Vehicle Trail	Bicycle Trail	Snowmobile Route	Cross-country Ski Trail	Cabin Rental	Hotel, Motel, Lodge	Groceries, Ice	Restaurant, Snacks	Campsites	Restrooms	Visitor Center (Handicap Access)
Buck Island Reef Natl. Monument, P.O. Box 160, Christiansted, St. Croix, VI 00820		●	●	●	●		●				●			●		●			●												
Christiansted Natl. Historic Site, P.O. Box 160, Christiansted, VI 00820	●	●	●	●	●		●																							●	●
Virgin Islands Natl. Park, 6310 Estate Nazareth, St. Thomas, VI 00801		●	●	●	●		●	●			●		●	●		●			●							●	●	●		●	●

WEST VIRGINIA

	Entrance Fee	Visitor Center	Museum/Exhibit	NPS Guided Tour	Self-guiding Tour/Trail	Guide for Hire	Picnic Area	Campground	Group Campsite	Backcountry Use Permits	Hiking	Mountain Climbing	Horseback Riding	Swimming	Bathhouse	Boating	Boat Rental	Boat Ramp	Fishing	Hunting	Off-road Vehicle Trail	Bicycle Trail	Snowmobile Route	Cross-country Ski Trail	Cabin Rental	Hotel, Motel, Lodge	Groceries, Ice	Restaurant, Snacks	Campsites	Restrooms	Visitor Center (Handicap Access)
Appalachian Natl. Scenic Trail (Me. to Ga.), P.O. Box 807, Harpers Ferry, WV 25425	●	●		●						●	●																				●
Bluestone Natl. Scenic River, 104 Main St., Glen Jean, WV 25846	●										●								●												
Gauley River Natl. Recreation Area, 104 Main St., Glen Jean, WV 25846										●	●					●			●							●					
Harpers Ferry Natl. Historical Park, (W.V., Md., Va.), P.O. Box 65, Harpers Ferry, WV 25425	●	●	●	●	●					●	●								●			●								●	●
New River Gorge Natl. River, 104 Main St., Glen Jean, WV 25846	●	●		●	●						●	●	●			●			●									●		●	●

WISCONSIN

	Entrance Fee	Visitor Center	Museum/Exhibit	NPS Guided Tour	Self-guiding Tour/Trail	Guide for Hire	Picnic Area	Campground	Group Campsite	Backcountry Use Permits	Hiking	Mountain Climbing	Horseback Riding	Swimming	Bathhouse	Boating	Boat Rental	Boat Ramp	Fishing	Hunting	Off-road Vehicle Trail	Bicycle Trail	Snowmobile Route	Cross-country Ski Trail	Cabin Rental	Hotel, Motel, Lodge	Groceries, Ice	Restaurant, Snacks	Campsites	Restrooms	Visitor Center (Handicap Access)
Apostle Islands Natl. Lakeshore, Rt. 1, Box 4, Bayfield, WI 54814	●	●	●	●	●		●	●	●	●	●			●		●	●	●	●	●			●	●					●	●	●
St. Croix Natl. Scenic Riverway (Wis., Minn.), P.O. Box 708, St. Croix Falls, WI 54024	●	●	●	●	●		●	●	●	●	●			●		●	●	●	●	●			●						●	●	●

ABOUT THE AUTHORS

DAVID AND KAY SCOTT reside in Valdosta, Georgia, where the winters are mild, the humidity is high, and the people are friendly. They have spent twenty-five summers touring the United States and Canada in a series of Volkswagen campers. The first VW bus they owned was a 1967 model that looked like a relic from World War II. During their first cross-country trip in it, in 1970, the VW was barely able to make headway against the wind blowing across a Wyoming interstate. Their two- and three-month trips have taken the couple through all the states, the Canadian provinces, and to nearly all the areas administered by the National Park Service. The Scotts drove from Georgia to Alaska and back during the summer of 1982. David and Kay have appeared live from Yellowstone National Park and Grand Canyon National Park on NBC's *Today* show, offering tips on visiting the national parks. In addition to their domestic travels, the Scotts spent two summers carrying backpacks while riding trains through Europe.

David Scott was born in Rushville, Indiana, attended Purdue University and Florida State University, and received a Ph.D. in economics from the University of Arkansas. During most of the year, he is a professor of accounting and finance at Valdosta State University. He has written numerous books on accounting, finance, and investing, including nine titles in Globe Pequot's Money Smarts series of personal finance books. In addition to travel, he is interested in amateur radio, computers, and the Atlanta Braves. His e-mail address is dlscott@grits.valdosta.peachnet.edu.

Kay Woelfel Scott was born in Austin, Minnesota, and was raised in Yankton, South Dakota. She graduated from Clearwater (Florida) High School and earned degrees at Florida Southern College and the University of Arkansas. During the academic year, she is assistant principal at an elementary school in Valdosta, Georgia. She is interested in a wide variety of crafts, including stained glass and designing and painting T-shirts. She drew all the maps that appeared in the earlier editions of this book.

Also of Interest from The Globe Pequot Press

If you have enjoyed **Guide to the National Park Areas: Eastern States**,
please be sure to read the following Globe Pequot books.

Guide to the National Park Areas: Western States
More than 170 areas East of the Mississippi Operated by
the National Park Service, $15.95
by David L. Scott and Kay W. Scott

Camp the U.S. for $5 or Less: Eastern States
Quality Campgrounds East of the Mississippi, $12.95
by Shuford and Mary Helen Smith

Camp the U.S. for $5 or Less: Western States
Quality Campgrounds West of the Mississippi, $12.95
by Shuford and Mary Helen Smith

Camping Made Easy
A Manual for Beginners with Tips for the Experienced, $15.95
by Michael Rutter

The Camping Sourcebook
Your One-Stop Resource for Everything to Feed Your Camping Habit, $18.95
by Steven Griffin

Campfire Songs
A Classic Collection of Tunes, $9.95
Edited by Irene Maddox and Rosalyn Blankenship

Campfire Chillers
The Classics, $9.95
Edited by E.M. Freeman

Campfire Thrillers
The Short and Scary Ones, $9.95
Edited by Rebecca Rizzo

The Globe Pequot Hiking and Nature Walk Guides

The Complete Line of Appalachian Mountain Club Books

Woodall's Campground Directories and Guides

Available from your bookstore or directly from the publisher.
For a catalogue or to place an order, call toll-free, 24 hours a day, (800) 243-0495
or write to P.O. Box 833, Old Saybrook, Connecticut 06475.
Prices and availability subject to change.